Hypnosis and Stress

Hypnosis and Stress
A Guide for Clinicians

Peter J. Hawkins
ISMAI, University Institute of Maia, Portugal

John Wiley & Sons, Ltd

Other Wiley Editorial Offices

John Wiley & Sons Inc., 111 River Street, Hoboken, NJ 07030, USA

Jossey-Bass, 989 Market Street, San Francisco, CA 94103-1741, USA

Wiley-VCH Verlag GmbH, Boschstr. 12, D-69469 Weinheim, Germany

John Wiley & Sons Australia Ltd, 42 McDougall Street, Milton, Queensland 4064, Australia

John Wiley & Sons (Asia) Pte Ltd, 2 Clementi Loop #02-01, Jin Xing Distripark, Singapore
129809

John Wiley & Sons Canada Ltd, 22 Worcester Road, Etobicoke, Ontario, Canada M9W 1L1

Wiley also publishes its books in a variety of electronic formats. Some content that appears in
print may not be available in electronic books.

Library of Congress Cataloging-in-Publication Data
Hawkins, Peter (Peter John)
    Hypnosis and stress : a guide for clinicians / Peter J. Hawkins.
      p.   cm.
    Includes bibliographical references and index.
    ISBN-13: 978-0-470-01951-1 (pbk) 978-0-470-02687-8 (hbk)
    ISBN-10: 0-470-01951-4 (pbk) 0-470-02687-1 (hbk)
    1. Hypnotism–Therapeutic use.   2. Memory.   I. Title.
    [DNLM: 1. Hypnosis–methods.   2. Stress, Psychological–therapy.
WM 415 H394h 2006]
RC495.H385 2006
616.89'162–dc22

                                                                                2005024424

British Library Cataloguing in Publication Data

A catalogue record for this book is available from the British Library

ISBN-13: 978-0-470-01951-1 (pbk)   978-0-470-02687-8 (hbk)
ISBN-10: 0-470-01951-4 (pbk)   0-470-02687-1 (hbk)

Typeset in 10/12pt New Baskerville by SNP Best-set Typesetters Ltd., Hong Kong
Printed and bound in Great Britain by TJ International Ltd, Padstow, Cornwall, UK
This book is printed on acid-free paper responsibly manufactured from sustainable forestry in
which at least two trees are planted for each one used for paper production.

Dedicated to my granddaughter Ellie.
May she have a happy and successful life.

Contents

List of Clinical Hypnosis Scripts

About the Author

Peter Hawkins is a founder director, and currently President of the European School of Psychotherapy. He is also a visiting professor in hypnosis and psychotherapy at ISMAI in Portugal. Peter has been involved in hypnosis and psychotherapy training in many countries during the past 30 years, and is presently teaching courses for clinicians in Italy, Spain and Portugal. He has written several books on hypnotherapy, which have been translated into several languages including Russian, Chinese, Greek and Spanish, as well as numerous clinical and research papers. He is Co-Director of two Erickson Institutes, in Madrid and Northern Portugal (Porto), and a member of the Editorial Advisory Board of the European Journal of Clinical Hypnosis. He is a former Chartered Counselling and Health Psychologist and has directed several European Union projects in counselling and health psychology in Romania, Uzbekistan and countries of Western Europe. He has frequently presented papers and workshops at international conferences.

Foreword

It appears that Dr Hawkins adheres to Hippocrates' proposition, which states that: 'Nothing should be omitted in an art which interests the whole world, one which may be beneficial to suffering humanity and which does not risk human life or comfort'. In fact, hypnosis, when applied properly by experienced clinicians, may be beneficial to many suffering individuals and may improve human well-being. There is no evidence that hypnosis is harmful in any way to human life. It is true that through the years hypnosis has been misconceived. However, despite the controversies surrounding it, there has been a renewed interest, especially during the second part of the twentieth century, in the scientific study and clinical applications of hypnosis.

Dr Hawkins has been engaged in the scientific study and application of hypnosis for many years, as well as teaching in many universities. Travelling widely to participate in scientific congresses and to teach the art and science of hypnosis in many parts of the world, he has given lectures, conducted seminars and demonstrated the application of hypnosis to undergraduate and graduate students of psychology, and also to practising and in-training psychotherapists, physicians and other healthcare professionals. He has visited most European countries, from Ireland to Portugal and Spain, from central Europe to Finland, as well as Italy and Greece. He has also taught in the Balkans, Central Asia, North America and the Far East.

Dr Hawkins has coordinated many European inter-university programmes in psychological therapies, is the co-founder of the European School of Psychotherapy. Upon the suggestion of his Greek colleagues, he prepared an introduction in clinical hypnosis that was published in Greek and very well accepted by the Greek scientific community and general readership. Although this book is intended for the practising clinician and, especially, for those with a professional interest in psychotherapy, it may be useful and enlightening to the sophisticated reader and those interested in knowing more about the process of healing.

With the book, Dr Hawkins skilfully presents, both to the neophyte as well as to the experienced clinician, an integration of traditional approaches based on suggestion and the more facilitative approaches of Erickson and Rossi, which lead to new learnings and understandings. He presents sophisticated and useful hypnotic techniques for the induction and management of a variety of stress-related problems, and also stresses the importance of metaphors and storytelling in therapy, as these can facilitate rapport, stimulate unconscious activity and allow the individual to develop a greater sense of self-esteem and comfort.

The six case studies and wealth of scripts included in the book are of special interest as they represent different therapeutic approaches to specific problems and offer many useful ideas to the clinician for ego-strengthening, managing and encouraging catharsis, finding inner resources, stress management, pain control, sexual and sleeping problems, enuresis, post-traumatic stress disorder, and so on. Throughout the book, the main emphasis is on the value of hypnotherapy in stress management as it relates to a wide range of problems. Indeed, all the problems discussed are stress related, and all have been carefully selected to demonstrate appropriate psychotherapeutic approaches. Dr Hawkins' reference to psychoneuroimmunology is particularly interesting, presenting ample evidence of contemporary research relating stress to the immune system.

The author focuses on, and addresses, important issues that are usually overlooked or ignored in other books on hypnosis. Such issues include the management of catharsis and the curative factors in psychotherapy. He convincingly supports the view that each individual has the potential to engage in an unconscious search and to draw forth existing unconscious resources and capabilities to solve his or her problems. The answer to the problem is within the individual. The therapist acts only as the facilitator, whose role is to encourage the individual to relinquish his or her role as patient and assist the individual to uncover and utilise these inner potentials by taking an active role in his or her own treatment. Clinicians themselves will find in this book a wealth of material containing a rich treasure of psychological insights to aid them mark out and utilise their own creative resources in their therapeutic work.

It should be pointed out that Dr Hawkins' review of the available literature is up to date and thorough. It covers important theoretical issues and debates as well as interesting and enlightening reports of clinical and experimental work. His interest to examine the appropriateness and validity of different therapeutic interventions should be commended because it helps to dispel any misconceptions of the possibilities and limitations inherent in hypnosis. Such a critical approach is important not only for the scientific status of hypnosis, but also for therapists who wish to evaluate and/or apply reliable and effective hypnotherapeutic interventions in their clinical practices.

Although the author refers extensively to quantitative research studies in order to support the application of effective hypnosis interventions, he raises serious questions when such unilateral approaches are deified and used exclusively, especially in psychotherapeutic research. He emphasises the benefits from the application of more qualitative models of research, which are predominantly hermeneutic or interpretative in style, as they involve the actions and subjective experiences of the patient in a collaborative context with the therapist. However, he recognises the complementary role of the two approaches, and encourages clinicians to utilise both qualitative and quantitative research methods to evaluate their therapeutic work.

Many of us have witnessed and were impressed by the author's effective use of hypnosis with psychodynamic and cathartic procedures in helping patients uncover and illuminate the origin of traumatic events and experiences. In his therapeutic work, Dr Hawkins also demonstrates the effective use of a technically integrative approach for the treatment of a wide variety of stress-related problems. I believe that the reader of this book will get a flavour of the author's ingenuity and will gain a better understanding of the important role of modern hypnosis in the hands of the trained clinician.

Nikitas Polemikos, PhD
Professor of Psychology, University of the Aegean, Greece

Preface

I cannot profess to know very much about gardening. However, I do know that careful preparation of the soil and tendering of young flora can achieve much healthier plants. The seeds are best planted in a nurturing growing environment where there is an appropriate balance of soil constituents and where water and heat are optimally available. When the conditions are correct, the seed germinates and a small green shoot appears from beneath the soil. As the young plant is watered by the spring rains, and then enjoys the early summer sun, it grows stronger and stronger and, in time, tiny buds appear that eventually flower. As summer progresses the fruits ripen, changing from green to yellow to red, and eventually drop to the ground where the seeds germinate once again and flourish in the nurturing soil. And so the growth process begins again, as winter changes into spring, and spring changes into summer, and summer changes into autumn and into winter again – a continuous cycle of often imperceptible change. In the same place yet a different place in time and space and evolution!

This book is written primarily for practising clinicians (psychologists, physicians, dentists, counsellors and psychotherapists) and does not intend to debate current theories of hypnosis, although requisite attention is given to the theoretical basis of the interventions as well as to research issues. In order to assist the clinician who is beginning to learn the techniques of hypnosis, a number of abridged 'clinical scripts' are provided throughout the text, not only for 'trance' inductions, but also for the ensuing psychological interventions. It should, however, be remembered that these abbreviated scripts are not necessarily to be followed verbatim. They are to be used as a 'template' in order to construct innovative and, usually lengthier, interventions that are appropriate for the patients and their problems. Experienced hypnotherapists soon learn to trust in the creativity of their own 'inner therapist', as well as utilising the 'patient as therapist'. Eventually, it is hoped that the clinician will forget the transcripts entirely and just 'do therapy' in a similar way to musicians who improvise and just 'play music from their heart'. However, musicians' extemporisations are based on a sound knowledge of musical structures and techniques along with many hours of experience. As a consequence, it is implicitly recognised that there is no standard way of doing hypnotherapy and hence it is impossible to write a 'do it yourself' text for clinicians or patients.

The major purpose of this text is to hopefully stimulate the inner creativities and imaginations of practising clinicians so that they are better able to assist patients to utilise their own resources to find solutions to their stress-related problems. It should be emphasised, however, that adequate training in psychotherapy is a prerequisite for practising hypnosis, regardless of whether the professional is a psychologist, physician, psychiatrist, dentist or social worker. In the light of this assertion, considerable attention is given to a discussion of issues that are often ignored in books on hypnosis; for example, the management of catharsis, and the importance of common curative factors in psychotherapy.

In the context of clinical interventions, an attempt is made to provide an integrative and holistic perspective that combines both traditional and Ericksonian approaches. Although there are few 'scientific' studies to support many of the clinical interventions proposed, it can be argued that they are clinically valid in that patients often get well without knowing why this is the case. Nevertheless, the number of studies reporting the efficacy of clinical hypnosis is rapidly increasing, and reference will be made to recent research wherever possible.

The approach to practising clinical hypnosis adopted in this book, both within psychotherapeutic as well as more traditional medical contexts, is an attempt to apply a democratic and reciprocal principle involving choice and self-determination where patient and therapist work together to find solutions. This view promulgates the idea that patients have the conscious and unconscious resources available, but require assistance from a caring facilitator to help them 'sing their song'. It also implies that individuals participate in their own 'illness' and hence their own health, through a combination of mental, physical and emotional factors. The influence of the work of Erickson and Rossi is evident throughout, although it is important to recognise that the theories, practice and research drawn from generic psychotherapy have also made a significant contribution. Importantly, experiential learnings provided by my patients and students over many years of practice as a hypnotherapist have been extremely significant in the development of clinical protocols.

Some of the case studies presented in the book took place in a single workshop demonstration session. Demonstrations in front of a professional group provide an excellent environment for clinical hypnosis as engaging in private work in public is inherently exciting and stimulating. Mesmer must have recognised this fact, as he performed his healing 'miracles' in front of a group. However, it should be recognised that for the majority of patients experiencing stress-related problems, often with complex histories, psychotherapy requires more than one session and maybe a considerable number. No attempt has been made to offer prescriptions with respect to the number of sessions required for specific problems, as there are too many variables involved that relate to the patient, the problem, the general milieu and the overall treatment strategy. Each individual clinician, in collaboration with the patient, is the best judge of the number of sessions, their frequency and duration to include in an initial contract, as well as the number and frequency of 'follow-ups'. At the end of the day the therapy will take 'as long as it takes', bearing in mind that 'you can't win them all'. Erickson (1977) sums it up as follows:

> You've got to do it slowly, you've got to do it gradually, and you've got to do it in the order in which he can assimilate it. A certain number of calories of food per day are necessary, but don't cram them all down at breakfast; if you do, you'll have stomach ache. You spread them out and you don't cram them all down in one mouthful. You take a number of mouthfuls. It's the same way with psychotherapy, as any analytically trained person will tell you. You go into some matters slowly, easily, and gently. In the matter of hypnotic psychotherapy you approach everything as slowly and as rapidly as the patient can endure the material. (p. 20)

The title *Hypnosis and Stress* is so inclusive that almost the whole field of clinical hypnosis could have been included, which would have made the book an overwhelming tome. It could be argued that all psychological and physical problems that reflect the human condition have a stress element with respect to aetiology, coping, diagnostic examinations, waiting for and receiving the diagnosis, treatment and fear of reoccurrence. Jung (1938/1969) reminded us of this in a rather tongue-in-cheek manner when he wrote:

> You can say, for instance, that life is a disease with a very bad prognosis: it lingers on for years, only to end with death; or that normality is a general constitutional defect; or that man is an animal with a fatally overgrown brain. This kind of thinking is the prerogative of habitual grumblers with bad digestions. (pp. 64–105, para. 167)

The issues discussed, and the stress-related problems described, have been chosen primarily because they are a reflection of my own clinical work with patients over a period of almost three decades. There are omissions with respect to specific issues and problems (e.g. addictions, cardiovascular problems), of course, but I hope that sufficient guidelines have been provided that can allow clinicians to use hypnotherapy with their own patients. Though the text is not offered as a complete clinical guide to replace what practitioners are already doing, hopefully it will allow clinicians to become more creative and intuitive professionals within their own spheres of expertise.

Throughout the book, the individual being hypnotised or being discussed in the context of a problem is referred to as a patient. Initially, the use of 'patient' rather than the nominally less pejorative 'client' may seem to be at odds with the overall phenomenological-humanistic stance described above.

However, many of the symptomatologies addressed and the interventions suggested are as relevant to physicians as they are to counsellors and psychologists, who usually prefer 'client'. Moreover, the 'patients' referred to are considered to be responsible for their own health and lives. Indeed, one of the major tenets of the overall philosophic approach is self-hypnosis and self-determination.

I was recently walking in the old port of Chania in Crete when I noticed the following written on a wall in the old part of the city: 'I'm sure of only one thing that I know. The one thing that I know is that I know nothing'. This statement, which was inscribed in Modern Greek, was a paraphrase of the famous old dictum attributed to Socrates. I consider this to be an appropriate attitude for all psychotherapists both before their training as well as afterwards. After a lifetime of practising therapy it is still true, since one realises even more the limits of one's knowledge. Training in psychotherapy never ends. Hopefully this book will provide information to allow clinicians to become better 'technicians', but above all to become creative, compassionate and ethical clinicians who are able to utilise their inner inspirations and resourcefulness to assist in the facilitation of patient healing.

As you read or consult this book you will probably become aware of contradictions, paradoxes, inconsistencies, confusions, repetitions and unanswered questions. Indeed, it might be argued that the book is a metaphor for the way in which our personal lives and the world in general are organised. This assertion might also apply to the field of psychotherapy and hypnotherapy.

There are times when, like all 'artists', we recognise that our inner creativities and inspirations do not flow, creative improvisation is lacking, and innovation and spontaneity are in a quiescent state. At these times we may feel like giving up and becoming long-distance lorry drivers, taking a holiday, or simply doing nothing. Perhaps this is a good thing – to be able to recognise that we are not gods and cannot walk on water, that we cannot facilitate the healing process in every patient. To take some time out from what, after all, is a very stressful pursuit, is valuable, since if we do not look after ourselves who will? A time for restoration, a couch to relax on can allow the inspiration to flow from the heart again, as it eventually will, but we can't make it happen. At some time in the future, sooner or later, the creativity will once again flow like the improvisatory notes of a musician or the words of a poet. However, in the meantime, whilst waiting for the passion to be rekindled and flow forth again, we can be psychotherapy 'technicians' utilising a range of techniques from our repertoires that may still be of considerable benefit to our patients. It is my contention that all therapists at some time should consider retiring from the profession through feelings of tiredness or simply because they feel that their therapeutic work is satisfactory but rather pedestrian, lacking in flair and creativity. If you never feel like this, maybe you should leave the profession or alternatively try walking on water. Please let me know whether you get wet or not!

A decade ago I wrote:

I would like to suggest that the use of hypnosis in health care is alive and well. It has a well-established pedigree, which has not always been recognised. It has an ill-founded reputation that is still promulgated today by the popular media and also, unfortunately by some departments of psychology and medical schools. There is a lively theoretical debate, and many reports of clinical and experimental work. But it is important for both academic and practising psychologists and physicians to enter this debate by engaging in more sustained empirical and clinical research, both quantitative and qualitative, and for institutions to introduce the study of hypnosis into their curriculum (Hawkins, 1994a, p. 6).

These assertions still hold true today. During the past 10 years a significant number of research papers and clinical studies have been published, and the majority of those referred to in the ensuing pages are post-1994. However, such is the wealth of published material that only the most relevant studies have been referenced. I'm sure that there are omissions, but hopefully you will be inspired to trace these and keep up to date with future publications. Indeed, this is part of the process of ongoing professional development.

I wish all students of clinical hypnosis, as well as experienced clinicians, who read this book a long life of creative and enjoyable endeavour.

Peter J. Hawkins
ISMAI, University Institute of Maia, Portugal

Acknowledgements

To list everyone who has made a contribution to the ideas and inspiration behind this book would fill a volume in itself. However, there are some who command a special thanks. Judith, my wife, for her patience and understanding, and the following colleagues who have provided stimulating environments for me to discuss and disseminate my hypnotherapeutic work: Antonio Capafons, Jose Gongora, Agostinho Almeida and the ISMAI Hypnosis Group in Portugal, Ana Almeida, Richard Page, Joannis Nestoros, Nikitas Polimikos, Eleanor O'Leary, Adriana Baban, Marcella Matucci and the Rome Hypnosis Group, Jarl Wahlstrom, Geoff Graham, Filippo Petrucelli, Guillem Feixas and the hypnosis group in Barcelona, Ana Paula Relvas, Laura Barnaby, Juan Abellán and the hypnosis students in Castellón, Spain.

Special thanks must also go to all those students and professionals who have attended my workshops throughout the world, in Russia, China, Central Asia and most European countries, and from whom I have learned so much. Last, but not least, a tribute to all my patients from whom I have learned much of what I know about psychotherapy.

Chapter 1
Contextual Understandings

A man drove to a bar one evening and parked his car alongside the pavement nearby. He went into the bar and had several drinks and left after a couple of hours. He walked to his car and searched his coat and trousers pockets for the keys, but could not find them, so he started to look around the car and further along the pavement. A policeman noticed him, went over and asked what he was doing, to which the man replied that he was just looking for his lost keys. Being a very friendly policeman he offered to help and the two of them searched for the lost keys. After a short while, with no sign of the keys, the policeman asked the man whether he was sure that the keys had been lost in that particular place. The man replied that he had not lost the keys near the car, but in the bushes, which were some distance away. The policeman was rather surprised and a little angry to hear this since he had wasted considerable time looking for the keys. 'Then why are we looking here?' asked the policeman, to which the man replied, 'Because it's lighter here!'

Introduction

The clinical interventions made by psychotherapists are usually based, at least to some extent, on the theoretical and philosophical beliefs that the therapist holds, along with the important learnings that develop through his or her experience of working with patients. This can sometimes lead to a degree of inflexibility where the locus of the intervention is the school or faith adhered to rather than the patients themselves. The 'map', or 'story', is presented as the current view of the field – for example, hypnotherapy – and is constructed by the therapist from his or her training and the reading of books and journals that present contemporary research. However, what constitutes 'good' research in the context of psychotherapy is controversial (Salmon, 1983; Murcott, 2005), as will be discussed later. It is therefore most likely that the 'map does not constitute the territory'. In other words, there are always alternative ways of construing the clinical reality. The approach adopted in this book is essentially built around the concept of 'utilisation' where the starting point is the patient rather than the theoretical and philosophical frameworks or 'stories'. It should also be recognised that therapists cannot always act from reflection and deliberation, and that much of their contribution to the therapy session will be spontaneous and intuitive interventions based on the utilisation of the patient's verbal and non-verbal behaviours. It is only after the session that it is possible to make some theoretical sense of the interventions.

Although there is a sense in which the emphasis of this book is on the development of clinical approaches in hypnotherapy, it is important to recognise the importance of the contextual aspects of psychotherapy in general and hypnotherapy in particular. The remainder of this chapter will be devoted to an examination of the major contexts in which clinical hypnosis is practised.

The Political Context

Even though the emphasis in hypnotherapy is on personal change – for example, in managing stress and its psychosomatic consequences – it is important to recognise the political dimensions of psychotherapy. For a start it could be argued that hypnotherapy and psychotherapy are political activities in that they recognise the power relationship that is both implicitly and explicitly defined with respect to professionals and their patients.

Acknowledging that patients are rational, intelligent and creative human beings with the capacity to find solutions to their problems redresses the conventional medical view that the professional has the answers. The tendency for the professional to give advice, prescribe, assess, diagnose, interpret and analyse, although sometimes appropriate, should not be carried out compulsively in the manner that 'the doctor knows best'. As Heron (1998a) eloquently puts it:

> Diagnosis, labelling, interpretation, analysis, assessment – a kind of endless intellectual prodding and poking of the client – is the favoured device of the helper to keep both the client's distresses conveniently at bay and repressed, and above all to keep the helper's own distresses firmly battened down, so that at no time will the issue of the helper's cathartic competence be allowed to come to the fore. A diagnosis a day keeps distress at bay. Helper and client are locked into complementary distortions, and so sustain from without what was originally set up from within. (p. 10)

The view adopted in this book is that patients have the answers to their problems, but that the actualisation of these potentials often requires professional assistance. However, this view does not alter the fact that, often, some extrinsic medical or social intervention is required. Nor does it subscribe to any idea that implies that the methods of hypnotherapy and personal development are a panacea for positive change. Nevertheless, as Madanes (2001) reflects, 'Therapy makes it possible to talk about the unacceptable. Therapy is about change and rebellion' (p. 23).

One important corollary of the view that the patient has the resources to find solutions to his or her problems is that he or she can learn to 'do it themselves'. Teaching the patient self-hypnosis is one of the most significant aspects of the politics of hypnotherapy, as it transfers the power from the professional to the patient. It is a profound act of deprofessionalisation, which recognises the essential quality of human beings to be self-directive and in control. It is now increasingly appreciated that individuals participate in their own (ill) health to a considerable degree, and once they recognise this they can be encouraged to play a significant role in their own 'treatment'. Often, health professionals, including psychologists, physicians and counsellors, undermine the potential of people to deal with their own lives in a personal and autonomous way. This can reduce people to the status of passive 'consumers' who are no longer taking part in their own treatment and healing, a process which Illich (1975) referred to as 'structural iatrogenesis'.

It should be recognised that the relationship between the clinician and the patient is implicitly (i.e. politically) defined. Bannister (1983) states this succinctly as follows:

> Psychotherapy happens within the context of an institution (with or without walls) and the institution happens within the context of a society. It follows that, in psychotherapy, the political themes of institution and society, their power structures, are immanent. Therapists and clients swim in political waters. (p. 139)

Bannister argues that the doctor–patient relationship is the most traditional style of relationship and accords with the medical model implicit in psychiatry. However, the patient usually views the therapist as an important and significant person where a positive transference develops. Nevertheless, the therapeutic alliance can be positively or negatively influenced by the therapists' social status, appearance (height, weight, clothing, facial expression), office furniture (e.g. psychoanalytic couch), face-to-face therapy, paintings, plants, framed diplomas, and so on.

Although many of the examples provided in the book suggest approaches that assist the patient in finding solutions to his or her individual stress, it is recognised that many of the problems are the result of wider political situations; for example, poverty, geography, education, housing, racism, sexism, street crime, job insecurity, financial debt, lack of perceived democratic process and disenfranchisement, centralisation of decision making, and so on. Many 'counselling consumers' require material help rather than, or as well as, psychotherapy. Their distress is more closely linked with environmental situations rather than deep internal longings and dissatisfaction. It should be recognised, though, that patients are not the passive victims of psychological or political determinism, but agents in a social world. Of course, there is a major paradox here in that psychotherapeutic experience suggests that individuals are both responsible for their actions and, yet, not able to account for them on a personal level. This view justifies an approach that involves both the personal and political dimensions (Halmos, 1978). Pirsig (1974), in the *Zen and the Art of Motorcycle Maintenance*, states it expressively in the following way:

> Programmes of a political nature are important and products of social quality that can be effective only if the underlying structure of social values is right. The social values are right only if the individual values are right. The place to improve the world is first in one's own heart and head and hands, and then work outside from there. (p. 121)

Therapists have the necessary skills to help an individual deal with stress as well as possible psychosomatic and behavioural consequences, but they are not usually in a position where they can act as political change agents. It is important that they recognise the limitations of their professional interventions and work with other health professionals, social workers and policy makers in promulgating change at both personal and political levels.

Individuals need to manage personal stress successfully in order to avoid negative consequences. However, there are also important economic reasons. In both Europe and the US, many millions of working days are lost each year because of stress. Stress at work also provides a serious risk of litigation for all employers and organisations, which can ultimately be very costly. Hence there are strong economic and financial reasons for organisations to manage and reduce stress in the work place, aside from the obvious humanitarian and ethical considerations.

The Personal Context

It is recognised that psychotherapy is a very demanding and stressful occupation that can lead to 'burn out' and consequent psychosomatic problems. Madanes (2001) contends that many therapists become limited by negative emotions such as anger, frustration, fear, disappointment and hopelessness. She advocates the cultivation of positive emotions such as love, gratitude, curiosity, compassion, determination, flexibility, confidence, vitality and the wish to contribute. It should also be remembered that therapists lead very similar lives to their patients, in suffering, ill health and, eventually, dying. Consequently, it is essential that clinicians develop ways in which they can remain 'healthy' and continue functioning at an optimal level. If this is not done then their health suffers, and they are unable to give their patients the service they require.

The psychological well-being of the clinician can be maintained and enhanced by, for example, the development of peer-support networks (co-counselling or peer counselling). This is a personal-development method used by the author on psychotherapy and clinical hypnosis-training courses organised for professionals. Co-counselling (Heron, 1998b) is a method of self-directed therapy that allows the clinician to deal with the stress of his or her everyday life with the cooperation of a supportive peer. In this way a degree of psychosomatic health is maintained. It should be noted here that co-counselling is not the same as supervision. Every therapist should have regular supervision (Clarkson, 1996), but from someone other than his or her co-counsellor. It is also clear that co-counselling is not the same as non-reciprocal therapy, as this is 'one way', and is usually conducted on a financial/business basis.

In order to become, and continue to be, an effective therapist, two essential items of equipment are also necessary: a couch and a waste-paper basket.

A couch is a valuable asset for the therapist, as it can be used to:

• Lie down on when exhausted, when struggling or taking things too seriously – to relax, to restore, to meditate, to engage in self-hypnosis and psychophysiological healing, to receive a massage.
• Retire to when we think that we know – to let go of our assumptions.
• Co-counsel – to work through the stress (historical/current) in our own lives; to dream of our own hopes and aspirations, to celebrate our own strengths and achievements; to validate peers and colleagues (they need praise and encouragement); to work through our own 'grief', feelings of impotence, existential anxieties, of worries about illness, incapacity, senility, old age, death, and so on.

The waste-paper basket enables clinicians to dispose of all their assumptions about patients in their care, along with the theories and techniques that get in the way of being 'co-present' with patients, in order to ensure maximum rapport and empathy. Such explanations for our patients' behaviours, thoughts and feelings, as well as our own, only partially represent the truth. They are the 'stories' in which we attempt to make sense of our patients' problems. Psychotherapy may be defined as a subject in which we never know what we are talking about, or whether what we are saying is true, or whether what we are doing works. In other words, the paradigms (or stories) that we employ constrain our visions and hence limit our creativity and the potential of our therapeutic effectiveness, and consequently patient functioning. If we know what a patient should be doing/experiencing with respect to given social/developmental normative models, then we are likely to 'struggle' to

understand what is happening, and also struggle to determine specific therapeutic outcomes. In 'non-struggle' the clinician does not necessarily leave the
patient entirely alone, but utilises what is happening. This involves being co-
present with the patient – listening, holding, touching, challenging, confronting, allowing, informing, empathising, curtailing, laughing, and so on.
In being co-present with the patient we are with the patient as he or she
engages in the process of autonomous rebirth, the latter being defined in
terms of the potential functioning of the individual. In engaging in our role
as 'midwife', we satisfy the three basic psychological needs of all human
beings: the need to be loved, respected and cared for as unique individuals;
the need to understand what is going on in our lives (including our physical
functioning); and the need to be self-directed and to have a sense of control
over our own lives (Heron, 1998a).

When the therapist is co-present with the patient, changes occur *festina
lente* (literally, hasten slowly), without either the patient or the therapist trying
to do anything or make anything happen. Remember the tortoise and the
hare! Essentially, this means that the therapist empties his or her mind of any
fantasies he or she may have regarding the nature of the problems (diagnoses,
prognoses, preferred therapeutic strategies, etc.). Only then can the therapist
really listen with what Reik (1948) calls the 'third ear'. The patient is then
able to tell his or her story. By listening to the patient 'speak', of telling and
retelling, the 'speak' meanders like a novel with a ragbag of concerns. It concerns the simple events that give continuity and context to life, and provides
its essential meaning. As the stories unfold, a different perspective develops
as the patient 'works through', often with associated pain and anguish, his
or her fears, anger, guilt, sadness, sorrow, remorse and loneliness, as well as
hopes and dreams.

In addition to emptying the assumptions, prejudices and biases into the
waste-bin, therapists also need to throw away the debris in their own lives. This
means putting themselves in the position of patients. In order to do this effectively, someone, for example, a co-counsellor, has to be co-present with the
therapist – to listen non-judgementally, so that he or she can tell his or her
story. As therapists we must also remember that we are not indispensable. It
is arrogant to believe that the patient needs us. How can the therapist be co-
present with the patient if the therapist believes that the patient really does
need him or her!

> As therapists we need to keep our optimism, and our faith in the tremendous
> resources that sick and frightened people have for getting well. We need to
> show them that we have confidence in this potential, and yet at the same time
> remove ourselves from the role of feeling that we are the healers and they are
> the pitiful victims. We are all potential patients, we are all human beings, none
> of us are indispensable, we are all vulnerable. To be maximally effective as a
> therapist it is important to look after ourselves. Is it time out, or burn out?
> (Hawkins, 1994b, p. 852)

Supervision and the scientist-practitioner model

The scientist-practitioner model is a method of enhancing reflective learning as well as providing a creative assessment of personal and professional functioning. Clarkson (2003) offers a metaphor for self-supervision based on the scientist-practitioner model. She discusses five elements, which comprise the model (pp. 295–96):

- an idea or goal, purpose, contract, direction or outcome measure;
- a scientific paradigm;
- units of analysis or attention, for example, transactions, dream images, type of relationship;
- an attitude of interest, curiosity about one's skills and process;
- a desire to make a contribution to the common stock of clinical knowledge.

For further discussion of the scientist-practitioner model and supervision issues refer to Clarkson and Aviram (1998).

The Research Context

It is important for hypnotherapists to recognise that the research evidence for the efficacy of hypnosis interventions is limited, and generally does not satisfy the criteria for evidence-based medicine and psychotherapy, even though the clinical evidence is often compelling. It should also be noted here that the methods by which medical science evaluates the efficacy of healthcare interventions is wholly inadequate. Funding is an important issue in that clinical trials are inordinately expensive, and only the pharmaceutical business can generally afford them. Consequently, the majority of research projects are concerned with the efficacy of drug interventions rather than psychotherapeutic ones.

The randomised controlled trial (RCT)

The randomised controlled trial (RCT) is the quintessential research method (Murcott, 2005; Roberts, 2005; Iphofen, Corin & Ringwood-Walker, 2005). Put simply, in the RCT patients are randomly assigned to clinical interventions where groups are treated equally apart from the one under investigation. As long as there is a sufficient number of patients in the trial, it is possible to say that any differences between the groups are due to the intervention rather than other factors. In clinical trials, the RCT design is further improved by the use of placebos and blinding (for further discussion refer to Roberts, 2005). However, it is logically clear that such methods are not appropriate for the evaluation of hypnotherapy, which may also explain the paucity of published research in the fields of complementary and alternative medicine more generally. Reasons for the problematic nature of the RCT for evaluating hypnotherapy are summarised by Roberts (2005) as follows:

> The concept of randomisation, that is, allocating patients to a therapy on the basis of a coin toss has been argued to be in direct conflict with the nature of many complementary therapies whereby joint decision making and the patients' choice and beliefs are fundamental. Ethical issues also come into play with the concept of randomisation. Typically it is argued that for a patient to enter a trial where they will be allocated to a treatment by chance, both the patient and the doctor must be in a state of equipoise. By this we mean that they genuinely are uncertain about which treatment would be most efficacious. If either the doctor or patient believe that one treatment option would suit them better than another, they should receive this treatment and should not be entered into a trial. The ethical requirement for trials conflicts with belief systems implicated in treatments such as hypnotherapy, whereby optimal care can only be achieved when both the patient and the treating therapist have belief in the treatment. This is not to say the treatment works only through faith but that the belief in benefit is a fundamental concept in the delivery of high quality effective treatment. (p. 18)

Arguably, it would be extremely difficult to find psychotherapists or patients who were genuinely equipoised. Also, it would be virtually impossible to standardise hypnotherapeutic interventions because the fundamental tenet of the personalisation of treatment would be compromised. It has already been emphasised that the clinical scripts presented in this book must be adapted and individually tailored to the patient's needs. Also, it must be remembered that hypnotherapy takes place in the context of a profound therapeutic relationship. Roberts (2005) argues that the partially randomised trial or preference trial may be a suitable methodological compromise. She writes:

> It is possible to recruit patients to a trial where they receive their choice of therapy where a preference exists but are randomly allocated where they do not express a treatment preference. This allows us to build into the study design that concept that choice and belief is a fundamental concept in treatment but will also allow us to look separately at the benefits accrued in groups who did not state a preference, thus helping to unpick somewhat the difference in benefit experienced by those who would not choose the therapy themselves. There remains the risk that we end up with different groups and we lose some of the methodological benefits of the RCT design but dependent on our question this may be an acceptable compromise.
>
> Trials are the best way of demonstrating effectiveness and cost-effectiveness, but they must be designed in a way that allows for the mechanisms of the therapy to work as they would in practice, and using outcomes that are sensitive not only to changes in the disease, but also holistic change, which may be accrued by the therapy.
>
> Trial design should therefore be something undertaken by teams with methodological expertise but also with an understanding of hypnotherapy – its

delivery and mechanics. Trial design should allow for the incorporation of multiple methods to address all aspects of therapy. (pp. 18–19)

Murcott has also argued that it is likely that the randomly controlled trials conducted thus far have been insufficiently sophisticated properly to measure outcomes in complementary therapy. The paucity of evidence in favour of complementary therapies probably says more about naive research methodology than it does about the treatments under study.

The current practice of trying to carry across the methods of exploration and research that have been developed in general psychology, and to apply these in a psychotherapeutic domain, is essentially a hopeless task (Mair, 1989). Wilson and Barkham (1994) contend that: 'There is an over-reliance on the logic of the randomised clinical trial, which is distant and alien to the rich experience of psychotherapy' (p. 49). They also assert that comparative outcome trials are rarely suited to individual practice unless carried out in collaboration with colleagues and a well-equipped research centre. This is a strong argument in the context of individual practice where hypnotherapists want to evaluate the effectiveness of their work. On another level, it can be argued that outcome studies are based on a false scientific premise that pieces of reality can be captured and quantified. This is important when set in the context of the issue of non-specific curative factors to be discussed later in this chapter. If there are certain factors common to therapies, there is a clear need to be able to identify which of these factors is effective. Rice and Greenberg (1984) express this well when they suggest that in order to answer questions about treatment effectiveness, a clearer understanding of what happens between patient and therapist must be gained. One way to attempt this is to examine qualitatively the process of the sessions rather than to focus exclusively on outcomes. In any event, outcome research should be related to process research, and there is no reason why the two should not be combined together (Treacher, 1983). Laing (1983) captures the essence of the problem when he writes:

> Experience is not an objective fact. A scientific fact need not be experienced. The differences or correlations, similarities and dissimilarities that we experience as events only sometimes correspond to those differences or correlations we regard as objectively real. Every schoolboy and schoolgirl knows that appearances are deceptive.
>
> We have to clear a space for the discussion of experience as such, because the methods used to investigate the objective world, applied to us, are blind to our experience, necessarily so, and cannot relate to our experience. Such blind method, applied blindly to us, is liable to destroy us in practice, as it has done already in theory. (p. 9)

Of course, the lack of scientific evidence for the effectiveness of most complementary and alternative medicine (CAM) approaches can lead to the possibility of erroneous conclusions and other reasons for their continued lack of recommendation for use within the National Health Service (House of Lords Select Committee, 2000).

Evidence-based medicine

Evidence-based medicine is the conscientious, explicit and judicious use of current best evidence in making decisions about the care of individual patients (Sackett, Rosenberg & Gray, 1996; see www.cebm.net for further information). However, 'current best evidence' is generally based on the use of the RCT which, as we have seen, is problematic in the context of evaluating hypnotherapy. Nevertheless, Sackett et al. offer a somewhat more optimistic view of evidence-based medicine in the context of CAM:

> The practice of evidence-based medicine means integrating individual clinical expertise with the best available external clinical evidence from systematic research. By individual clinical expertise we mean the proficiency and judgement that individual clinicians acquire through clinical experience and clinical practice. Increased expertise is reflected in many ways, but especially in more effective and efficient diagnosis and in the more thoughtful identification and compassionate use of individual patient's predicaments, rights and preferences in making clinical decisions about their care. By best available external clinical evidence we mean clinically relevant research, often from the basic sciences of medicine, but especially from patient-centred clinical research into the accuracy and precision of diagnostic tests (including the clinical examination), the power of prognostic markers, and the efficacy and safety of therapeutic, rehabilitative and preventative regimes. External clinical evidence both invalidates previously accepted diagnostic tests and treatments and replaces them with new ones that are more powerful, more accurate, more efficacious and safer. (p. 71)

Although this extended definition refers to the practice of medicine, it can also be applied, with modification, to the practices of psychotherapy and hypnotherapy. Good therapists use both individual clinical expertise and the best available external evidence, which promotes them as evidence-based practitioners. Even where there is good external evidence, judicious clinical judgement with respect to the individual needs of patients is still an essential requirement. In this respect, Sackett et al. state:

> External clinical evidence can inform, but can never replace, individual clinical expertise, and it is this expertise that decides whether the external evidence applies to the individual patient at all and, if so, how it should be integrated into a clinical decision. (p. 71)

Inherent in these views is an assumption that an evidence-based psychotherapy need not adhere rigidly to a research-based positivism, but can embrace a philosophical, scientific, political and social shift towards an expanded view of what constitutes scientific evidence (Chwalisz, 2003). However, the development and implementation of pluralistic methodologies for the evaluation of hypnotherapy is extremely expensive and time consuming, and support from funding bodies is unlikely. The major dilemma posed here is that between carrying out small-scale qualitative research projects, which do not satisfy the requirements of currently accepted evidence-based criteria, and those that ostensibly do. Methodological 'compromises' have been criticised by Wilson (2005) who contends that:

> I would encourage researchers to develop methodologically robust evaluations of this complex intervention and seek resources to undertake the comprehensive large-scale evaluations that will be taken notice of by the healthcare establishment. (p. 20)

One important issue to address with respect to evidence concerns the question of 'successful treatment'. This should not be equated with 'cure', which implies a 'total' elimination of pathology and an induction of a healthy state of well-being. To be hopeful of such a goal in hypnotherapy with stress-related problems is probably idealistic in many cases, and to offer a cure to patients may be naive and irresponsible. Issues relating to therapeutic objectives should obviously be discussed with the patients in the initial session and some agreement reached with respect to realistic gaols. It should, of course, also be a major consideration when planning any research project.

Alternative methodologies

Some of the criticisms of the RCT and outcome studies can be surmounted by the development of more qualitative phenomenological models of action research, which focus on the experiences of patients and the therapeutic relationship. Reason and Bradbury (2001a) define action research as:

> a participatory, democratic process concerned with developing practical knowing in the pursuit of worthwhile human purposes, grounded in a participatory worldview.... It seeks to bring together action and reflection, theory and practice, in participation with others, in the pursuit of practical solutions to issues of pressing concern to people, and more generally the flourishing of individual persons and their communities. (p. 1)

Such methods are differentiated from quantitative methodologies in that interpretations of actions and experiences are involved. Both the therapist and the patient can reflect on designated actions and experiences and attempt to make sense of them, with respect to mutually agreed therapeutic goals. In this way, knowledge about what is happening in therapy (process), the effects of therapy (outcome), and the meaning that this has for both therapist and patient is 'constructed'. Debatably, this approach to research is a more egalitarian mode of inquiry that generates 'local contextual understandings' on the grounds that the meaningfulness of actions and events is an intrinsic part of the 'naturalistic context' (Henwood & Nicolson, 1995). Importantly, too, it could be asserted that the development of experiential methods of research based on subjective experience is more consonant with the humanistic-oriented theoretical frameworks and hypnotherapeutic approaches presented in this book. This is particularly true with respect to cooperative inquiry (Reason & Rowan, 1981; Reason, 1988, 2001; Reason & Heron, 1995; Heron, 1996, 2001; Heron & Reason, 1997; Reason & Bradbury, 2001a; for further papers by Reason see www.bath.ac.uk/carpp/papers.htm), which involves the collaborative participation of both experimenter (i.e. clinician) and subjects (i.e. patients).

Most traditional psychotherapy research involves little authentic collaboration where the patient is passive and dependent and is the recipient of a therapeutic programme unilaterally designed and managed by the therapist. The methodology of cooperative inquiry draws on a fourfold-extended epistemology (Heron, 1992, 1996) namely:

• experiential knowing – through empathy, compassion and resonance;
• presentational knowing – expression through narrative, drawing, movement and aesthetic imagery;
• propositional knowing – drawing on theoretical concepts and ideas;
• practical knowing – a consummation of the other forms of knowing in clinical intervention.

Within the domain of clinical practice these participative forms of inquiry have a political dimension in that they empower people through the process of constructing and using their own knowledge (Reason & Bradbury, 2001a). Such a political dimension is implicit in the general clinical approach adopted in this book. Further information on action research in professional practice can be found at www.bath.ac.uk/~mnspwr/ and www.human-inquiry.com.

An example of a partial cooperative research approach into the use of hypnosis in the treatment of sleeping problems in children is provided in Chapter 8.

As well as cooperative inquiry methods there are many other qualitative methods that could be useful in evaluating psychotherapy, including observation, interviewing, personal construct approaches, ethnography, task analytic procedures (Greenberg 1991), clinical case studies (Hilliard, 1993), grounded theory (Henwood & Pidgeon, 1995; Glaser & Strauss, 1967) and interpretive phenomenological analysis (Smith, Jarman & Osborn, 1999). These are systematically reviewed in Bannister, Burman, Parker, Taylor and Tindall (1994), Denzin and Lincoln (1994) and McLeod (1994).

One question that needs to be asked concerns the complementarity of the quantitative, largely positivistic, traditional approaches and the qualitative approaches mentioned above, which are predominantly hermeneutic or interpretative in style, and heavily influenced by classical phenomenology (see Stevenson & Cooper, 1997). What is required in psychotherapy research is an intensive study of the individual patient (or groups of patients) so that both idiographic and nomothetic perspectives can be developed within a methodological pluralism. This does not mean that qualitative methods replace the more traditional quantitative methods, but that the two approaches are combined in ways that are complementary and synergistic.

Rennie and Toukmanian (1992) argue that the two ways of knowing, the paradigmatic and the narrative, can be combined in research in two major ways:

- by ensuring that each research team includes researchers who are expert in each mode;
- employing data from both narrative and paradigmatic methods at different phases of the research programme.

Bergin and Garfield (1994) have actively encouraged this development of methodological pluralism in psychotherapy. They write:

> The growing endorsement of narrative, descriptive and qualitative approaches represents a rather significant shift in attitude that is likely to become more and more manifest in the conduct and reporting of inquiries. We find ourselves endorsing a kind of pluralism that does not throw out the virtues of the traditional approaches to research, but complements these with a variety of more flexible techniques for getting at the complexity of the phenomena we deal with. (p. 828)

Throughout the book references are made to research studies, mainly quantitative, that support the use of hypnosis interventions. Details of recent hypnosis research literature can be found at www.hypnosis-research.org, and in a recent paper by Solloway (2004a). There is little 'scientific' research evidence to support Ericksonian interventions apart from numerous individual case studies, which in themselves are ultimately compelling.

The Psychotherapy Context

Although this book is primarily concerned with the use of hypnosis for helping people deal with stress-related problems, there are other therapeutic factors that play an important role in the healing process. It is therefore necessary for the hypnotherapist to have some understanding of these 'extra' factors, for reasons that will be obvious. Relevant research has shown that:

(i) different therapies have, in general, similar outcome results and
(ii) there is no single therapeutic approach that is clearly superior to any
     other for treating specific problems.

This has been stated as the dodo bird verdict that 'everyone has won and all
must have prizes' (Luborsky, 1995).

Common factors

Based on reviews of outcome psychotherapy research, Lambert (1992) concluded that 40% of therapeutic improvement can be attributed to 'extrathera-
peutic change' (e.g. fortuitous events, social support, ego strength, etc.),
30% to 'common factors' that are found in all therapies regardless of the therapist's theoretical orientation, and 15% to the 'techniques' of the specific
psychotherapies (e.g. systematic desensitisation, hypnosis). Although no psychotherapy is superior to any other, all are superior to no treatment (Lambert
& Bergin, 1994). The common factors approach (e.g. Frank, 1973; Lambert
& Bergin, 1994) seeks to determine the core ingredients that different therapies share in common, with the eventual goal of creating more parsimonious,
efficacious and integrative treatments based on those commonalities.

However, the various psychotherapeutic schools do not demonstrate all the
relevant factors equally. Usually, a school makes one or two factors central
(typically only one) and relegates others to secondary status. Although the
common factors are discussed separately below, it will be obvious that
that they are not discrete, with considerable overlaps occurring between
them.

The story

All psychotherapies are based on a theoretical 'story' or 'map', which usually
explains the aetiology of the presenting problem(s), as well as how the symptomatology is maintained and how it can be treated. Some therapeutic
'stories' are extremely elaborate (e.g. psychoanalysis), whilst others are more
parsimonious (e.g. radical behaviour therapy). Generally there are attempts
to justify the story in terms of research and clinical evidence, although the
research methodologies used are often part of the story! The above view also
applies to clinical hypnosis and it is therefore necessary for the clinician using
hypnosis for stress-related problems to relate the 'hypnotherapy story' as well
as the 'stress story' in a manner that is understood, consciously and unconsciously, by the patient, as this will considerably decrease any resistance and
increase the effectiveness of the interventions. Inherent in the story is a profound belief that the patient can get well if he or she engages in the associated therapeutic rituals. When the patient shares this belief with the therapist,
a strong expectation and hope for a successful therapeutic outcome is established, and this acts as a powerful placebo. Beecher (1959) contended that

up to 35% of a therapeutic response to any medical treatment could be attributed to the placebo effect.

The ritual

The therapeutic ritual essentially promulgates the 'story': for example, in psychodynamic therapies a key theoretical concept is the importance of early experiences, and hypnoanalytic 'rituals', such as ideodynamic finger questioning and ego state approaches, attempt to uncover these early experiences. In fact, much of the material presented in the remainder of this book is concerned with hypnosis rituals. Mesmer provides a good example of the importance of ritual and this is described in the next chapter.

The therapeutic relationship

Research has shown that one of the most influential factors in the outcome of psychotherapy is the relationship between therapist and patient (Bergin & Lambert, 1978; Luborsky, Crits-Christoph, Alexander, Margolis & Cohen, 1983; Clarkson, 1998). Mutual and ethical affection between patient and therapist is one of the most powerful therapeutic factors affecting change. It is important to recognise that therapists cannot help but influence their patients; sometimes patients improve because they want to please their therapist. Therapists should also communicate to patients that they care and that it is worthy for the patient to invest in the therapeutic relationship. Murcott (2005) summarises research on the therapeutic relationship in the context of complementary medicine and concludes that the quality of the relationship between practitioner and patient concretely influences the outcome.

Arguably, too, the most powerful hypnotic tool in the treatment of any individual is the hypnotherapeutic relationship. Because hypnosis is a collaborative experience rather than something that is done to a patient unilaterally, it is crucial to devote time and effort to developing a positive relationship rather than concentrating solely on developing technical expertise with hypnosis. The therapeutic alliance is fostered by certain characteristics of the therapist's personality; for example, empathy, warmth and genuineness (Truax & Carkhuff, 1967). A further discussion of these 'core conditions' is provided below. Furthermore, in order to change, patients need courage, which may only be found in the context of an affirming relationship. If the patient doesn't want to get well or is not ready to improve, it is impossible for him or her to be helped by any therapist; that is, the patient should always have the motivation to be cured. In the context of hypnotherapy the willingness of the unconscious to engage in the therapeutic endeavour should be ascertained ideodynamically (refer to Chapter 5 for a detailed explanation).

Clarkson (2003, p. 7) has identified an integrative psychotherapeutic framework that contains five possible modalities of the client–psychotherapist relationship, namely:

- the working alliance;
- the transferential/countertransferential relationship;
- the reparative/developmentally needed relationship;
- the person-to-person relationship; and
- the transpersonal relationship.

Clarkson writes:

> The five-relational Clarkson framework provides an integrative principle, which focuses on similarities and differences between different approaches to psychotherapy and differentiates which relationships each approach tends to favour. It is designed to facilitate this recommended flexibility and range in every psychotherapist – whatever their training. (p. 7)

According to Clarkson, these relationships are present in all psychotherapeutic relationships, although at different times depending on a number of factors (e.g. the phase of therapy, nature of the problem, and the therapeutic focus). Clarkson's analysis is equally applicable to hypnotherapy as to any other psychotherapy, and provides an insightful examination of the importance of relationships in hypnotherapeutic contexts.

Catharsis

The terms 'catharsis', 'abreaction' or 'emotional discharge' may be used in cognitively synonymous ways, although catharsis will be adopted as the preferred term in the following discussions. Definitions vary, but the two provided below are representative.

> An emotional release or discharge after recalling a painful experience that has been repressed because it was consciously intolerable. A therapeutic effect sometimes occurs through partial discharge of desensitisation of the painful emotions and increased insight. (American Psychiatric Association, 1980, p. 1)

> A complex set of psychosomatic processes by means of which the human being becomes purged of an overload of distress due to the cumulative frustration of basic human needs. As defined it is thus a peculiarly human phenomenon, attributable to a somatic being with capacities for love, understanding and self-direction. The assumption is that the high vulnerability of such capacities active in a physical body and world, is compensated for by a restorative process, which relieves the person of disabling tension. (Heron, 1998a, p. 6)

Arguably, it is an aspect of psychotherapy for which many therapists are insufficiently prepared, although catharsis commonly occurs in all psychotherapeutic approaches. Catharsis derives from the Greek *katharsis*, meaning 'to clean or purify', and has always played an important part in various societal rituals as well as in drama, religion and sport (Scheff, 1979). These activities provide a culturally sanctioned occasion for experiencing and expressing significant but taboo thoughts and feelings.

Many approaches to psychotherapy have emphasised catharsis to varying degrees within their respective systems (Nichols & Zax, 1977; Hawkins, 1986; Heron, 1998a). Catharsis was considered to be the essence of psychoanalytic treatment, as demonstrated in the famous case of Anna O. described by Breuer and Freud (1895/1955) in *Studies in Hysteria*. At the heart of these therapeutic systems is a belief that the emotional discharge of repressed traumatic material brings relief to emotional tension, thereby resulting in an alleviation of physical and psychological symptoms. However, it should be noted that insight is also regarded as an important component of therapeutic change, at least in the majority of the approaches. Catharsis is generally believed to be a necessary, but not sufficient, condition, for therapeutic change to occur.

It is likely that at some time in working with patients using hypnosis an emotional abreaction or catharsis will occur even though this may not have been the intention of the therapist. Often, therapists are unprepared to deal with such emotional outbursts and mismanage the situation because they do not have any training or sufficient understanding of these events. The two most common forms of mismanagement are premature closure and 'too deep too soon'. The author promotes the view that therapists should accept emotional expression in almost any therapeutic context. In this way, patients learn to recognise, accept and express their feelings. Even if catharsis is not the major focus of the therapy, it is generally a good idea to permit patients to cry or say angry things whenever these feelings emerge. Indeed, whenever a patient tells and retells his or her story, the emotion is discharged through verbal and non-verbal expression.

Issues related to the effective management of catharsis in the context of hypnosis are discussed in Chapter 5, where hypnoanalytical approaches to stress management are discussed, although it should be remembered that patients can become emotionally upset in any situation; for example, when making the appointment or during the initial interview.

Anxiety reduction and emotional support

This is probably one of the most important processes in psychotherapy. When the patient speaks about stressful life events this usually causes anxiety and other negative feelings directed towards relatives and friends. However, this does not happen when speaking to the therapist. Alexander (Alexander & French, 1946) has called this process a 'corrective emotional experience'. It is important that therapists remain calm and able to endure unpleasant affective states generated either in their patients or in themselves. When a person is stressed this causes a malfunction in concentration, memory and attention. Consequently, the reduction of anxiety liberates these important cognitive functions and enables the individual to make use of his or her resources in order to solve problems. It should also be emphasised that the alleviation of anxiety often causes the reduction or even the elimination of psychopathological symptoms in the majority of psychosomatic disorders.

Provision of new cognitive contexts

Every system of psychotherapy provides the patient with a new cognitive context, which enables the patient to interpret and understand his or her own behaviour and psychosomatic functioning, as well as that of others. With the therapist's support, life situations and people are interpreted as less threatening to the patient. In hypnoanalysis, patients are often able to re-evaluate early experiences, and this provides them with a new cognitive context in which they can be more intentional with respect to making important life decisions and formulating key therapeutic goals.

Persuasion and suggestion

The persuasions of the therapist about the effectiveness of his or her particular therapeutic methods, and the suggestion to the patient that therapy will succeed, are major elements in all psychotherapies. Jerome Frank (1973) refers to the 'raising of morale' and to the 'increase of hope' as necessary prerequisites in changing ways of thinking and behavioural habits. Instilling a sense of realistic hope in the patient is one of the most important ingredients of successful therapy (McDermott & Snyder, 1999; Snyder & Taylor, 2000). If patients can foresee a possibility of resolving their stress-related problems, they will often feel more positive about their predicaments. Interestingly, Lynn & Hallquist (2004) have recently contended that Erickson's success in using hypnosis interventions in psychotherapy may be due to the way he developed positive response sets in his patients, as well as facilitating a therapeutic environment.

Identification with the therapist

The patient normally identifies with the therapist's value system. The tone of the therapist's voice informs the patient about what is considered normal or abnormal by the therapist. Therefore, it is extremely important that the psychotherapist's personality is characterised by flexibility and freedom from extreme ideological and moral positions. It should always be remembered that psychotherapy primarily aims to satisfy the needs of the patient and not the needs of the therapist.

Development of self-control and autonomy

According to Strupp (1983), acquisition of self-control and autonomy are common targets of all types of psychotherapy. As we noted earlier, to be self-directive is one of the basic psychological needs of human beings. In the context of hypnotherapy, teaching the patient self-hypnosis early on can help to give him or her this much needed sense of independence and autonomy.

Rehearsal and confrontation

Finally, the rehearsal and the confrontation of the actual problem constitute common features of all psychotherapies (Strupp, 1983). Whatever happens in the clinician's office is of no significance if it cannot help patients cope with the actual problems in their lives. In the context of hypnotherapy, asking the patients to imagine themselves at sometime in the future when the problem is solved is an often-used technique. Only when they can do this without difficulty should they be encouraged to 'do it for real', if that is appropriate with respect to the presenting issues.

Core conditions

Rogers (1971, 1980) placed the emphasis on the person, or client, rather than on his or her presenting problems. He argued that in order for the client to become self-directed within the therapeutic relationship, the therapist needed to show empathy, congruence and unconditional positive regard.

Empathy

In empathy, therapists examine, with patients, the accuracy of their under-standing. Paying attention to the body language of patients can facilitate this checking. Non-verbal cues such as a blush, stammer, a change in breathing, clenched teeth, a closed fist or hugging oneself can be valuable cues in assist-ing the establishment of empathy. Tone of voice is another valuable indicator: for example, in anger it may raise in pitch and increase in volume; in fear it may be high and gasping; in sadness, low, faint or broken; in love, warm and accepting. Empathy has more to do with attitude than technique. It requires creativity on the part of the therapist to enter the many different worlds of patients from the patients' points of view. O'Leary (1993) states:

> Empathy may be likened to two tuning forks in the same key. When one is struck the other picks up the sound emitted by the first while losing none of its own essential nature. Empathy is tuning into the wavelength of the client. Counsellors must attune themselves to that particular wavelength. (p. 113)

Congruence

Congruence refers to the therapists' ability to be their true selves. They do not depend on their professional role, but rather use their personality to create genuineness and authenticity in the relationship. To achieve congruence, therapists must know how they are responding during counselling and make this known to clients if appropriate. O'Leary writes:

> Congruence is not self-disclosure. Therapists do not express everything that they are experiencing in the particular moment on the grounds that they are being congruent. Rather congruence occurs in the context of the therapeutic relationship and ensures that it is the needs of the clients rather than those of therapists, which are the primary focus. (p. 135)

Unconditional positive regard

Unconditional positive regard refers to a positive, non-judgemental and accepting attitude on the part of the therapist towards patients. Unconditionality allows patients the freedom to reveal themselves in the therapeutic relationship, since they know that therapists will accept them without judgement. It is through this experience of feeling unconditionally accepted by therapists that patients learn to accept themselves. By its very nature, unconditionality is opposed to diagnosing and labelling; therapists think of their patients as individuals who are experiencing particular difficulties in their life at this particular time. Unconditionality involves the unconditional worth of patients. Therapists achieve this through listening to what patients have to say. Pietrofesa, Hoffman and Splete (1984) indicated that, for many patients, it might be their first experience of being accepted in an unconditional manner 'with no strings attached' (p. 105).

Compassion

Apart from the three core conditions elucidated by Rogers, there are other related therapist factors that should be considered as important. According to Brandon (1976):

> The real kernel of all out help, that which renders it effective, is compassion (p. 6) ... Without it relationships between people are like dry leaves in the wind. Openness, intimacy and sensitivity are the herbs of compassion. Those qualities are concerned with seeing deeply and directly into the other person and feeling his needs and wants. The beginning of compassion both to oneself and to others is in decreasing the number of judgements. Compassion means giving people room; opening doors rather than closing them; asking questions rather than giving answers. Compassion is the process of deep contact with the primordial source of love. It is the direct communication from the innermost recesses of one's existence (pp. 48–9).

Fromm (1956) pointed out that compassion contains the ingredients of care, responsibility, respect and knowledge (p. 20). Erickson (1965) also reminds us that it is important to recognise the patient's needs as a human personality. He writes:

> Merely to make a correct diagnosis of the illness and to know the correct method of treatment is not enough. Fully as important is that the patient be receptive of the therapy and cooperative in regard to it. Without the patient's full cooperativeness therapeutic results are delayed, distorted, limited, or even prevented. . . . To attempt therapy upon a patient only apparently sensible, reasonable, and intelligent when the patient may actually be governed by unconscious forces and emotions neither overtly shown nor even known, to overlook the unconscious mind for possible significant information, can lead easily to failure or to unsatisfactory results. . . . Nor should therapists have so little regard for their patients that they fail to make allowance for human weaknesses and irrationality. . . . Therapists wishing to help their patients should never scorn, condemn, or reject any part of the patient's conduct simply because it is obstructive, unreasonable, or even irrational. The patient's behaviour is part of the problem brought into the office; it constitutes the personal environment within which the therapy must take effect; it may constitute the dominant force in the total patient–doctor relationship. (p. 57)
>
> The therapist's task should not be a proselytising of the patient with his own beliefs and understandings. . . . What is needed is the development of a therapeutic situation permitting the patient to use his own thinking, his own understandings, his own emotions in the way that best fits him in his scheme of life. (p. 65)

Six Category Intervention Analysis

Heron (2001) has 'operationalised' many of the essential elements discussed above into a number of basic categories of intervention skills referred to as Six Category Intervention Analysis. The six categories are grouped under two designations:

Authoritative interventions

(i)   Prescriptive – giving advice, being judgemental/critical/evaluative.
(ii) Informative – being didactic, informative, interpretive.
(iii) Confronting – challenging, providing direct feedback.

Facilitative interventions

(iv) Cathartic – encouraging the patient to release tension in laughter, crying, trembling and storming.
(v)   Catalytic – being reflective, encouraging self-directed problem solving.
(vi) Supportive – being approving, confirming and validating the patient as a human being. A supportive intervention affirms the value and worth of the patient.

This model provides the clinician with different forms of helping behaviour, which can be adopted when working with a patient.

Although this book is primarily about hypnosis and its application with patients who are experiencing stress-related problems, it is obvious that clinicians need to be cognisant of all the factors that affect clinical outcomes. Being aware of the therapeutic factors that are common to all therapies, including the core conditions necessary for effective helping, is important in this respect. In order to be a good hypnotherapist, it is first necessary to be a good clinician, with appropriate skills in each of the six categories elucidated by Heron. Hypnotherapists are not merely technicians, but creative clinicians who are able to use their skills in imaginative ways that allow the patient to 'sing their song'. Much of what is written in this book is concerned with techniques and strategies, but these must be applied in parsimonious, creative and ethically sensitive ways that respect the integrity and autonomy of the patient.

Chapter 2
Hypnosis and Stress

There is a Zen story about a woman who could not make up her mind out of which door she would leave a particular room, since both doors led to the outside world. After some hours of indecision she piled up some mats against one of the doors and fell fast asleep. In the morning she got up early and contemplated the whole problem once again. One door was free, but the other was blocked by a heap of mats. She sighed and exclaimed that she now had no choice!

Stress

We now live in a world that, although supposedly more civilised, creates increasing stress for individuals. The highly commercial and competitive consumer-oriented society demands that people look good, achieve status through belongings and qualifications, and have the latest technology and fashion accessories. As a consequence there are few opportunities for individuals to satisfy their spiritual and transpersonal needs. Many fall by the wayside because of lack of financial, social and personal resources that frustrate their efforts to satisfy their social and psychological needs. Paralleling these demands are increases in street crime, bullying, pollution and traffic congestion, to name but a few. Is it any wonder that stress and stress-related problems are on the increase?

The term 'stress' means different things to different people. Contemporary definitions of stress regard the external environmental stress as a stressor (e.g. problems at work, family conflicts, commuting), the response to the stressor as stress or distress, and the concept of stress as something that involves biochemical, physiological, behavioural and psychological changes. Researchers have also differentiated between stress that is harmful and damaging (distress) and eustress that is positive and beneficial (Ogden, 2000,

p. 232). Hanson (2004) talks about 'nice stress' and 'nasty stress'. She writes:

> Nice stress probably includes ruling the world, earning a fortune, having a tight schedule, knowing what you are doing for every minute of the day, having a purpose, and knowing where and what you are. This is the lovely, buzzy-type stress – the sort that produces a hormone called dehydroepiandrosterone, or DHEA-S for short. This leads to better brain and memory function, it strengthens the body's defences, boosts the immune system, improves the complexion, and lengthens life. Nasty stress is the sort that drudges on forever with no end in sight: endless debt, bereavement, relationship breakdown or bullying can bring it on, and this stress will give you high blood pressure, despair, palpitations, headaches, bowel upsets, insomnia and an increase in minor infections. It's the people in low-grade, low-paid jobs and in endless powerless situations who are likely to suffer the more destructive type of stress. (p. 8)

Stressors

There are many stressors that can affect the individual, some of which are current, whereas others may be historical (i.e. related to experiences earlier in an individual's life). Current stressors are commonplace in most individuals' lives and are related to life experiences, as well as to physical and environmental situations (see Figure 2.1). Holmes and Rahe (1967) developed the schedule of recent experiences (SRE), which provided a list of possible life changes or life events. These were ranked in terms of objective 'stress', from high severity (e.g. death of a spouse, death of a close family member, divorce, moving house and retirement) to low severity (e.g. holiday, change in eating habits, change in sleeping habits). It was assumed that scores on the SRE indicated the person's level of stress and concomitantly his or her health status. However, there are numerous problems associated with the SRE, which are reviewed by Ogden (2000, pp. 234–6). One significant issue concerns the chronicity of the life experiences, which is not recognised by Holmes and Rahe. There are many life experiences that are ongoing and chronic. Moos and Swindle (1990) identified the following:

- physical health stressors (e.g. medical conditions; medical interventions);
- home and neighbourhood stressors (e.g. safety, cleanliness, pollution);
- financial stressors;
- work stressors (e.g. interpersonal problems, workload, deadlines);
- spouse/partner stressors (e.g. emotional problems with partner);
- child stressors;
- extended family stressors;
- friend stressors.

They argued that life events should not be evaluated in isolation, but should be integrated into two facets of an individual's life: ongoing social resources,

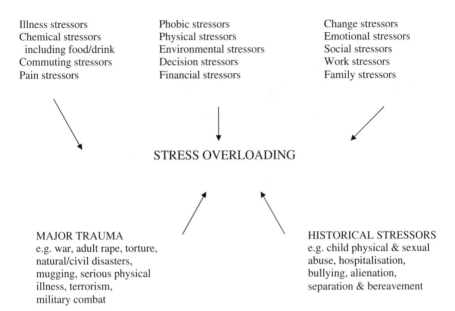

COMMON EVERYDAY STRESSORS

Illness stressors	Phobic stressors	Change stressors
Chemical stressors	Physical stressors	Emotional stressors
including food/drink	Environmental stressors	Social stressors
Commuting stressors	Decision stressors	Work stressors
Pain stressors	Financial stressors	Family stressors

STRESS OVERLOADING

MAJOR TRAUMA
e.g. war, adult rape, torture,
natural/civil disasters,
mugging, serious physical
illness, terrorism,
military combat

HISTORICAL STRESSORS
e.g. child physical & sexual
abuse, hospitalisation,
bullying, alienation,
separation & bereavement

Figure 2.1: Current and historical stressors.

such as social support networks and financial resources, and ongoing stressors.

It has now been recognised that not all stress comes from major life events. Lesser events, such as missing the bus, catching a cold, or that it's raining, can also be stressful and are referred to as daily hassles. Kanner, Coyne, Schaefer and Lazarus (1981) measured these minor stressors with a Hassles Scale, which indicated that the most frequently reported hassles were:

• concerns about weight and body shape;
• health of a family member;
• rising prices of everyday goods;
• home maintenance;
• too many things to do;
• misplacing or losing things.

They also found that positive experiences made the hassles more bearable, reducing their impact on health. Reported positive experiences, as measured by the Uplifts Scale, included the following:

• relating well with partner;
• relating well with friends;

SOMATIC	BEHAVIOURAL	EMOTIONAL	COGNITIVE
e.g. increased muscle tension, elevated blood pressure & rapid heart beat, sweating, intestinal distress, headache, nausea & vomiting, sighing, tremors, tics, incoordination	e.g. overeating & excessive alcohol consumption, increased caffeine & sugar intake, smoking, sleeping problems including nightmares, sexual problems, emergence of uncharacteristic behaviour interests diminish	e.g. increased anxiety, depression & anger, helplessness, hopelessness, lowered self-esteem, agitation, tiring easily, irritability, panicky feeling, increase in hypochondria, existing personality problems increase	e.g. increased distractibility, decreased concentration, memory impairment, worry, dread increased mistakes

Figure 2.2:   Short-term effects of stress.

- completing a task;
- feeling healthy;
- getting enough sleep;
- eating out;
- pleasant home environment.

In a recent study, Steptoe, Wardle and Marmot (2005) showed that positive states, that is, happiness, are protective and directly related to health-relevant biological processes. Their research demonstrated that positive effects in middle-aged men and women are associated with reduced neuroendocrine, inflammatory and cardiovascular activity.

The effects of stress

Where stressors are intense and prolonged, they can lead to stress overload with immediate physiological, behavioural, emotional and cognitive effects (Figure 2.2). These are characteristic of the so-called 'fight or flight' reaction, a term coined by Cannon (1932), who described the primitive reflexes of sympathetic and adrenal activation in response to perceived danger and other environmental pressures. Hans Selye (1956) further defined the deleterious effects of stress on health.

Individuals can usually cope with a degree of stress by using a range of strategies. However, some of these may be ineffective or even stress enhancing; for example, overeating, smoking, and so on. If the person continues to be stressed, then more serious psychosomatic problems may result, such as cardiovascular morbidity, along with possible lifestyle consequences and a diminution of quality of life (Figure 2.3).

SOMATIC DISORDERS	BEHAVIOURAL PROBLEMS	EMOTIONAL DISORDERS	COGNITIVE PROBLEMS
e.g. headaches hypertension, gastrointestinal problems, skin disorders, bronchial asthma, diabetes mellitus, immune dysfunction, muscular problems	e.g. alcoholism, over work, obsessive behaviour, obesity, sleep disorders, relationship problems sexual problems	e.g. chronic anxiety, depression, phobias, personality change, mental illness	e.g. memory problems. obsessive thoughts, academic problems

Figure 2.3:   Long-term effects of stress.

An interactive view of stress

The discussion so far has conceptualised stress as an automatic response to an external stressor. This view is also reflected in the life-events theory, which suggests that individuals respond to life experiences with a stress response that is therefore related to their health status. A somewhat different view suggests that individuals do not passively respond to stressors, but interact with them (Lazarus & Cohen, 1973, 1977; Lazarus, 1975). Lazarus argued that the individual appraises the potentially stressful situation as being either stressful or not, a process he referred to as primary appraisal. The individual also engages in a secondary appraisal, which involves evaluating the pros and cons of his or her coping strategies. The form of the primary and secondary appraisals determines whether or not the person shows a stress response. If the event is appraised as a stressor, then psychophysiological changes may be elicited (Figure 2.2). Some of the psychophysiological effects of stress can be seen as adaptive, in that they prepare the individual to respond, or non-adaptive, in that they may be damaging to health.

Stress has also been conceptualised as a result of a person's capacity for self-efficacy (Lazarus & Folkman, 1987), hardiness (Maddi & Kobasa, 1984) and mastery (Karasek & Theorell, 1990). It follows that successful coping and self-management reduces stress, whereas failed self-regulation results in a stress response with concomitant psychophysiological changes. Prolonged failure at self-regulation is considered to produce stress-related illness and, of course, being ill itself could be a stressful event. If illness is perceived as stressful, this could exacerbate it and reduce the chances of recovery.

Stress-related illness

Stress-related illness can be a result of behavioural or physiological changes, or an interaction of the two. Research has shown that stress can affect specific health-related behaviours as well as more general behavioural change. Specific health behaviours that may be affected are:

- smoking (e.g. Lichtenstein, Weiss & Hitchcock, 1986; Carey, Kalra, Carey, Halperin & Richard, 1993);
- alcohol (e.g. Herold & Conlon, 1981; Violanti, Marshall & Howe, 1983; Cappell & Greeley, 1987);
- diet (e.g. Michaud, Kahn & Musse, 1990; Conner, Fitter & Fletcher, 1999);
- unsafe sexual practices (e.g. Irons & Schneider, 1997);
- psychoactive substance abuse.

On a more general level, research suggests that individuals who experience high levels of stress show a greater tendency to engage in harmful behaviours that potentiate illness or injury (Wiebe & McCallum, 1986; Irons & Schneider, 1997). In particular, the individual may increase his or her consumption of alcohol, cigarettes, coffee and confectionary, as well as reducing the amount of exercise taken. All such behaviours are linked to the development of various illnesses (Baer, Garmezy, McLaughlin, Pokorny & Wernick, 1987) and injury through accidents (Johnson, 1986).

Illness may also be related to stress via physiological pathways. This is summarised by Ogden (2000, p. 242) as follows:

- Stress may cause an increase in acid secretion in the stomach, which can cause ulcers.
- Stress causes an increase in catecholamines, which cause an increase in blood clot formation thereby increasing the chances of a heart attack.
- An increase in catecholamines can lead to kidney disease.
- Heart attacks and strokes can be promoted by stress via an increase in cardiovascular response and the increased chances of injury or damage to arteries via plaque formation and fat deposits.
- Stress causes an increase in corticosteroids, which can lead to arthritis.
- Stress causes increases in catecholamines and corticosteroids, which affect the immune system, thereby making the individual more susceptible to infection.

Psychoneuroimmunology

Psychoneuroimmunology is based on the prediction that a person's psychological state can influence his or her immune system and therefore his or her health. A number of psychological factors play a role in immune-system functioning. These include mood, thought suppression and stress. A positive mood appears to increase immune functioning, while a negative mood decreases it (Stone, Cox, Valdimarsdottir, Jandorf & Neale, 1987; Cohen, Doyle & Turner, 2003). Stress may affect an individual's immune system and can lead to a prolongation of any problems and further psychosomatic symptomatology (Adler, Felton & Cohen, 1991; Walker, Johnson & Eremin, 1993; Black, 1994; Walker & Eremin, 1995; Gruzelier, Levy, Williams & Henderson, 2001; Kiecolt-Glaser, Marucha, Atkinson & Glaser, 2001). A number of recent studies have also shown that stress can compromise the immune system, which makes it more vulnerable to opportunistic infections (Glaser, Lafuse, Bonneau, Atkinson & Kiecolt-Glaser, 1993; Castes et al., 1999; Dhabhar, Satoskar, Bluethmann, David & McEwen, 2000; Kiecolt-Glaser et al., 2001). Conversely, hypnosis can effectively modulate immune-system functioning by altering hypothalamic activity (Rossi, 1986/1993, 2002; Rossi & Cheek, 1988; Kiecolt-Glaser & Glaser, 1992; Ruzyla-Smith, Barabasz, Barabasz & Warner, 1995; Solloway, 2004b).

There is evidence that thought suppression is related to the development of illness, whereas thought expression may increase immune activity (e.g. Gross & Levenson, 1997; Petrie, Booth & Pennebaker, 1998). There are also controversial data that stress can affect tumour growth (Laudenslager, Ryan, Drugan, Hysen & Maier, 1983) and lymphocyte activity (Kiecolt-Glaser & Glaser, 1986). More recently, Rossi (2002) presented evidence that suggests that a special class of genes are often expressed (behavioural state-related gene expression) in a wide range of human experiences, associated with changing states of arousal, including waking, sleeping and dreaming. These genes may be associated with stressful experiences. Rossi also suggests that the 'conscious experience of novelty, environmental enrichment and voluntary physical exercise can modulate gene expression to encode new memory and learning' (p. 12). He refers to this process as 'experience- or activity-dependent gene expression', which can turn on genes that code for proteins leading to neurogenesis, that is, the generation of new neurons and their connections in the brain. Rossi (2003a) proposes the creation of a new discipline, 'psychosocial genomics', to explore how the experiences of everyday life can turn on activity-dependent gene expression and neurogenesis in ways that optimise performance, health and well-being. Of central interest to psychosocial genomics are a special class of immediate early genes (or 'third messengers') that can be activated within seconds to a minute or two in response to important signals. They have a special role in mediating psychological arousal and optimal performance as well as the stress response (Morimoto, 2001). Several research studies have demonstrated how psychosocial stress can impair cellular-genomic functioning in the immune system (Glaser et al., 1990, 1993; Malarkey, Glaser, Kiecolt-Glaser & Marucha, 2001).

Research evaluating the use of hypnotic interventions to enhance cellular-genomic functioning is encouraging, though as yet inconclusive (Castes et al., 1999). It is now important that more is discovered about the 'third messengers' and their association with stress, pain and healing responses (Samad et al., 2001). One hypothesis is that traumatic life experiences and chronic stress can result in the desynchronisation of circadian and ultradian dynamics of the 90–120-minute basic rest-activity cycle at the cellular-genomic level (Kaufer, Friedman, Seidman & Soreq, 1998; Cho, 2001; Rossi, 2002, 2005).

Rossi, Lippencott and Bessette (1995, p. 11) hypothesise that the mild stress of 'free associating' about one's problems during the period of ultradian rest can occasionally reactivate the state-dependent encoding of trauma/stress-induced problems that lead to recovery of memory about their sources.

While the field of immunology continues to advance rapidly, it must be borne in mind that the current methodological techniques for evaluating the immune system are still relatively unsophisticated. It is important that each study is critically evaluated within the context of the current limitations. However, as the research literature expands, the clinician must respect the increasing contribution of psychoimmunology to our understanding of stress-related illness and psychosomatology, and the implications for psychotherapy in general and hypnotherapy in particular.

Mediating factors

A number of mediating factors between stress and illness may also be postulated (McDaniel, Moran, Levenson & Stoudemire, 1994), including exercise (e.g. King, Blair & Bild, 1992), gender (Stoney, Mathews, McDonald & Johnson, 1990), coping styles (Moos & Schaefer, 1984), life events (Schmale & Iker, 1966; Greene, 1966; Engel, 1971), personality (Kissen, 1967; Greer & Morris, 1975; LeShan, 1977; Friedman, Thoresen & Gill, 1986; Grossarth-Maticek, Eysenck, Vetter & Frentzel-Beyme, 1986) and social support (e.g. Wills, 1985). It is important for the clinician to acknowledge these factors when working with patients with stress-related issues.

Catharsis and stress

Heron (1998a) developed a useful explanatory approach to understanding stress based on both psychodynamic and humanistic principles. He assumed that the individual person starts life with inherent positive tendencies and resources, including a number of dialectically organised basic needs. These include the need to be loving and caring towards others, the need to be self-directive and self-affirming, with a capacity for self-actualisation and 'healing', and the need to understand both our internal and external environments. A fourth need has been suggested by Madanes (2001); namely, the need to repent for mistakes, wrongdoings, harm caused to others, and to forgive others for harm caused to oneself. These basic assumptions are derived from the work of humanistic psychologists, in particular Carl Rogers (1951) and Abraham Maslow (1973). However, for the human being to become 'fully functioning' or 'self-actualised', it is essential that optimal environments occur often at critical stages of development (Erikson, 1950). This is impossible to achieve since distorted societal and political practices (parental, educational, medical, legalistic) occur throughout our lives at both overt and covert levels and block the fulfilment of basic psychological needs. Heron suggests that if the needs are satisfied through healthy interaction with other people and society, the individual will develop into a psychosomatically healthy and fulfilled human being. An important task of the therapist should be to assist the patient in satisfying his or her personal needs, not only through the therapy process itself, but also through the therapist–patient relationship.

When basic psychological needs are frustrated then the person will experience 'stress'. Such negative and distorting practices are arguably most influential during the early years of life. For example, the need to be loved unconditionally (and its active form, the need to love others) is not met because love (approval) is only given conditionally, that is, before love is given it is necessary for the child to engage in behaviours that are approved by parents, teachers and other significant adults. Separation experiences occur throughout life – for example, hospitalisation and divorce – resulting in negative emotional experiences, that is, a grief response. The need for information is often frustrated by alienating educational, medical and legal practices, and so on. The frustration of psychological needs results in negative emotions such as sadness, anger, fear, embarrassment and shame, which would naturally 'discharge' in physiological and behavioural reactions (catharsis). However, such emotions are often repressed where they, and the associated experiences, become dissociated from consciousness, but continue to act as a dynamic affecting psychosomatic functioning. Heron refers to this process as encysting: 'The distress is occluded, so that the pain – which would be too great for the child to experience and resolve – does not enter consciousness or (disrupt) distort behaviour but is still latent as a line of stress in the system. This is a strong form of automatic protective inhibition'.

Modern 'civilised' societies are essentially non-cathartic, and emotional outpourings are not encouraged except in anything but abbreviated forms with respect to place, time and intensity. Heron (1998a) summarises this view as follows:

> It is not too extreme to characterise our society as non-cathartic. Child-raising practices are largely anti-cathartic: from the earliest years children are conditioned to deal with their distress emotions of grief, fear and anger, by controlling and containing them, by holding them in. Little boys don't cry, little girls don't get angry; little boys and girls soon learn that social acceptance is only won by the complete hiding away and burying of their personal hurts. (p. 8)

However, some 'essential' catharsis is socially sanctioned, as in the expressive arts (drama, music, poetry), sport and religious practice (Scheff, 1979), as well as in dreaming, laughter and intimacy. The repressed dynamic or 'historical stress' continues to affect the psychosomatic plane with respect to both physical and psychological functioning, and may be a contributory factor in the development of some major illnesses such as cancer (e.g. Kissen, 1966, 1967; Kissen, Brown & Kissen, 1969). On the other hand, according to Heron (1998a), discharge of distress has a profound therapeutic effect:

Discharge of distress has the effect of breaking up the distorted construct, liberating the mind to make a truly discriminating appraisal of what was really going on in the early critical incidents and in subsequent replays. The person's intelligence, previously occluded and inhibited by emotional tension, will, as the tension discharges off, spontaneously re-evaluate the tension inducing situations and their subsequent effects. The basic insight here is a dynamic one: the person sees clearly what it was she as an authentic person really needed, sees how this need, interrupted and frozen, has together with the associated pain been the hidden motive force behind an elaborate set of distorted behaviours. Associated insights liberate other figures in the early drama from oppressor stereotypes so that they are seen in the round, as humans with all their facets. (p.22)

The theory developed by Heron stays remarkably close, in terms of its central propositions, to the theory propounded by Breuer and Freud (1895/1955):

(i)   Neurosis is caused by '. . . psychical traumas. Any experience which calls up distressing affects – such as that of fright, anxiety, shame or physical pain – may operate as a trauma if there has not been an energetic reaction to the event that provokes an affect sufficient to discharge it . . .' (pp. 6 & 8).

(ii)   Neurosis is cured by successfully '. . . bringing clarity clearly to light the memory of the event(s) by which it was provoked and in arousing its accompanying affect; the patient must describe the event(s) in the greatest possible detail and 'put the affect into words'. (p. 6)

(iii)   The task of the therapist '. . . consists solely in inducing him (the patient) to reproduce the pathogenic impressions that caused it (the neurosis), giving utterance to them with an expression of affect . . .'. 'To do this the therapist must overcome the resistance, or defence, a psychical force in the patients . . . opposed to the pathogenic ideas becoming conscious'. (pp. 268, 278 & 283)

(iv)   Neurosis is essentially a 'splitting of consciousness' between memory and affect and the cure of neurosis, is, therefore, the healing of this split – which 'brings to an end the operative force of the idea which was not abreacted in the first instance . . .'. (pp. 12 & 17)

This view laid the foundations for many short-term psychotherapeutic approaches (e.g. Alexander & French, 1946; Moreno, 1946; Davanloo, 1978; Reich, 1961; Perls, 1969). At the heart of these therapeutic systems is a belief that historical stressors are unconscious and dynamic stressing mechanisms resulting from repressed traumatic early experiences (e.g. an occluded bereavement, sexual abuse, etc.), which are 'pressing for resolution'. The natural repression may be augmented by the development of so-called coping strategies such as compulsive and addictive behaviours (e.g. food, alcohol, drugs, smoking), which can lead to major physical and mental health problems that have been discussed earlier. Illness may result from the processes of hysterical conversion or somatisation, that is, where emotions such as anger and guilt become somatic.

Heron (1998a) contends that there are four major thrusts to the reintegration process:

- emotionally provocative imagery from outside;
- progressive opening up of associations and images from within;
- physical pressure from outside;
- voluntary energisation of the body from within.

The first two strategies can be prosecuted with hypnotherapy whereas the latter two generic interventions are essentially bioenergetically oriented. However, there is no reason why an integrative approach to hypnotherapy should not incorporate each of these four approaches.

Hypnosis

A brief history

Although it has never had a major impact on healthcare philosophies and technologies, hypnosis has always been part of the medical culture, influencing it at a covert level. Its popularity has waxed and waned (Gauld, 1992). From the 'healing temples' of ancient Greece, for example at Epidaurus (Nestoros, Vasdekis, Patakou-Parassiri & Sfakianakis, 1998), to more recent times, particularly in the work of Mesmer, Braid, Elliotson, Charcot, Freud and Erickson, to mention but a few, hypnosis has played a part in clinical and medical endeavours.

Mesmer

The father of modern hypnotism is usually acknowledged to be Anton Mesmer (1733–1815). Mesmer obtained some rather startling and dramatic cures, often with individuals who were incurable by traditional medical approaches. During the 'hypnotic rituals', up to 30 patients were 'magnetised' by holding iron rods between 10 and 12 inches long that projected from a large oaken tub filled with iron filings, water and powdered glass. He passed among patients, stroking their arms and ailing parts, making 'passes' at others with his wand, and occasionally fixing patients with a stare and commanding them to sleep. Gradually, individual patients became restless and agitated until a 'crisis' occurred. One patient would scream, break into a sweat and convulse, and others would follow this until most of those present would be emotionally ventilating. Mesmer argued that animal magnetism produced the crisis, but that the 'cure' was affected by the crisis itself. It should also be noted that Mesmer created a very trusting atmosphere by establishing a good relationship with his patients, thereby allowing them to 'drop their defences', so that discharge was free to occur. He must also have realised that emotional states are 'contagious', and that some degree of expectancy is required.

In 1784 a Commission of Inquiry on animal magnetism concluded that magnetic fluid did not exist and that the therapeutic effects were a result of imagination, physical contact and imitation – in fact, the conditions necessary for any modern psychotherapy. Hoareau (1998) suggests that Mesmer provided the conditions (i.e. common factors) necessary for any psychotherapy, namely: a theoretical base (the universal fluid); a clearly defined technique (the reorganisation of fluids in the sick body); a 'psychotherapist' practising within a ritualised structure; and 'patients' who are in a state of 'receptive belief'.

Elliotson and Esdaile

Later, in the 19th century, Elliotson and Esdaile, amongst others, popularised the anaesthetic properties of magnetism, rather than the 'crises' induced by Mesmer. Elliotson (1791–1868) published his own journal, the *Zoist*, in which the claims by doctors to have performed numerous painless surgical operations using mesmerism were extensively written up. Unfortunately, he believed in phrenology and clairvoyance with the consequence that his researches in hypnotism were largely neglected. Nevertheless, he had a wide practice and left a great many records of bona fide cures (Erickson, 1934).

Esdaile (1808–59) was stimulated in the study of hypnosis by reading Elliotson's reports (Erickson, 1934). He successfully operated on hundreds of patients under 'mesmeric trance' and continued to use mesmerism as an analgesic until chloroform came into general use in 1847. However, the theory of 'animal magnetism' was totally rejected by the Abbé de Faria, a Portuguese priest (Faria, 1906), and later by James Braid (1843). Faria realised that hypnotic susceptibility does not depend upon any special power of the hypnotist, but almost entirely upon the natural ability of the patient. He realised that suggestion alone was required to place susceptible members of the audience into a somnambulistic state. In his Vaudeville-like performances he suggested in a quiet but authoritative voice that a person should go to 'sleep'. He demonstrated that there was no need to assume the existence of animal magnetism and, furthermore, that trance could be achieved through suggestion, so laying the foundation for the typical induction procedures adopted today.

Braid

Braid rejected the idea of magnetism and developed his own theories of increased susceptibility and suggestibility. In 1843 he published his book *The Rationale of Nervous Sleep Considered in Relation with Animal Magnetism*, and 'from neurypnology through hypnology the word hypnosis was derived' (Waxman, 1986, p. 4). Initially, Braid brought on the artificially induced state by eye fixation on a bright object. However, he later realised that the same result could be obtained by sustained concentration on the hypnotist's voice. In his later writings, Braid (1846, 1855/1970) abandoned much of his earlier physiological theories and dealt more with the psychological aspects of hypnotism, demonstrating that the observed phenomena are the product of the imagination of the patient powerfully influenced by the suggestions of the therapist, given either deliberately or accidentally.

Charcot and Bernheim

During the 1880s, controversy raged between two schools of hypnotism represented by Charcot at the Saltpêtrière and Bernheim at the University of Nancy. Bernheim argued that hypnosis was the result of suggestion, and insisted that normal people could be hypnotised. He originally took his views from Liébault (1823–1903), who had considerable success by treating patients by suggestion in hypnosis. He suggested to his patients very quietly that they were ready to go to sleep, and many of them entered the trance state. When in the 'trance' he would give them suggestions that would help in removing their symptoms. In his view it was the suggestions made that were important and not the means of achieving the hypnotic state. Liébault's approach was probably the clearest change from negative to positive hypnosis; the use of quiet suggestion activated the patient's parasympathetic nervous system and produced a trance state that was calm rather then hysterical (Shone, 1994).

Bernheim (1886/1957) described hypnosis as the:

> exaltation of the ideo-motor reflex excitability, which effects the unconscious transformation of the thought into movement, unknown to the will. . . . The mechanism of suggestion in general, may then be summed up in the following formula: increase of the reflex ideo-motor, ideo-sensitivity and ideo-excitability. (p. 138)

He introduced the concept of degrees of hypnosis: a subject could be lightly, moderately or deeply hypnotised, and he gave a scale of nine degrees of hypnosis. For Bernheim the phenomena of suggestion 'were a function not of a magnetic state (Mesmer), nor a hypnotic state (Braid), nor induced sleep (Liébault) but of certain physiological characteristics of the brain triggered off in the waking state' (Hoareau, 1998, p. 63).

Charcot, on the other hand, developed a pathological theory and suggested that hypnosis was a pathological condition of passivity that progressed from lethargy and catalepsy to somnambulism, rather than one of heightened activity. In 1882, Charcot delivered a paper on hypnotism at the Académie des Sciences in which he provided a detailed description of the trance state. This event brought about a radical change in the negative attitude towards hypnosis in France. In 1884 and 1885, Charcot succeeded in 'artificially' reproducing non-organic paralyses with the use of hypnosis. He also pioneered the uncovering of unconscious memories in his studies of dynamic amnesia, in which he showed that forgotten memories could be recovered under hypnosis. Charcot's demonstrations at the Saltpêtrière exerted a profound influence and motivation on Freud during his stay in Paris. Charcot died in 1895, after which hypnosis was treated with considerable scepticism in France, except for the research work of Pierre Janet who had considerable influence on researchers in the US. Janet understood the hypnotic state as a suppression of personal control leading to a reduction of the critical faculty, and the increased probability of the implantation of a (therapeutic) suggestion and its transformation into an action or belief.

Freud and Breuer

Freud, who with Joseph Breuer established the ideas of hypnotic regression and dynamic psychotherapy, later rejected hypnosis in favour of the new school of psychoanalysis, a development that had a profound negative effect on the development of hypnosis. Sigmund Freud had originally studied under Charcot and had a deep interest in hypnosis for much of his life. In 1889, he shifted from Charcot's view to that of the Nancy school's emphasis on suggestion rather than hysteria, believing that patients often remembered repressed memories in a beneficial process under hypnosis. Freud was reportedly a very poor hypnotist, being limited to a simple authoritarian style of induction and, in 1896, he rejected hypnotic induction ritual as unnecessary and too likely to foster unwanted amorous advances by patients. However, it could be argued that although Freud gave up direct authoritarian approaches to hypnosis, his procedure of allowing patients to lie on a couch and free associate may be understood as an indirect form of hypnotic induction. He replaced the hypnotic procedure with simply placing his hand on the subject's forehead to help establish what he believed was the proper social relationship of doctor in dominance over patient. Freud describes his use of the Bernheim model to access the unconscious and remove symptoms by direct suggestion as follows:

> This astonishing and instructive experiment served as my model. I decided to start from the assumption that my patients knew everything that was of any pathogenic significance and that it was only a question of obliging them to communicate it.
>
> Thus when I reached a point at which, after asking a patient some question such as: How long have you had this symptom? or, What was its origin?, I was met with the answer, 'I really don't know'. I proceeded as follows:
>
> I placed my hands on the patient's forehead or took her head between my hands and said: 'You will think of it under the pressure of my hand. At the moment at which I relax my pressure you will see something in front of you or something will come into your head. Catch hold of it. It will be what we are looking for. Well, what have you seen or what has occurred to you?' (Breuer & Freud, 1895/1955, p. 110).

He then goes on to explain his hand-pressure method as a form of 'communication that could be replaced by any other signal or by some other exercise of physical influence on the patient for a 'momentarily' intensified hypnosis'. This emphasis on communication rather than suggestion is the main shift of focus from hypnotherapeutic suggestion to hypnotherapeutic work (i.e. the ideodynamic use of language and mind–body signalling) that has been the focus of attention in the last three decades (Rossi, 1996, p. 184). The concept of hypnotherapeutic work is discussed in detail in Chapter 3.

During the first part of the 20th century there was a decline in the use of hypnosis in psychiatry. Ellenberger (1970) discusses the many cultural, social, political and scientific changes that led to this decline in what he calls 'the first dynamic psychiatry'. However, a temporary revival of interest was brought about by the occurrence of a large number of functional disorders during the First World War. Brown (1920, 1921) used Freudian-type regression, allowing soldiers to relive their battle experiences under hypnosis, and invented the term 'hypnoanalysis'.

What qualified acceptance of hypnosis in medicine we have today is largely due to the efforts of pioneers in the experimental study of hypnosis, starting in the 1920s and 1930s. Foremost early researchers were Clark Hull and his then student Milton Erickson. Hull (1933/1968) maintained that hypnosis is a state of arousal – a view consistent with current perspectives. In clinical hypnosis there was a gradual move away from direct induction techniques. This was not only evident in the work of Freud, but also in that of Jung (1902/1957) and Perls (Perls, Hefferline & Goodman, 1951). Rossi (1996) comments:

> We see each of their major innovations – free association, active imagination and Gestalt dialogue – as mild rituals of induction that evoke a special state of therapeutic communication and expectation that shifts the locus of control from the authority of the therapist to the inherent creativity of the patient. These newly named rituals of induction, however, all retain some of the tell-tail signs of naturalistic hypnosis. (p. 191)

Erickson and Rossi: the implied directive

Although Erickson used many varieties of direct suggestion throughout his career, he pioneered the use of indirect suggestions for 'utilising the patient's own belief system and inner resources' (Erickson & Rossi, 1979, p. 119). Erickson and Rossi regarded 'implication' as the essence of the dynamics of suggestion because it is not what the therapist says that is important as much as what the patient does with what the therapist says. It is important in formulating psychological implications to realise that the therapist only provides a stimulus; the listener creates the hypnotic aspect of psychological implications on an unconscious level.

Erickson explained that his approach was naturalistic in the sense that he very carefully observed his patients' natural behaviour and continually utilised their own language, worldview and inner resources to help them solve their own problems in their own way. In this regard, an Ericksonian approach is strategic and the therapist is actively responsible for setting goals, treatment planning and delivering interventions designed to accomplish those goals. Erickson believed that people have all the resources within themselves that they need to solve their problems. However, in certain contexts they are unable to access those resources, perhaps because they didn't believe the resource existed or because the social network didn't encourage or permit its occurrence in a particular context. Because resources are usually retrieved and reassociated using indirect techniques, the patient (and the therapist) are often unaware how much therapy has accomplished until some time and experience with significant others has provided an opportunity to notice changes.

Milton Erickson died in 1980, but left a legacy of often zealous followers, a number of important contributions to the field and several offshoot schools of applied psychology based on his core principles of indirect strategic therapy and suggestion, and based on hypothetical unconscious processes and indirect forms of human communication (e.g. Haley, 1973, 1976; Lankton & Lankton, 1983; Rossi, 1996).

What is hypnosis?

There have been many definitions of hypnosis, which vary according to theoretical perspective, but the two provided below are representative of many of those currently proffered:

> Hypnosis typically involves an introduction to the procedure during which the subject is told that suggestions for imaginative experiences will be presented. The hypnotic induction is an extended initial suggestion for using one's imagination, and may contain further elaborations of the introduction. A hypnotic procedure is used to encourage and evaluate responses to suggestions. When using hypnosis, one person (the subject) is guided by another (the hypnotist) to respond to suggestions for changes in subjective experience, alterations in perception, sensation, emotion, thought or behaviour. Persons can also learn self-hypnosis, which is the act of administering hypnotic procedures on one's own. If the subject responds to hypnotic suggestions, it is generally inferred that hypnosis has been induced. Many believe that hypnotic responses and experiences are characteristic of a hypnotic state. While some think that it is not necessary to use the word 'hypnosis' as part of the hypnotic induction, others view it as essential.
>
> Details of hypnotic procedures and suggestions will differ depending on the goals of the practitioner and the purposes of the clinical or research endeavour. Procedures traditionally involve suggestions to relax, though relaxation is not necessary for hypnosis and a wide variety of suggestions can be used including those to become more alert. Suggestions that permit the extent of hypnosis to be assessed by comparing responses to standardized scales can be used in

both clinical and research settings. While the majority of individuals are responsive to at least some suggestions, scores on standardized scales range from high to negligible. Traditionally, scores are grouped into low, medium, and high categories. As is the case with other positively-scaled measures of psychological constructs such as attention and awareness, the salience of evidence for having achieved hypnosis increases with the individual's score. (American Psychological Association, 2005)

The term 'hypnosis' denotes an interaction between one person, the 'hypnotist', and another person or people, the 'subject' or 'subjects'. In this interaction the hypnotist attempts to influence the subjects' perceptions, feelings, thinking and behaviour by asking them to concentrate on ideas and images that may evoke the intended effects. The verbal communications that the hypnotist uses to achieve these effects are termed 'suggestions'. Suggestions differ from everyday kinds of instructions in that a 'successful' response is experienced by the subject as having a quality of involuntariness or effortlessness. (From Draft BPS Statement prepared by BSECH, September 2000; www.ucl.ac.uk/hypnosis)

Spiegel and Spiegel (2004) point out that 'the authentic hypnotic experience can be defined as formal hypnosis only when it is knowingly induced by the operator; responded to by the subject in a sensitive, disciplined way; and terminated by the operator's signal' (p. 35).

When someone is 'hypnotised' they go into 'trance', which may be construed as an altered state of consciousness or a special state of mind. This 'state theory' of hypnosis is in contrast to the 'non-state' theories that propose a sociocognitive explanation rather than a more physiological one. Refer to Kirsch and Lynn (1995) for discussion of the debate between 'state' and 'non-state' theorists. Individuals often enter trance or become 'entranced' quite naturally and spontaneously when they are engaged in activities that are 'absorbing their attention', such as watching television, reading a book, having sex, listening to music or practising self-hypnosis. Formal hypnosis encourages patients to:

- focus their attention (e.g. by listening to the voice of the therapist);
- disattend to their surroundings (e.g. by closing their eyes);
- become absorbed in some activity, image or feeling (e.g. by imagining their favourite place).

This process is likely to be more successful if patients are motivated and co-operative, and have positive expectations of a successful result. There are also some clinicians who believe that some people, high hypnotisables, have a high capacity for entering trance, as compared with low hypnotisables. For example, Spiegel and Spiegel (1978) approach hypnotisability by using the Hypnotic Induction Profile, or HIP (refer to discussion and Script 1 in Chapter 3) along with a personality inventory. They conclude:

Three major personality types that emerge from the data are Dionysian, Apollonian and Odyssean. Dionysians are intuitive, feeling and trusting of others; they tend to be highly hypnotizable. Apollonians are logical, organized and prefer to lead rather than follow. They tend to be in the low range of hypnotizability. Odysseans fluctuate between action and despair and are more balanced in the dialectic between feeling and thinking. (p. 96)

When patients are in trance they are generally more open to direct suggestions provided by the therapist. Although most 'hypnotic phenomena' can occur spontaneously and outside of hypnosis, the following effects can be produced by suggestion, either in heterohypnosis or in self-hypnosis:

- relaxation;
- ideomotor behaviours (e.g. arm levitation);
- ideosensory behaviours (e.g. analgesia);
- amnesia;
- post-hypnotic suggestion;
- regression;
- hallucinatory behaviours.

Inherent in the above discussion of hypnosis is the view that it is not a type of psychotherapy per se, but a catalyst that enhances other types of therapies and treatments through the facilitating effects of increased suggestibility and consequent hypnotic phenomena. Within this 'traditional' approach, details of hypnotic procedures and suggestions will differ depending on the goals of the practitioner and the purposes of the clinical or research endeavour. Spiegel and Spiegel (2004) state: 'that hypnosis is therapy is also a troublesome myth. We avoid the term hypnotherapist because by itself hypnosis is not therapy. . . . It may enhance therapeutic leverage, but by itself is not a treatment' (p. 16).

Oakley, Alden and Degun-Mather (1996, p. 504) list a number of properties of hypnosis that are of relevance to clinical hypnosis:

- increased suggestibility, or at least an increased willingness to accept suggestions less critically;
- enhanced capacity for imagery and role enactment, so that imagined events are experienced as real;
- greater access to childhood memories, though not a literal return to an earlier stage of cognitive development;
- reduced reality testing. A greater tolerance of logical incongruities – so-called 'trance logic';
- enhanced relaxation responses, which can be learned and applied in everyday situations;
- increased rapport;
- increased expectancy of positive outcome of therapy;

- more focused attention and enhanced ability to disattend to extraneous thoughts and feelings;
- an opportunity to create, develop and control dissociative experiences.

It is obvious that these properties will enhance the therapeutic endeavour.

Hypnotherapeutic work

Erickson and Rossi (www.ernestrossi.com; erickson-foundation.org) consider that the 'hypnotic trance' can be healing in its own right and, further, that everyone is capable of developing appropriate levels of trance. Rossi (1996) asserts that hypnotherapeutic work, facilitated by the ideodynamic use of language and mind–body signalling, can be used to effect psychosomatic changes in the patient. Hypnotherapeutic work provides a way to access and facilitate psychobiological healing and creativity in stress management. Erickson recognised that patients would often enter natural periods of healing lasting between 10 and 20 minutes. He referred to these periods of healing as 'The Common Everyday Trance' and suggested that patients could utilise these periods of inner focus to gain better access to their emotions, intuitions and deepest thoughts. Rossi (1996) says that:

> Our natural Common Everyday Trance seems to be a period when the window between our conscious and unconscious opens up a bit. Because the inner mind is the source of our deepest intuitions, people may be at their most creative and experience insights, fantasy, and intuitive leaps during these meditative moments. The Common Everyday Trance can also be a period of openness and vulnerability to outside influences; suggestions made during this time are sometimes more easily accepted. (p. 130)

Erickson called this use of the common everyday trance his naturalistic or utilisation approach, because he believed that he was simply helping people utilise their own natural resources to solve their own psychosomatic problems during these ultradian periods. From this, Rossi developed a new theory of therapeutic hypnosis and self-hypnosis as well as mind–body communication and healing. He writes:

> Excessive and chronic stress cause symptoms by distorting our normal ultradian/circadian rhythms; hypnosis could ameliorate these symptoms simply by providing an opportunity for these natural mind–body rhythms to normalise themselves. Hypnotic suggestion might work because it entrains and synchronises our natural ultradian processes of ultradian and circadian rest, restoration and healing. The secret of transformation from illness to health to higher levels of performance and well-being lay in recognising and facilitating a person's own creative resources during these natural windows of inner focus and rejuvenation that arise periodically for about 20 minutes every hour and a half or so throughout the day (Rossi, 1982, p. 24).

Further, Rossi et al. (1995) write:

> When we are at our best we are flowing along in synchrony with these natural
> up periods of performance excellence as well as natural down (rest) periods of
> recovery and healing. Stress, bodily symptoms and psychological problems are
> often signals that we have pushed ourselves beyond our natural rhythms and
> have fallen out of synchrony with our psychobiological nature. (p. 6)
>   We speculate that in the ordinary course of everyday life most people have
> an 'ultradian rest-rejuvenation deficit', that is, they have skipped one or more
> of the natural twenty-minute rest-rejuvenation phases of the Basic Rest-Activity
> Cycle we typically experience every 90 minutes throughout the day. (p. 11)

Erickson used the term 'unconscious' to represent the core of the person. For
him, the therapeutic task was to arrange the conditions that would encourage and facilitate the emergence of the unconscious resources as a positive
force. He writes (1977): 'Thus, one tries to do hypnotherapy at an unconscious level but to give the patient an opportunity to transfer that understanding and insight to the conscious mind as far as it is needed' (p. 21).

An important aspect of Erickson's approach was to spell out the conditions
for optimising both direct and indirect suggestion by utilising the patient's
own belief system and inner resources (Erickson & Rossi, 1979). He believed
that hypnotic suggestion is actually the process of evoking and utilising the
patient's own mental processes in ways that are outside his or her usual range
of ego control. Erickson (circa 1950s) writes: 'Hypnosis is not some mystical
procedure, but rather a systematic utilisation of experiential learnings – that
is, the extensive learnings acquired through the process of living itself'. In
other words it is not what the therapist says that is important, but, rather, what
the patient does with what the therapist says. This was referred to as 'the
implied directive' (Erickson, Rossi & Rossi, 1976; Rossi, Lippencott & Bessette,
1994; Rossi, 1996).

> The implied directive is thus a way of facilitating an intense state of internal
> learning or problem solving. We may suppose that all of a subject's available
> mental resources (e.g. stored memories, sensory and verbal associational pat-
> terns, various forms of previous learning, etc.) are marshalled toward a creative
> state of learning and problem solving. (Rossi, 1995a, p. 11)

It is implicit in the above statement that the unconscious carries out the suggestion and also signals when it is accomplished by creating an ideodynamic
behaviour (e.g. a movement of a finger or hand). Later, Rossi speculated that
the implied directive facilitates the internal synthesis of new protein structures
that could function as the basis of new behaviour and phenomenological
experience in the patient. The implied directive became the cornerstone of
Rossi's hypnotherapeutic approach in so much as he reformulated it into a
three-stage dynamic referred to as the 'basic accessing question', whereby the
'directive' is changed into a question. Rossi says that this development added

an important degree of patient centredness as well as an activation of the patient's inner resources: 'Even when nothing seems to happen, it focuses the patient's attention on the essential processes of self-communication and buys time for continuing therapeutic developments in the future' (Rossi, 1995a, p. 12). Here are some examples (Rossi, 1995a, p. 13):

(i)   when your inner mind is ready;
(ii) to solve your problem;
(iii) will those hands move together all by themselves?

(i)   when the inner you is able to experience;
(ii) all the sources, memories and emotions related to your problem;
(iii) will one hand drift down all by itself?

(i)   when your unconscious knows;
(ii) it can continue that inner healing, and when your conscious mind knows it can co-operate by helping you recognize those periods during the day when you need to take a healing rest (a 15–20-minute rest break);
(iii) will you find yourself awakening?

Rossi believes that the basic accessing question, in its various forms, may be regarded as the sine qua non of psychotherapy in general and hypnotherapy in particular. He argues that the positive attitudes associated with Mesmerism (i.e. imagination, hope and faith) are: 'the more easily observable states associated with the more hidden inner psychobiological work of optimising mind–body communication and successful problem solving that is the basic stuff of stress reduction and healing in hypnosis' (1996, p. 120). This view recognises that emotional problems are dynamically pressing for resolution and that this can occur when the patient is in a safe and supportive environment. Rossi (1996) contends that:

> a major source of stress and psychosomatic illness may be found in the chronic abuse of our naturally occurring mind–body rhythms of performance and healing . . . it is speculated that most of our current approaches to holistic healing (hypnosis, meditation, imagery, ritual, prayer, biofeedback, etc.) share a common denominator in facilitating the complex adaptive periodicity of our chatobiological rhythms of performance and healing – particularly the 20-minute ultradian healing response that apparently plays a role in coordinating the major systems of mind–body self-regulation every 90–120 minutes throughout the day. (p. 180)

Rossi is pointing out here that suggestions are facilitators of creative experiences rather than a means of programming, a perspective that is consistent with the current neuroscience view of activity-dependent gene expression and neurogenesis in the creation and recreation of mind, memory and consciousness. This view contrasts strongly with the idea that hypnosis is a state of passivity.

Assumptions about hypnosis and hypnotherapy

The following assumptions are made throughout the book and are stated formally here because they have considerable influence on the way in which psychotherapy and stress management are carried out. Such fundamental postulates are present in all psychotherapies, although they are not always presented, and often as alternatives:

(i)   the hypnosis state, or 'trance' state is natural and occurs without formal induction by a 'hypnotherapist';
(ii) all hypnosis is self-hypnosis;
(iii) individuals have an unconscious mind which has resources for healing and self-realisation;
(iv) the patient is able to engage in the process known as 'unconscious search' to 'recover' their unconscious resources in order to find solutions to their problems;
(v)   the trance state facilitates the internal unconscious process of psychosomatic healing (including the processes of gene expression and neurogenesis);
(vi) an unconscious search for the repressed dynamics that are responsible for supporting and maintaining the symptomatology is also possible using various hypnoanalytical approaches, as well as being implicit in Rossi's hypnotherapeutic approach.

The strategies for stress management and prevention suggested in this book are essentially an integration of Ericksonian approaches, including those developed more recently by Rossi, and the more traditional approaches. In the traditional approach, hypnosis is usually regarded as a secondary or catalytic strategy that facilitates and enhances a primary strategy, such as cognitive behaviour therapy or psychodynamic therapy. In this case the patient is more suggestible (in hypnosis) and, as such, is more likely to accept the suggestions (instructions) given by the therapist. Suggestions can also be made to facilitate the expression of relevant hypnotic phenomena, although these may sometimes occur spontaneously. In a meta-analysis performed on 18 studies in which a cognitive behaviour therapy was compared with the same therapy supplemented by hypnosis, it was shown that the addition of hypnosis substantially enhanced treatment outcome (Kirsch, Montgomery & Sapirstein, 1995). Effects seemed particularly pronounced for treatments of obesity where patients treated with hypnosis continued to lose weight after treatment ended.

    The Ericksonian approach is more process oriented than content oriented because it is the therapist who facilitates self-exploration and self-healing in patients by encouraging them to utilise their own language, worldview and inner resources to help them solve their own problems in their own way.

Hypnosis and Stress Management

When individuals experience stress, there is often an initial tendency to adopt a stoical attitude, the 'stiff upper lip' syndrome. This comprises sentiments reflected in the following phrases: 'that's life'; 'it could be worse'; 'you just have to get on with things'; 'life goes on'; 'every cloud has a silver lining'; look on the bright side'; 'mustn't grumble', and so on. There may be times when such a stoical approach to life can be construed as a constructive approach to personal stress management.

Clinical interventions, including those utilising hypnosis, can be made at any of the levels described below (refer to Figure 2.4):

- assisting the patient to realistically appraise daily hassles;
- helping the patient recognise and enhance positive experiences and to create new ones;
- dealing directly with the 'stress response' by using general therapeutic techniques such as relaxation, ego-strengthening, reframing or cognitive restructuring;
- accessing unconscious healing resources for psychosomatic healing and reframing (i.e. Rossi's hypnotherapeutic work);
- dealing with the ineffective coping strategies often associated with stress – for example, smoking, problem drinking, food-related behaviours (e.g. overeating);
- dealing with the longer-term effects of chronic stress – for example, psychosomatic problems, alcoholism, obesity, diminished quality of life;
- identifying the stressors (current or historical), and dealing with them therapeutically ('working through', catharsis, reframing, restructuring, relationship counselling, family therapy, etc.);
- assisting the patient in identifying and changing mediating factors such as social support, exercise and coping styles;
- helping the patient to identify and change the way he or she appraises potential stressors;
- helping the patient to become more assertive so that he or she may engage in appropriate personal, social and political action.

A useful summary of hypnosis approaches in dealing with stress-related problems is provided by Gravitz and Page (2002).

Methods of hypnotherapy

It has already been noted that some practitioners of hypnosis (e.g. Rossi, 1996) assume that the patient has inner resources for change, and that

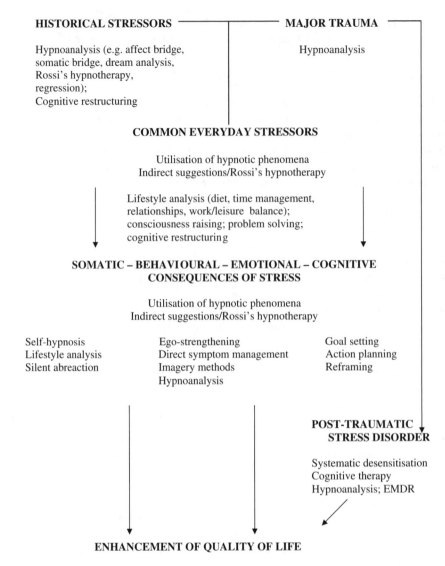

Figure 2.4: Hypnosis interventions with stress-related problems.

hypnosis is required in order for these unconscious resources (creativity, potentiality, healing) to be accessed. Consequently, the task of the therapist is to facilitate this process of unconscious healing in the patient using 'the language of the unconscious'; for example, by using metaphors, stories, the implied directive and the basic accessing question, as well as more explicit ideodynamic approaches (Cheek & LeCron, 1968; Erickson & Rossi, 1979; Rossi & Cheek, 1988; Hawkins, 1994c, 1997c; Rossi, 1995b, 1996).

The most commonly used hypnotherapeutic methods for managing stress-related problems are relaxation, ego-strengthening, direct and indirect suggestion, cognitive reframing and hypnoanalysis. The use of relaxation is a very simple and valuable method for anxiety and stress management that can be easily taught to patients. There are many approaches to developing the 'relaxation response', including hypnosis. These methods could be combined with passive progressive relaxation or autogenic training (Schultz & Luthe, 1959). Asking the patient to create 'imaginary scenes' is also a very common approach; for example, visiting a garden or a favourite outdoor place associated with peacefulness and calmness (Assagioli, 1965/1975; Singer, 1974). The therapist helps the patient to build up the images by making suggestions that ideally include all the sensory modalities (visual, auditory, olfactory, tactile and kinaesthetic).

When the patient is in trance, the therapist can provide therapeutic suggestions concerning the presenting problems. Such suggestions may be direct (the suggestion may simply be given for the symptom to lessen or disappear), or indirect (telling stories, using metaphors and other 'Ericksonian' techniques). The direct approach may be very effective in symptoms in which there is no underlying psychological dynamic. Instead of being suppressed, the symptom may be diminished to some degree, whilst leaving a 'residue' to remind the patient that there is some organic damage that requires careful attention. This is often the case with pain, since the total alleviation of organic pain could mask warning signs of further disease processes. If assessment reveals that the symptom has a serious dynamic meaning, the symptom may be reduced or substituted with a less pathological symptom. In some cases, the meaning of the symptom should be explored before any attempt is made to modify it with direct symptom management.

Psychodynamic (or hypnoanalytical) approaches assume that the presenting problems are being dynamically maintained by repressed historical experiences or current conflicts. In order to resolve the problems, the patient needs to access the repressed experiences in order to gain (unconscious) insight and to 'work through' the associated feelings in order to re-evaluate the conflictual material from an adult perspective in the context of the present time. A number of hypnoanalytical procedures have been described (e.g. Hartland, 1971; Rossi and Cheek, 1988; Cheek, 1994; Hawkins, 1994c; Heap & Aravind, 2001), and these will be discussed fully in Chapter 5.

Self-hypnosis

It is important that patients continue with their therapy between sessions. It is easy for them to 'put themselves into trance' and enjoy the benefits of the relaxation and healing that result. During the self-hypnosis they can also engage in therapeutic tasks such as positive thinking and ego-strengthening; for example, imagining successful outcomes to the therapy. Self-hypnosis for a wide range of problems can be easily taught to the patient during the normal therapy session (Alman & Lambrou, 1997), and several such strategies are presented in the next chapter.

A detailed examination of the clinical applications of these general stratagems will be discussed in the remainder of the book with respect to dealing with stress and its psychological, behavioural and somatic consequences.

Chapter 3
The Hypnosis Session:
Clinical Issues

Let me tell you the story of a Japanese master who was visited by a university professor who came to receive information about Zen. The master served tea to his visitor, but kept on pouring until the cup was full and overflowing. The professor watched the tea spilling over from the cup and then remarked with some consternation that the cup was full and no more tea could be poured in. The master replied that, like the cup, the professor was full of his own opinions and speculations, and that before he could be shown Zen he had to first empty his cup.

The Initial Interview

The therapist begins to determine whether hypnosis is an appropriate therapeutic modality for a given patient during the first interview. Caution must be exercised with patients who exhibit active suicidal symptoms, psychotic conditions, impairment with alcohol or other drugs, borderline personality disorder and other conditions that present with extreme dependency and emotional liability (Wester, 1984; Crasilneck & Hall, 1985), but this does not mean that hypnosis cannot be used successfully with such patients. I have had considerable success in using hypnosis with schizophrenic patients. Although many such patients can benefit from the use of direct and indirect hypnosis, the therapist must decide how hypnosis can best be introduced in these cases. If presenting symptoms are seen to impair the patient's full involvement in establishing a positive hypnotherapeutic context, the therapist may decide to postpone formal hypnosis until daily functioning is more stable and a solid therapeutic alliance has been established (Phillips & Frederick, 1995). Of course, this maxim applies with respect to all of our patients.

It is important to remember that the therapy commences 'before' the patient even meets the therapist, perhaps when the patient telephones to make an appointment (if someone telephones on behalf of the patient, then they should be encouraged to make the patient telephone themselves as this is a significant commitment to the therapeutic process). During the telephone conversation, statements expressing hope and optimism can be made, providing the patient with a positive mental set (i.e. 'seeding'). When the patient arrives at the clinic, more positive statements can be made during 'natural conversation'.

Before commencing with inducing the 'trance' state it is essential to prepare the patient for hypnosis and then provide the necessary therapeutic interventions required for the given patient problems. The preparation involves a number of interrelated factors:

- dealing with any resistance;
- providing the patient with information concerning the procedures;
- clearing up any misunderstandings concerning the nature of hypnosis.

This increases motivation and also facilitates the patient–therapist relationship. This phase can be considered to be the pre-induction phase, although it may be thought of as part of the induction procedure. It decreases the probability of the patient resisting the procedure and consequently increases the chances of success. The next stage is the hypnotic induction, for which there are many techniques.

It may be useful to have two chairs arranged in the clinic – one for the pre-hypnosis interview and another for the hypnosis per se (although it goes without saying that 'hypnosis' occurs in both chairs!). The patient can be told:

> I would like you to sit in this chair first so that we can have a discussion about the problems that you are experiencing, and I can ask you some questions about this and explain the way in which the treatment will proceed . . . then you will have the opportunity to ask me questions about hypnosis and the treatment approaches . . . afterwards when you are ready I will ask you to change chairs so that you are sitting in the other chair . . . the chair in which a hypnotic trance always happens . . . and many people experience a profound change in the way they feel when they change chairs . . . but don't go into a deeper trance until you sit in the other chair.

Notice the use of indirect communication here; for example, 'don't go into a deeper trance until you sit in the other chair' implies that the patient is already in a light trance. There is also the use of the paradoxical command '*don't* go into a deeper trance *until* you sit in the other chair', as well as the embedded command '*go* into a deeper trance'. A powerful expectation that trance will occur is also set up.

Using the 'word' hypnosis

There are some hypnotherapists who argue that for some patients it is inadvisable to use the word 'hypnosis' because of its negative connotations. Instead, they use words such as relaxation or sleep. It is probable that using the word 'hypnosis' does have an effect on behaviour as well as subjective experience. Whether the influence is positive or negative will depend on the patient's expectations, and it is the prerogative of the therapist to make an appropriate judgement. Shakespeare's comment in *Romeo and Juliet* that 'a rose by any other name would smell as sweet' does not apply to hypnosis as the efficacy of a 'hypnotic induction' seems to depend on the label 'hypnosis' (Gandhi & Oakley, 2005).

Taking the case history

This is more than just finding out about the problems the patient is experiencing – it is an essential part of the therapeutic process. Providing patients with the time to narrate their stories allows them to gain deeper understandings and to continue the process of finding meanings in their predicaments. The interview also provides the opportunity to create an appropriate climate in which the hypnotherapy can occur. During the interview, the therapist helps the patient to develop a sense of positive expectation and hope in the therapeutic process, which will prepare the patient for a successful hypnosis experience. As well as asking the normal questions that would be expected when taking the case history, it is important to ask questions that are relevant to the clinical hypnosis strategies. Some of the more important are randomly listed below. However, it should be recognised that there has been no attempt to provide an exhaustive list of possible questions. The relevance of the questions will be immediately apparent in the context of the discussions in the previous chapter as well as in the discussion of clinical applications later on.

- Who referred the patient?
- What are the motivations for the patient to seek help for the current symptoms?
- Are the current symptoms/difficulties being used to get needs met by others?
- Why is the patient seeking treatment at this particular time?
- How long has the patient been experiencing the problem?
- Are there times when the problem is better or worse?
- If they could experience a 'miraculous' cure, how would their life change?
- Do they have a story that explains the problem? It should be emphasised to patients that this is their own personal story and doesn't have to be based on absolute facts or evidence. The patients' stories are extremely important and can provide the therapist with important information and indi-

cations for therapeutic interventions. It should be remembered in this context that patients always know more than the therapist about their problems.

- Who provides them with emotional support?
- Is there anything that a patient wants to add that you haven't mentioned?

The answer to the question 'Are there times when the problem is better or worse?' is usually 'yes', in which case the therapist can respond by pointing out to the patient that he or she therefore has the resources to help alleviate the problem, though he or she may not know how do this consciously at this moment in time. The implication is that the patient can find these inner resources and use them at some point in the future. It is useful to ask the patient to imagine the time when the problem was a little better by using a Visual Analogue Scale (VAS), that is:

> When you are experiencing the problem, now that it is much better (*ask them to imagine the time when this occurred*), tell me where the pointer rests on a 10-point scale somewhere between 0 and 10, where 10 is the most uncomfortable (distressful) and 0 the most comfortable and relaxing.

The patient can also be asked to experience a time in his or her life when the symptoms were worse. This introduces the patient to the idea of regression, to using his or her imagination to recall experiences and evaluating such experiences. It provides the therapist with a useful device to monitor the progress of the therapy during the session or over the course of treatment. It also heightens the patient's sensitivity to his or her symptoms, so that he or she can better appreciate periods throughout the day when symptoms threaten to get worse and recognise therapeutic improvements that can motivate and reinforce his or her progress. It may also be valuable to have the patient produce the symptom (i.e. symptom prescription), as this helps the patient 'learn how to make the symptom better' by accessing the state-dependent encoding of mind–body problems (Rossi, 1986/1993). Often patients will say that the symptom feels worse at a particular time of the day, or when they are tired, hungry or stressed. This circadian problem periodicity often takes place in the middle of or late afternoon (Tsuji & Kobayashi, 1988). Rossi, Lippencott and Bessette (1995) write:

> By this time of day many people have already skipped two or three ultradian rest periods so that an accumulated ultradian deficit and stress syndrome is expressed with these common complaints: 'I'm exhausted by mid-afternoon'. . . . 'I get stressed, tense and irritable toward the end of the workday'. . . . 'My addiction gets worse later in the day when I have to have something'. . . . 'I get sleepy in the afternoon' . . . 'The worse time is when I have to go home after school and I'm too tired to do homework' . . . 'Just before dinner everybody is irritable and that's when arguments start'. Many of these acute and chronic

periodic problems may be ameliorated by taking one or two ultradian breaks earlier in the day or taking a nap after lunch or early in the afternoon. (p. 13)

Information concerning the nature of the presenting symptoms and difficulties, family background, health and medical history (including current medical treatment), employment and educational situation, current lifestyle, personal interests and previous experiences and beliefs about therapy and hypnosis should also be gathered. Information might also be ascertained with respect to favourite holidays, favourite animals, pets, and so on, as this might be useful in guided imagery and metaphor work.

During the assessment interview process, the therapist may want to use a slightly different style of communication oriented to eliciting unconscious responses. For example, when interviewing a patient with a severe back pain and consequently a restricted lifestyle, I suggested to the patient:

> Just allow your eyes to close and take your mind back to the time before you had the problem . . . and just experience life as it was then . . . allowing yourself to really experience that time again as if it were really happening right now . . . and just enjoy that for a moment longer . . . knowing that you can access these positive memories at any time that you wish.

This simple age regression provides a basic assessment of hypnotic responsiveness, and also introduces the patient to an ego-strengthening experience of 'good memory' (refer to further discussion of ego-strengthening methods in the next chapter). Yapko (1990a) points out that individuals have abilities and resources that they are oblivious to because they have no conscious awareness of, or access to, them.

Phillips and Frederick (1995) state that:

> These types of inner explorations, which can occur in the first interview, set the stage for more extensive inner-directed work throughout the course of therapy. . . . If the patient is uncomfortable with this type of approach, quickly moves onto a more regressed state with disoriented responses, or loses contact with the therapy situation, the therapist has received important diagnostic information. The therapist may hypothesise that the individual has a lack of internal boundaries for containment, so that hypnotherapy will need to proceed cautiously, and only after careful preparation. (p. 24)

Myths about hypnosis

Another essential aspect of the assessment process is an examination of the patient's beliefs and misconceptions about hypnosis (Erickson, 1932). Any previous experiences with an individual clinician, in a group setting, or with autohypnosis training, should be thoroughly explored, as well as the following myths about hypnosis:

- that hypnosis is the same as sleep;
- that the hypnotist has complete control over the patient;
- that hypnosis is an unusual and abnormal experience and therefore may be harmful (Udolf, 1981);
- that the patient may begin talking spontaneously and divulge personal and confidential information;
- that the patient will lose all conscious awareness of surroundings and have no memory of the hypnotic experience (Kroger, 1977);
- that the patient will not be able to exit from the hypnotic experience;
- that the patient may engage in strange behaviours suggested by the hypnotherapist.

There does not seem to be any evidence supporting the view that hypnosis is harmful in any way, although uninformed and misguided people can sometimes use hypnosis in the wrong way. I find it constructive to normalise hypnosis and consequent hypnotic phenomena by informing patients that many 'trance' behaviours often occur quite naturally. For example:

- Have you ever been so fascinated and absorbed in a television programme or a book that you have lost a sense of where you are or even who you are?
- Sometimes people become so engaged in an activity that they lose a sense of time.
- Have you noticed how people can become so fascinated with something that they do not respond when you ask them a question?
- Do you remember times when you have forgotten someone's name but then remember it later on?
- Sometimes people are reminded of a past experience by a particular song.
- I've often noticed that when I have an important decision to make it may take a considerable amount of 'for and against' before a decision emerges.
- Have you ever gone to bed with a problem on your mind and woken up in the morning and the problem has been resolved?
- Were you aware that you nodded your head in agreement when I asked you whether you were married?
- People sometimes notice that their face flushes quite involuntarily in some situations.
- I wonder whether you've ever experienced a feeling of deep relaxation, so comfortable that it's difficult to move?
- Sometimes when people are so relaxed and comfortable they can dream very pleasant thoughts and images.
- Even when people are asleep their unconscious mind is awake and allows them to dream and solve problems, as well as keeping their bodily processes functioning optimally.
- Have you noticed that when you are daydreaming you immediately respond if someone calls your name?

- Have you ever forgotten something, say a telephone number, and then later on without thinking about it, the number pops up into your head?
- Although there are regular sounds all around you, such as the ticking of a clock, you can put them out of your mind.
- Do you remember a time when your arm or leg went to sleep?
- Have you noticed how when you're enjoying yourself time passes very quickly, and when you're bored time goes so s l o w l y?
- Have you ever been alone and heard someone's voice, but there is no one there?

In order to assist patients to understand some of the processes of hypnotherapy, a computer analogy of the brain can be presented. However, it should be ascertained that the patient has some understanding of computers and, if he or she does not, then suitable alternatives could be offered. This may also be useful for more specific interventions (e.g. for sleeping problems).

Some patients believe that with hypnosis 'all their problems will be magically cured'. Although their high expectations and hopes should not be totally dismissed, it is important that, in collaboration with the therapist, the patient establishes realistic and achievable therapeutic goals.

It is also important in the first session to convey to patients that they have their own inner resources for creative problem solving and psychosomatic healing. This view is supported when they agree, often tentatively, that they are responsible for modulated and temporal changes in their symptomatology, as already stated. Rossi (1995a) writes:

> The therapist's major role is to 'arrange the conditions' so that the patient has an opportunity to learn how to recognise and facilitate their own natural ultradian creative processes as the agency of problem solving and healing. Psychotherapy becomes an experiential education wherein patients learn how to optimise their own natural rhythms of performance and healing. (p. 7)

In the first session, or the beginning of subsequent sessions, the therapist's task is to cooperate with the patient in searching for the problems and issues. Open-ended questions such as the following can be asked:

- What is causing the stress in your life?
- What is really bothering you right now?
- What is the most important issue in your life right now?
- What seems an appropriate agenda for this session?

Asking such open-ended questions tends to access the relevant state-dependent memories at the source of the patient's stress and uses his or her own mental preoccupations for trance induction and inner healing. Rossi again:

Such questions may initiate enough motivation and emotional arousal to evoke and/or heighten the patient's natural 90–120-minute ultradian psychobiological cascade from mind to gene that are typically involved in problem solving in everyday life as well as in emotional emergencies, trauma and stress. (p. 7)

During this initial stage the patient's major task is to identify what issues or stress-related problems are most pressing. It is usual for the patient to have a range of experiences at this stage, such as curiosity, hope, expectancy and confusion, although negative experiences sometimes occur. However, the key task of the therapist at this early stage is to help the patient to develop a trusting and collaborative relationship with the therapist in order that a sense of hope and expectancy (i.e. a therapeutic state of emotional arousal) is developed to enable therapy to continue.

Hypnotic capacity

In experimental research into hypnosis, various scales of hypnotic capacity and suggestibility have been developed (see http://socrates.berkeley.edu/~kihlstrm/hypnosis_research.htm). These scales include Spiegel's Hypnotic Induction Profile, or HIP (Spiegel & Spiegel, 1978), the Stanford Hypnotic Clinical Scale for Adults (Morgan & Hilgard, 1978a), which also has a children's version (Morgan & Hilgard, 1978b), Pekala's PC1-HAP (1995a, 1995b) and the Barber Suggestibility Scale (Barber, 1969; Barber & Wilson, 1978). Fellows (1988) provides a good review of the various scales. However, there is considerable controversy regarding the clinical value of scales of hypnotisability. Hilgard (1982) argues that some form of assessment is essential if the therapist is to adapt hypnotic psychotherapy to the individual patient. He states that:

> The choice lies between clinical judgement of responsiveness and measurement. Although measurement is desirable, care has to be exercised in selecting the appropriate measurement instrument, because an efficient scale must be based on sound psychometric considerations and avoid the illusions inherent in clinical intuition. (p. 394)

On the other hand, Waxman (1981) argues that tests of hypnotisability are neither necessary nor desirable, and that the best test is: 'The assessment and instinct and experience of the doctor, his positive decision to use hypnosis and the co-operation and motivation of the patient' (p. 73). However, as Gibson and Heap (1991) point out: 'Whether formal scales of measurement are administered or not, all clinicians will gain a great advantage by familiarising themselves with the details of a number of scales and by acquiring some practice in their administration' (p. 38). With reference to this issue, Oakley, Alden and Degun-Mather (1996) state the following:

Individual differences in hypnotisability are of potential importance clinically for two reasons. These are, firstly, because one might expect that only clients above a certain level of hypnotic susceptibility would benefit from hypnotic interventions and, secondly, because hypnotisability may have aetiological significance in some clinical psychological problems. . . . Even if a strong positive relationship were to be established between susceptibility and outcome it could still be argued that if hypnosis is an effective adjunct to established therapy even the most hypnotically insusceptible of clients would still gain the benefit of the underlying treatment, those who are even more susceptible would gain slightly more, and so on. (p. 503)

Key issues with respect to highly hypnotisable individuals have recently been discussed by Heap, Brown and Oakley (2004).

In practice, very few clinicians make use of such instruments because it is now assumed that even patients with very low capacity can still benefit from hypnosis by using the imaginal capacities they have, and particularly their 'skills' in producing specific hypnotic phenomena. In contrast to this view is that which suggests that the capacity test is an important formal tool to be used in the initial phase of the therapy. Spiegel argues that it is important for the clinician to have a diagnostic profile of the patient in order to determine the most effective therapeutic approach. Instruments such as the HIP introduce patients to hypnotic procedures and also help to develop the trusting relationship between therapist and patient, as well as providing important diagnostic information. The HIP also serves another important purpose – that of fulfilling the patient's expectations related to 'a diagnostic examination', which is consonant with those used in more conventional medical settings, and as a consequence the potency of the positive (archaic) transference may increase.

Furthermore, if the therapist is well aware of the capacity of the patient and the nature of the responses available, even if the instrument is not rigorously administered and scored, then it is possible to optimise the making of self-hypnosis exercises on tape for the patient to practise between sessions (Gibson & Heap, 1991, p. 37). A competent therapist who is made aware of the level of susceptibility of a patient, even if it is rather low, will adapt a programme of therapy to the individual case. For instance, Spiegel and Spiegel (2004) advocate using different pain-control techniques for different levels of hypnotisability. Highly hypnotisable patients are taught self-hypnosis for directly suggesting numbness or body dissociation; mid-range subjects are taught sensory alteration or fantasy techniques; and low hypnotisables are encouraged to use distraction techniques. There is also some evidence of a correlation between hypnotic ability and certain psychological disorders, such as eating disorders (Covino, Jimerson, Wolfe, Franko & Frankel, 1994; Everill & Waller, 1995; Wybraniec & Oakley, 1996).

The important clinical issue is whether an individual who does not respond well to standardised hypnotic assessment may be responsive to more flexible hypnotic approaches used within the interpersonal context of a developing therapeutic alliance. From an Ericksonian perspective (Erickson, 1952a; Gilligan, 1987), each individual is considered to have the capacity to respond experientially within the hypnotic relationship (i.e. all normal individuals can be hypnotised), so the task of the hypnotherapist becomes one of identifying and creating a context favourable for hypnotic development.

The hypnotic induction profile and the creative imagination scale

Two examples of standard assessment procedures, the HIP (Spiegel & Speigel, 1978; Spiegel, Greenleaf & Spiegel, 2000) and the Creative Imagination Scale (Barber & Wilson, 1978) are presented below. The HIP includes instructions to produce a sense of lightness in the arm and hand, with tests of response to this instruction. Response is characterised by dissociation, hand elevation after it is lowered, involuntariness, response to the cut-off signal and altered sensation. Spiegel and Spiegel (2004) contend that turning hypnotic induction into a test of hypnotic capacity transforms the initial encounter by:

- removing pressure on the clinician to successfully hypnotise the subject; and
- reducing patients' experiences of complying with the clinician's wishes, rather than exploring and discovering their own hypnotic capacity.

Script 1 – The Hypnotic Induction Profile (HIP) (adapted from Spiegel & Spiegel, 1978, pp. 35–78)

As with the other scripts presented in this book, there is no need to follow the prescription with the exact words. These should be adapted to the needs of the patient paying requisite attention also to the tone of your voice and pace of delivery.

This script is a considerably abbreviated adaptation of the original that was developed by Spiegel and Spiegel. The procedure and expected phenomena are explained to the patient prior to commencement.

> Firstly, allow your feet to rest flat and comfortably on the floor as you become aware of your breathing . . . letting the passage of air flow up your nose and down into your lungs (*N.B. this should match with what the patient is actually doing*) . . . and back out again . . . allowing all the discomfort in your body to flow out as you exhale . . . and the next time that you breathe in, turn up your eyes as if you were looking at something at the top of your head (*this is referred to as Speigel's Eye Roll Method of Induction – the patient is instructed in this approach prior to the exercise*) . . . and as you breathe out closing your eyelids to a point where you feel they just do not work . . . allowing that feeling of relaxation to spread right down to the tips of your toes . . . letting

your body float . . . and as you enjoy that floating sensation you may soon notice a sensation in one of your fingers . . . maybe your right hand . . . maybe your left hand . . . you may notice it first in the tip of the finger, just waiting for that to happen . . . all by itself, nothing you need do to make it happen . . . and when you notice it allowing that sensation to spread to the rest of your hand and to become lighter and lighter . . . flowing gently and effortlessly away from your leg . . . higher and higher as it becomes lighter and lighter . . . just imagine that your hand is tied to a beautiful coloured balloon which is gently pulling your hand even further into the air . . . enjoying that pleasant sensation. In a moment when I count from one to six, I want you to open your eyes and look at your hand, keeping the sensation that you have right now . . . and when you look at your hand you might notice that your hand becomes even lighter and is drawn up towards your eyes (*this procedure is then carried out*). Now close your eyes again and become twice as relaxed as you are right now . . . and in a moment when I count from one to six you can open your eyes keeping the sensations just as they are now until I give you the signal by touching your elbow (*therapist touches patient's elbow – this is a post-hypnotic suggestion*) when the normal sensations will return (*this procedure is then carried out*).

When the patient opens his of her eyes, and before the post-hypnotic suggestion is given, he or she is asked to say how his or her left and right arms and hands differ with respect to temperature, degree of control, numbness, and so on (the differential response). Throughout the procedure, the therapist observes the patient's behaviour very closely, as this provides significant information. It should be noted that during this initial assessment, the clinician is 'hypnotising' the patient. I often use this approach to teach the patient a method of self-hypnosis (refer to Script 7).

Script 2 – The Creative Imagination Scale (CIS) (adapted from Barber & Wilson, 1978, p. 85)

The scale consists of 10 discrete items that are read aloud to the patient, who sits relaxed in a chair with closed eyes, and imagines the scenes described. There is no prior hypnotic induction, although imagining the scenes is a form of induction (active imagination). It is explained to the patient that the purpose of the test is to establish what things they find easiest to imagine. It should be noted that this is not the full script and that the original script is strictly timed.

1. Hold your left arm out horizontally with the palm upwards . . . imagine that one . . . two . . . and then three heavy books are being placed on your hand. (*The clinician should note what movements of the hand and arm occur.*)

2. Hold your right arm out horizontally with the palm facing downwards
   ... now imagine a strong stream of water from a garden hosepipe pressing upwards onto the palm of your right hand. ...

3. Imagine that an anaesthetic is being injected into your left hand ... your
   hand is becoming numb, very numb ... just letting that happen ...
   nothing you need do. ...

4. Imagine that you are climbing in the mountains and you are getting hot
   and thirsty ... experience the sensations as you drink a cup of cold,
   refreshing water ... what are you feeling just now?

5. Imagine that you are peeling and eating an orange ... allowing yourself
   to experience all of the sensations connected with this ... the smell, the
   taste, the texture. ...

6. Imagine that you are listening to some very powerful and exciting music
   ... imagining that now and experiencing all the sensations and feeling
   that you have. ...

7. Imagine that your right hand is exposed to some warm comfortable sunshine and noticing how this makes your hand feel warmer ... becoming
   warm and comfortable ... feeling just right for you to enjoy. ...

8. By controlling your thinking you can make time slow down ... there is
   lots of time ... between each ... second as time s-t-r-e-t-c-h-e-s out ...
   slower ... and slower. (*The therapist should slow their speech down when
   giving this item.*)

9. Imagine that you are back in primary school ... you notice the teacher
   in the class ... the boy or girl sitting next to you ... in front of you
   ... the sounds ... you may even know the names of some of the
   children. ...

10. You are lying on the beach on a warm summer's day ... feeling com-
    fortably warm and relaxed ... allowing the warmth to bathe every part
    of your body ... warm, relaxed and comfortable. ...

The patient's experience can be rated formally, or relevant clinical information can be acquired by observation and questioning. An indication of the
patient's overall ability for imagination in response to suggestions as well as
their response style within each sense modality can be obtained. This can be
of considerable help to the clinician when deciding on induction approaches
and treatment strategies.

As well as testing patients for hypnotic susceptibility, it may also be useful
to teach them how to respond to hypnotic suggestions (Golden, Dowd &
Friedberg, 1987; Phillips & Frederick, 1995, pp. 45–60), as such training has
been found to be effective in increasing hypnotic responsiveness (e.g. see
Diamond, 1974, 1977; Katz, 1979). Self-control is emphasised in hypnotic skills
training, and patients have experiences similar to self-hypnosis prior to
experiencing heterohypnosis. Golden et al. (1987) argue that under these
conditions:

Patients are more likely to develop realistic than magical expectations about hypnosis. They see that hypnosis requires their co-operation and participation and that it is under their control. As a result of skills training, they are more likely to develop an internal locus of control and attribute success to themselves rather than to the hypnotist or the 'powers of hypnosis' . . . almost all individuals can learn to become adequate subjects with skills training, although they might not be able to experience all hypnotic phenomena. (p. 14)

Philips and Frederick (1995, pp. 45–6) discuss several useful 'training' strategies, developed by a number of clinicians, which introduce the patient to formal hypnosis (Jencks, 1984; Wester & Smith, 1984; Wright & Wright, 1987; Yapko, 1990a; Alman & Lambrou, 1997). These include:

- active and passive relaxation;
- comfortable eye closure;
- developing an internal focus;
- ability to deepen a light trance in a safe and comfortable way;
- comfortable responses to suggestions of imagery;
- comfortable responses to other sensory suggestions, especially kinaesthetic and auditory;
- ability to initiate and stop internal experiences at will;
- ideomotor/ideosensory signalling (refer to Chapter 5 for a detailed discussion);
- affect/somatic bridging (a regressive technique to focus on positive experiences);
- reorientation to the outside room at the end of the formal induction.

Engaging in these experiences allows the patient to develop a sense of mastery and self-control and, with this emphasis on ego-strengthening, builds confidence and helps to overcome any initial resistance to engaging in the therapeutic process. The focus is on helping the patient achieve comfort and control, starting and stopping inner experiences at will, and achieving a sense of internal stability and safety. Adopting these approaches also helps to establish the therapeutic relationship between the therapist and the patient, an important component in the developing 'therapeutic alliance'.

Hypnotising the Patient

Before exploring some specific methods of induction, the importance of the relationship of the therapist and patient within the general hypnotherapeutic context will be further examined. It was Erickson's belief that one of the most important aspects of effective hypnotherapy are the therapists themselves. He sums it up in the following way:

An induction technique is not a series of words, phrases, sentences, nor is it just a matter of suggestions, intonations, inflections, pauses and hesitations. An induction technique is both simply and complexly a matter of communication of ideas and understanding and attitudes by the doctor to his patient. (1962, p. 1)

Erickson discusses a number of issues in relation to what the hypnotist should communicate to the patient in order to develop a good climate for an induction. These include the following:

- to be aware that patients are seeking help because they cannot understand or cannot help themselves solve their problems, and believe that the therapist can help them;
- the need to be continuously aware and alert to patients' own needs to communicate in some way – for example, by verbalisation, facial expression, gesture, something that they consider important to both themselves and the therapist;
- therapists need to be aware of their own ability, knowledge and skill, and convey a sense of confidence and self-respect, and to realise that they are well prepared and competent to deal with the situation;
- the therapist should have a profound understanding of hypnosis as an experience common to everyone.

Implicit in the above statements are important issues related to the adequate training and preparation for practising psychotherapy, as well as to the necessity for continuing personal development and professional training.

Induction methods can be broadly divided into two categories: direct 'formal' methods of induction, and indirect 'naturalistic' methods. However, it should be stressed that these approaches are not discrete and can easily be integrated in clinical work.

Direct methods of induction

There are numerous techniques for hypnotising. According to Hilgard and LeBaron (1984a), there are three main components of the process of inducing hypnosis:

- relaxation (suggestions of relaxation, peace, calmness, etc.);
- imagination (use of guided imagery, e.g. favourite place, pleasant scenes);
- enactment (e.g. eye fixation, hand levitation).

You will notice that many of the scripts below include more than one of these components.

Direct induction techniques generally involve patients in fixating their attention. As they concentrate and narrow their field of attention, there is, as a result, a reduction in peripheral consciousness and, consequently, a blocking of the critical faculty. Standard eye-fixation approaches include focusing on an object (e.g. the tip of a pen, a spot on the wall or a coin). Other fixation of attention approaches include: imagination and visualisation, hand levitation, relaxation and all forms of inner sensory, perceptual or emotional experience including focusing on the symptom (e.g. pain, describing the problem), listening to stories that are absorbing, motivating and fascinating.

There are many more traditional techniques and the reader is referred to Heap and Aravind (2001) for a comprehensive account of such induction methods. It is important to recognise that the focusing techniques described above occur 'naturally' – for example, when absorbed in a book, watching an interesting film or listening to music.

Indirect techniques can also be made part of a formal method of induction; for example, some suggestions can be 'embedded' by making changes in voice tonality or emphasis. Examples of such embedded suggestions are highlighted in the following standard 'focusing of attention' script.

Script 3 – Eye fixation with distraction (counting backwards)

First of all, tell the patient what you are going to do and what you expect him or her to do.

> In a moment I am going to ask you to find something (*for example, an object or part of an object*) that is slightly above the level of your eye-gaze so that you will have to turn your eyes upwards in order to look at it. I want you to focus on that, and at the same time count backwards from 300 in threes. When your eyes have closed, you should stop counting. Whilst you are doing this I will be talking to you about *relaxation*. You will hear this but it won't interfere with your task. Any questions? Then we'll begin.
>
> Focus on the spot and start counting backwards. . . . Your feet are becoming warm and heavy and relaxed as you continue to breathe slowly and *effortlessly* . . . with every exhalation your feet becoming warm and heavy . . . allowing the warmth and heaviness to spread up into your legs massaging away all of the residual tension . . . nothing you need do to make that happen . . . it can happen *effortlessly* all by itself . . . your legs are warm and heavy and totally relaxed as these sensations spread up into your thighs, allowing them to become warm and heavy and relaxed. (*These suggestions are continued so that all the areas of the body are mentioned – abdomen, chest, arms, hands, face and, eventually, the eyelids. It is most probable that at some earlier time in the progressive relaxation the patient will begin to experience heaviness and relaxation in their eyelids, that is, they will blink their eyelids and these may also show a cataleptic 'flutter'. When this happens it can be suggested that they can close their eyes*). And the next time your eyelids close just allow them to stay closed and you will find that experience very *relaxing* and *comfortable*

. . . allowing that feeling of *relaxation* to flow down to the tips of your toes just letting your body float.

When this stage has been reached the therapist can proceed with more formal ego-strengthening (refer to scripts in Chapter 4) or with whatever interventions are appropriate at this time.

Script 4 – Eye fixation with active progressive relaxation

Begin in the same way as with eye fixation with distraction. In this induction, however, there is no distraction task, that is, counting backwards, for the patient to perform. Instead he or she engages in progressive relaxation in an active manner his- or herself.

Focus on the spot that you have selected and then concentrate your attention on your feet noticing the sensations that you are experiencing there . . . allowing your feet to become warm, heavy and relaxed . . . , and so on.

The same procedure then continues as with Script 3 until the patient closes his or her eyes.

Script 5 – Hand and arm levitation (ideodynamic movements)

Once again the patient is told what he or she has to do and what he or she can expect to happen.

Just look at your hand and, sooner or later, you will notice a sensation, maybe in the tip of one of your fingers, perhaps sooner than you expect . . . just waiting for that to happen and when it happens noticing this experience . . . you may already be wondering in which finger and on which hand this sensation is going to occur and you may be surprised when it really does happen . . . and maybe you can really enjoy noticing those important changes . . . and when they do occur just allowing those sensations to change into a movement so that the finger may, to your surprise, move upwards away from where it is resting right now . . . (*as soon as you notice this, comment on it and lightly and briefly touch the finger*) . . . and those sensations and movements can gently flow to the rest of your hand so that the whole hand and forearm becomes light, as light as a feather, and can begin to float effortlessly into the air all by itself, nothing you need do to make this happen . . . and I wonder if you will enjoy how naturally and easy and relaxing you will find this experience as your hand floats towards your eyes . . . and as this happens you may be surprised to find that your eyelids are becoming very heavy and relaxed . . . and are already beginning to close.

As soon as you see the patient's eyelids closing or blinking, you can suggest eye closure. This can be achieved by using the words:

> . . . and it's okay to close your eyes now and leave them closed, finding this experience comfortable and relaxing,

or

> . . . is it okay to close your eyes now and leave them closed, finding this experience comfortable and relaxing?

Alternatively, this can be done non-verbally, by simply drawing two fingers down above the patients eyelids. In my experience this technique always works successfully. Once eye-closure has been established, the therapist can proceed with ego-strengthening or another appropriate intervention.

Indirect methods of induction

'Naturalistic' methods (or 'Ericksonian techniques') are informal because there is no apparent induction, as in the more formalised, ritualistic procedures just described. Erickson (1958a) defined the naturalistic approach as:

> The acceptance and utilization of the situation encountered without endeavouring to psychologically restructure it. In so doing, the presenting behaviour of the patient becomes a definite aid and an actual part in inducing trance, rather than a possible hindrance. (p. 3)

> The adaptation of hypnotic techniques to individual patients and their needs leads readily and easily to effective therapeutic results. (p. 11)

Because the approach is natural and the patient is not consciously aware of what is happening, there cannot, therefore, be any resistance, as might be the case when more direct techniques are being used. Given that the process is natural, then, any critique with respect to ethical procedures cannot be logically argued. Indeed, the patient is engaging in a collaborative therapeutic relationship and has agreed to cooperate in the hypnotherapeutic process.

In Erickson's approach to hypnosis, hypnotic induction is achieved through utilisation of the patient's own personal associations and natural response tendencies (i.e. experiential learnings), instead of relying on standardised hypnotic induction procedures. Everyone has a large number of unrecognised psychological and somatic learnings and conditionings, and it is the intelligent use of these that constitutes an effectual use of hypnosis. Erickson believed that the purpose of clinical induction is to focus attention inwards and, as a consequence, depotentiate a person's everyday conscious sets. Patients are increasingly absorbed in this process as they become fascinated with stories, images, paradoxes and experiences. As a result, spontaneous hypnotic phenomena (e.g. dissociation, age regression, catalepsies, amnesia, etc.) frequently occur (Erickson & Rossi, 1976a).

The approaches Erickson used to depotentiate consciousness are inter-woven with the processes of induction and suggestion and are difficult to distinguish. It is important to recognise that Erickson always accepted the patient's immediate reality and frames of reference, thus creating a strong alliance with the many different and, often contradictory, sides of the patient.

Most indirect approaches are discussed in the paper by Erickson and Rossi (1976a), where the microdynamics of induction and suggestion (i.e. fixation of attention, depotentiating conscious sets, unconscious search, unconscious processes and hypnotic response) are presented. Because trance does not ensure the acceptance of suggestion, indirect forms of communication are necessary to: 'Evoke, mobilize and move a patient's associative processes and mental skills in certain directions to achieve certain therapeutic goals' (Erickson & Rossi, 1976a, p. 169).

Indirect forms of communication include, among others: utilisation (Erickson, 1959), metaphor and analogy (Hammond, 1990a; Kopp, 1995; Battino, 2001), jokes, implication, tonal shifts, implied directive and the basic accessing question, double binds (Erickson & Rossi, 1975), open-ended suggestions, pantomime (Erickson, 1964a), covering all possibilities of response, compound statements and dialectical processes.

Indirect suggestions for beginning the session

Below are some examples of indirect communications for beginning the session, although they may also be appropriate at other times:

- I wonder if you experience yourself ready to begin?
- I wonder whether you would like to experience a light, medium or deep trance?
- It's fine to take your time at the beginning of therapy because we might finish it even sooner.
- Would you prefer to go into trance with your glasses on or off, or would you rather just close your eyes?
- Some people prefer to go into trance with their eyes open, whereas others prefer to close their eyes. I wonder which you prefer?
- People usually go into trance when they sit in your chair.
- You can go into trance now or later.
- When your unconscious mind is ready to work, will your eyes close all by themselves?
- Does your unconscious mind want to work on the problem you've just told me about or on a more important one?
- Sooner or later you will decide what problem to resolve.
- Do you want go into your past now or later, or after you've decided what problem to resolve?

- People often find that they can solve a problem whilst they are asleep.
- As you sit there, close your eyes and develop whatever degree of trance is necessary.
- If your unconscious wants you to enter trance, your right hand will lift. Otherwise your left will lift.
- Before the session is finished your unconscious mind will find an appropriate way of communicating something important to your conscious mind. And you may be fascinated with this idea and wonder how and when this will happen.
- You don't need to bother to listen, but you can understand everything that I say, utilising everything for your own personal needs.

The script below shows how questions can be used to induce a trance.

Script 6 – Rossi's basic accessing questions

Now, what you have just told me about the way in which your problem follows a rhythmic pattern during the day is very interesting . . . and did you know that you are responsible for allowing that to happen? . . . And when you know that you have these resources, and that healing can now take place, will your eyes close all by themselves? . . . That's fine! And will it be alright to keep all of your inner explorations and experiences a secret that you don't have to share with anyone? . . . And when your unconscious mind knows that it can continue with that inner healing, and when your conscious mind knows that it can cooperate by helping you to recognise those periods during the day when you need to take a healing rest (a 15–20-minute rest break) will you find yourself awakening, allowing your eyelids to float open all by themselves?

Other examples of the use of indirect suggestions are provided throughout this book, and they are fully discussed in Erickson (1958a, 1977), Erickson and Rossi (1976a, 1976b, 1979) and Erickson, Rossi and Rossi (1976).

Self-hypnosis

It is important that patients continue with their therapy between sessions as this:

- allows the relationship with the therapist and the therapeutic process to continue;
- facilitates the process of self-help and ego-strengthening;
- strengthens the therapeutic process itself.

It is easy for them to 'put themselves into hypnosis' and enjoy the benefits of the relaxation that is induced, as well as the natural healing processes that occur. During self-hypnosis, they can also engage in therapeutic tasks, such as positive thinking and ego-strengthening; for example, imagining successful outcomes to the therapy. Self-hypnosis can be easily taught to the patient during the normal therapy session, as at the end of therapy, and whilst still in trance, they can be given the following instructions:

Script 7 – An illustration of self-hypnosis (1)

... knowing that you can easily do this for yourself at home. All you need do is to sit or lie in a relaxing place and be aware of your breathing, saying to yourself 'relax' every time you breathe out ... noticing that you are becoming more and more relaxed with every exhalation ... and the next time you breathe out just allowing your eyes to close to the point where you feel they just will not work ... allowing that feeling of relaxation to spread right down to the tips of your toes, just letting your body float ... enjoying that floating sensation as you float to your favourite outdoor place ... noticing what you can see ... hear ... feel ... and maybe, if you wish, you can meet your friendly animal, to give away your problems, to learn something positive about yourself (*refer to Script 17 in Chapter 4*) ... knowing that when you open your eyes (*after a predetermined time*) you will be feeling relaxed and alert, knowing that important positive changes are occurring within you, even though you may not be aware of them just yet, but trusting in your unconscious mind to allow that to happen ... knowing that you will only go into this pleasant and healing state of hypnosis if it is safe and appropriate for you to do that at this moment in time. If, for any reason, it becomes inconvenient or unsafe whilst you are in hypnosis, you will immediately open your eyes and become totally alert.

Script 8 – An illustration of self-hypnosis (2)

And you can use this approach for yourself at times when you want to feel more calm and relaxed (*or it may be 'prescribed' by the therapist as a homework task that is followed by a specific therapeutic task, such as positive thinking and ego-strengthening; for example, imagining successful outcomes to the therapy*) ... all you need do is to sit down in a comfortable chair at home and look at your hand ... and allow the changes to occur just as they have now ... and you can enjoy that experience of deep relaxation until you are ready to open your eyes. You can decide beforehand how many minutes you continue in this pleasant relaxed state of mind and body (*I sometimes explain to the patient at this point that we have a biological clock that we can set, which wakes us up at the appropriate and previously decided time, as they may have anxieties about staying in this comfortable state for too long or even that they may not 'wake-up'!*). And your hand and arm will only change in this way when you decide that it will for strictly 'therapeutic' purposes ... it will not happen when you casually glance at your hand and arm at any other and inappropriate time. As you practice self-hypnosis everyday, you will find that the feelings of relaxation and peacefulness become stronger and stronger . . . and that when you open your eyes that sense of relaxation and peace will remain with you for longer and longer. You will find that you are better able to deal with issues in your life and you will feel increasingly a sense of well-being.

Overcoming resistance in hypnotherapy

According to the traditional psychoanalytic position, resistance is inevitable because it is inherent in the defences the patient uses to ward off anxiety and guilt, and is overcome through interpretation and insight. However, careful preparation of the patient during the first interview will obviate most of the difficulties related to resistance, that is:

- dealing with the myths about hypnosis;
- establishing positive expectations;
- assessing the patient using a formal scale such as Spiegel's HIP (see Script 1);
- building a good collaborative relationship involving respect and trust;
- paying attention to boundary issues (e.g. frequency of sessions, length of sessions, fees and the therapeutic contract).

Nevertheless, even when the above guidelines are adhered to, the patient may still resist hypnosis. As already discussed, Erickson developed a number of indirect methods that would bypass or overcome patient resistance. These include paradoxical prescriptions, therapeutic binds, indirect suggestions, pantomime, confusion techniques, utilising the patient's symptoms, as well as the resistance itself (Erickson, 1952b, 1956, 1973; Erickson & Rossi, 1975).

'My Friend John' technique

A brief description of Erickson's 'My Friend John' technique (1964b) will be provided here as I consider it to be a very valuable approach to hypnotising the resistant patient. Typically, the therapist tells 'My Friend John' to sit comfortably in the chair, to place his hands comfortably on his legs, and to notice, sooner or later, a sensation in one of his fingers, which may be his left or maybe his right, followed by finger, hand and arm levitation. As the therapist makes these suggestions, each step is illustrated by a slow continuing demonstration of such movements (i.e. pantomime). The therapist then adds that, as the hand floats towards the face, the eyes will close when the fingers touch the face, and that they will remain closed for the period of the clinical work. Erickson writes:

'My Friend John' Technique is an excellent measure of teaching resistant subjects to go into trance. I demonstrate it to the resistant patient who comes to
therapy but resists, and I demonstrate it so thoroughly and carefully that as he
watches me induce a trance in my purely imaginative friend John, he resents
so much the waste of his time and money, and becomes so unwittingly responsive while I am hypnotizing 'John', that he follows 'John's' example and develops trance without needing to offer resistance. . . . I also use it to teach
self-hypnosis in the heterohypnotic situation, and with subjects who are to
rehearse at home in relation to study, migraine, obesity, etc. (1964, p. 5).

When using this approach with children, imaginary or real dolls and stuffed
toys can be used with good effect.

Utilisation

In working with resistant patients, Erickson stressed the importance of utilising patients' symptoms and general patterns of behaviour. He writes: 'By using
the patients' own patterns of response and behaviour, including those of their
actual illness, one may affect therapy more promptly and satisfactorily, with
resistance to therapy greatly obviated and acceptance of therapy facilitated'
(1973, p. 217).

Ending the Session

At the end of a clinical session, it is important that the patient is functioning as a rational, intelligent adult, and fully grounded in the present. By
using 'present-time' techniques, the therapist is usually able to assist the
patient in reorienting to the present time. This is particularly important where
the patient has spent some of the session working with past negative experiences. There are many techniques that can help the reorienting process,
including:

• literal description (e.g. describing the room or the journey home);
• ego-strengthening (e.g. something the patient is looking forward to later
  in the day, or that he or she can celebrate about his or her life);
• validating the patient;
• discussing the homework required of the patient.

I am often asked how to 'bring the patient out of hypnosis', and whether any
difficulties might be encountered. It is not likely that there will be any difficulties in bringing a patient out of trance, but in the unlikely event that
this happens, the worst scenario is that the patient will go into a natural
sleep. The trance is usually terminated by the request to 'awaken', for
example:

When I count from one to six, on the count of six open your eyes feeling relaxed and refreshed.

However, sometimes it may be necessary to arouse patients in a gradual manner, for example:

And with every breath that you take, allowing the feeling of alertness to spread up from your feet into your legs . . . the alertness spreading throughout your whole body . . . up into your face and your eyelids . . . allowing your eyelids to gently open . . . as you come back into this room, feeling fresh and alert and knowing that important things are happening in your unconscious mind right now, even though you may not be aware that it is happening.

Using the implied directive as well as the basic accessing question is also a very useful way to finish a session, for example:

As soon as your unconscious knows that it can return to this state comfortably and easily to do constructive work the next time we are together, will you find yourself awakening feeling refreshed and alert? (Erickson & Rossi, 1976b, p. 13)
   When your unconscious mind knows that it can continue with the healing work after you've opened your eyes, even whilst you're asleep later today, will you find yourself awakening feeling relaxed and refreshed?
   And when your other mind knows that it can utilise all the learnings from this session in assisting you in resolving issues in your life, will your eyes open?
   When your inner self knows that it has completed enough inner work for today, will you find your feet moving first, or will your arms stretch first as you awaken ready to discuss whatever is necessary? (Rossi, 1996, p. 198)
   When your unconscious knows it can continue that inner healing, and when your conscious mind knows that it can cooperate by helping you recognise those periods during the day when you need to take a healing rest (a 15–20-minute break), will you find yourself awakening? (Rossi, 1996, p. 194)
   And when you become aware that you can awaken with a full memory of all you need to know about your situation, will your eyes open as you come fully alert with a comfortable stretch? (Rossi, 1996, p. 200)
   Have you decided when you'll use the learnings from the session?
   Your conscious mind can be interested in what you learn from the experience and your unconscious mind can take care of really learning from it, or perhaps your unconscious mind only allows you to develop interest as your conscious mind develops a learning (Lankton & Lankton, 1986, p. 249).

You may be surprised that you can either learn from this experience or understand yourself differently.

When your unconscious mind knows that it can utilise the learnings from this experience or to understand yourself differently, will you find your body becoming more alert so that your eyes open?

And as you wonder whether you will be able to incorporate all these learnings into a healing dream later today, or tomorrow or at the weekend, will you find yourself awakening in a fascinated anticipation?

Another approach that assists the patient in linking the work and unconscious learnings of the session with later dreams and insight is the 'imaginary crystal ball'.

Script 9 – Crystal-ball gazing

And now, when you're ready and with the help of your unconscious mind, you can imagine a special crystal ball . . . In this crystal ball, your unconscious mind can project your future self, as you will be when you have integrated the experience from the past that you have discovered today, when it is an asset to you . . . free of the distressing feelings and reactions you experienced just a few moments ago . . . when it truly is a help to you. . . . Just take a few moments now to allow this to occur. . . . When you have something in mind, just let your head nod 'yes' or allow your 'yes' finger to move, to let me know . . . but you may not know this consciously just yet, even though your unconscious mind knows . . . and you may know later when it is more appropriate . . . perhaps in a dream later tonight . . . or tomorrow. And you may be wondering whether this will happen tonight or tomorrow night or perhaps sometime next week, but when your unconscious mind knows that healing is happening will your eyes open as you become fully aware of where you are?

In general it should be recognised that many of the techniques, both direct and indirect, used for trance induction can be used for 'trance exit'.

Termination of Therapy

Ideally this should be discussed with the patient in the first session. The predetermined number of sessions should be explained, as often the ending of the therapeutic relationship can be threatening. Usually, the ending of therapy is not a problem. However, there may be occasions where the patient has had past difficulties with separation experiences, which might confound the situation. Of course, resistance to termination may also affect the therapist, and vigilance of personal reactions is important. The reasons for resistance may be related to monetary factors as well as failing to reach unrealistic therapeutic goals. It should be emphasised here that the therapeutic change often occurs after the formal therapy sessions have finished. The work done in the hypnotherapy sessions should have prepared the patient to utilise self-hypnosis approaches in dealing not only with his or her specific problem, but also with stressful problems in general. Most patients will have learnt techniques of relaxation, ego-strengthening, self-observation of destructive behaviours and, hopefully, a more positive philosophical outlook on life.

Chapter 4
Ego-Strengthening

Are you sitting comfortably? Then I'll begin. Once upon a time there was a man who was out hunting when he suddenly realised that there was a tiger close by. In panic he started to run as fast as he could. Although he couldn't see the tiger, he could feel its hot breath on the back of his neck, which made him run even faster. He ran faster than he'd ever run before, and eventually came to a precipice, which he blindly tumbled over. As luck would have it, he managed to grasp hold of a small shrub and was left dangling precariously above the ground. As he looked up, he saw the tiger, clearly in a ferocious mood, looking down on him; and as he looked down, he noticed another tiger looking up at him, its jaws wide open, waiting for him to fall. But this was not all. Two small mice were nibbling away at the stem of the shrub that was saving him. It was then that the man noticed a strawberry plant close by. He reached over and picked a couple of red-ripe fruits, put them into his mouth and savoured the luscious sweet taste – upon which he exclaimed: 'Ah, the delicious taste of wild strawberries!'

Introduction

Many people in therapy (and out of therapy) are distressed and experience feelings of hopelessness, helplessness and a loss of self-direction and (perceived) control. In other words, they feel 'stressed'. Patients need to find the strength and motivation to take up the difficult task of solving their stress-related problems. Ego-strengthening and relaxation may be valuable here, and may, by themselves, be sufficient to help the patient deal with some of his or her problems (Hartland, 1971; Calnan, 1977; Stanton, 1979; Johnson, Walker, Heys, Whiting & Eremin, 1996). Hartland recognised that most patients in therapy are unwilling to give up their symptoms until they feel strong enough to do without them. It therefore makes sense to devote considerable time to using ego-strengthening approaches with patients, particularly at the beginning of therapy, and at the beginning and end of each session. As was noted in Chapter 2, positive well-being is also directly related to health-related biological processes (Steptoe, Wardle & Marmot, 2005).

As well as carrying out ego-strengthening procedures, it is useful to encourage a patient to disclose any minor distresses (i.e. current 'daily hassles') that he or she might be experiencing, as these can often occlude the positive experiences (think about mice and strawberries!). The following two procedures (Scripts 10 and 11), Stanton's five-step approach to ego-enhancement (described later in this chapter), and that described in Script 16, might also be effective in helping the patient deal with minor distresses, and in liberating the occluded positive emotion and cognition. After successfully appraising minor distresses, the patient is able to view these 'stresses' in his or her life as essentially irrelevant, or even farcical, in the context of the enormity of other issues in the individual's life. It is sometimes valuable to encourage the patient to laugh about his or her inanity, although this should be done with care and respect. Laughter provides a good start to the cathartic process and is, in itself, fundamentally de-stressing.

Script 10 – Dealing with minor distresses (1)

Be aware of where the tension is in your body and, as you exhale, allowing that tension to flow out in your breath . . . with every exhalation you can enjoy the experience of becoming more relaxed. Have you begun to notice that yet? I'd like you to let yourself become more and more aware of how relaxed you are becoming. . . . That's fine! And I wonder whether you can begin to allow all those trivial upsets in your life to float away, just as if a cool breeze picked them up on a warm summer's day, blown far away so that they won't bother you anymore . . . that's fine! Noticing your breathing, slow and effortless . . . and your body in contact with the chair . . . and the sound of my voice . . . allowing the lightness to spread up from your feet into your legs and body, healing every cell . . . up to your eyelids . . . as they gently open.

Script 11 – Dealing with minor distresses (2)

When you are ready to deal with all those current minor distresses in your life, just close your eyes and allow your unconscious mind to find positive experiences and memories in your life . . . and you may be surprised to discover that you will begin to notice positive feelings and sensations . . . allowing those to flow gently down into your dominant hand, filling your hand with healing energies and resources . . . and as you squeeze your hand into a fist those positive feelings can become stronger and stronger . . . and as you hold onto those feelings, focus on your other hand and put all those distresses in your life into that hand . . . that's right. And now squeeze your positive hand even tighter and as you do, pushing all those positive feelings and resources up your arm, across your shoulders and down your other arm . . . that's fine! And as that positive energy continues to flow down your arm, so it pushes the distresses out through your fingertips . . . and you may be wondering whether this is really happening as you notice fascinating sensations in your fingertips . . . that's right, just give your hands a little shake so as to shake away any residual distress! And I'd like you to know that whenever you wish to access those positive resources and feelings, then all you need do is squeeze your dominant hand. Perhaps you'd like to try that now before you open your eyes and tell me how you're feeling . . . that's fine!

A similar approach to ego-strengthening was first described by Stein (1963) and is referred to as the 'clenched fist technique', where the stress is collected in the clenched fist and then released as the fist opens, perhaps with an associated utterance as the person exhales. Of course, these approaches are also relaxation and ego-strengthening techniques.

There are three general approaches to ego-strengthening (Phillips & Frederick, 1995, p. 83):

• direct suggestion facilitated by heterohypnosis or self-hypnosis;
• projective/evocative ego-strengthening;
• Ericksonian approaches.

Direct Suggestion and Self-Hypnosis

Hartland used ego-strengthening with patients who were on the waiting list for hypnoanalytical treatment. His suggestions were authoritarian, directive, future-oriented and broadly supportive. Hartland's purpose was primarily to increase the patients' confidence and self-esteem, as well as their coping skills, and to minimise anxiety and worry. He argued that only a few patients would let go of their symptoms before they felt confident and strong enough to function without them. This approach may be eminently apposite for patients who have a great need for structure and thrive on instructions and directions. Phillips and Frederick (1995) state: 'Direction and direct suggestion may create a familiar place for such patients to begin their quest for growth and autonomy'. (p. 84)

Positive suggestions for self-worth and effectiveness can be given to both individuals and groups within hypnosis. The techniques described below can easily be taught to the patient, who can then practise them at home, perhaps by using an audiotape made by the therapist. Some patients like using a specially prepared tape, but should be encouraged to dispense with this as soon as possible as they become more independent in managing their own stress.

Script 12 – Direct suggestions for ego-strengthening

The patient is first hypnotised and then the following, or a similar, intervention is given:

> As you sit there, close your eyes and develop whatever degree of trance is necessary for you to feel better, and that is all you have to do as I talk to you. The only thing that is important is what I have to say, so please listen intently with both your conscious and your unconscious minds . . . especially with your unconscious mind, which will take over more completely as you continue to listen attentively to my voice. There is nothing you have to do or to remember, simply to be fascinated by my words and to allow whatever I say to float effortlessly into your unconscious mind. With every breath that you take you will continue to feel more confident, more self-assured, knowing that you can deal with your problems in an effective manner, and so lead your life in a more satisfying way. Now listen even more intently. A greater feeling of control over all those areas of your life that are important to you . . . your relationships, your health, your sexuality, your work, your family . . . and these positive feelings will continue to grow stronger with each passing day, even when you are asleep . . . and you can anchor those strong feelings of confidence and self-worth by gently rubbing your thumb and forefinger together . . . that's fine. And now I will count from one to six, and as I do, allowing the feelings of alertness to flow up through your legs, up through your body and into your face, and as the lightness flows into your eyelids letting your eyes open. You will be fully alert, awake and oriented in the present, knowing exactly where you are and what your immediate intentions are . . . knowing that this is something that you can do by yourself in your own home later on. In the future, whenever you wish to access those feelings of confidence and self-worth, then all you need do is to rub your thumb and forefinger together.

Visualisation and imagery

Direct suggestion in ego-strengthening has been modified by adding visualisation and imagery (Stanton, 1979, 1989). The experience of mastery has also been found to have excellent ego-strengthening results (Gardner, 1976; Dimond, 1981). Techniques aimed at eliminating anxiety-filled thoughts and feelings, as well as those that 'accentuate the positive' through accessing past mastery experiences and successes, can also be used, such as hypnotically visualising the disposal of the day's anxieties and problems by tossing them into an imaginary rubbish container (Phillips & Frederick, 1995, p. 84). A review of past accomplishments can often be an excellent preface and preparation for future challenges.

Projective/Evocative Ego-Strengthening

Past positive experiences

Ego-strengthening methods are designed to evoke unconscious material relevant to the patient's problems, so as to activate relevant inner resources. This approach emphasises that, although a patient's past may contain unknown problems, it also holds unknown resources. The success of the exercise revolves around the use of hypnosis to help the patient concentrate and focus on successes and achievements in the past. This can include reference to everyday experiences such as learning to ride a bike, to read, to walk, to pass examinations, and so on. One way of accomplishing this is to ask the patient to imagine a photograph album or scrapbook containing past positive experiences and events.

Script 13 – Photograph album for ego-strengthening and goal setting

When the patient is in 'trance', the following suggestions can be made:

> Just imagine that you have in front of you, or on your lap, a photograph album . . . now, a photograph album is where we put all of the positive experiences and memories that we have in our lives . . . of our holidays . . . celebrations, such as birthdays, weddings, parties, graduations . . . which, when we look at the pictures remind us of these happy and enjoyable times . . . and also makes us feel good. I would like to invite you to open the album at today . . . there is no photograph there yet, but I would like you to paste one in there now . . . a photograph of something good in your life today . . . that makes life worth living right now on (*state the actual date*) . . . this doesn't have to be a 'special' happening in your life . . . in fact it may be something that is quite trivial, but nevertheless something that makes life worthwhile . . . maybe a relationship, related to work . . . and so on . . . and hold onto those positive feelings . . . and do you know when you first felt like that? . . . Find that time in your photograph album and notice the images there . . . where is it? what is happening? who is there? . . . how does that make you feel? And hold onto that feeling, allowing it to become stronger and stronger . . . turning the page and finding the next event in your life that was a positive experience . . . and turning the pages into the future and putting a photograph there that represents a positive experience in your life at some point in the future when you have achieved a goal or dream that you have . . . knowing that you have the resources to enable that to happen . . . and there may be things that you need to do sooner or later to make that happen, even though you may not know that until later tonight . . . or sooner or later. . . .

By imagining the photograph album, the patient is encouraged to find positive experiences from the past and to take them into the future. In this way patients can experience themselves dealing effectively with current problems as well as experiencing the fulfilment of the agreed therapeutic goals at some hallucinated future date. Assisting the patient to set goals in this way is an important aspect of ego-strengthening, as well as being important in decision making and stress management. This method of working can be built into simple or complex imagery sequences using a variety of scenarios.

Positive age regression

Positive age regression can be facilitated in many ways: for example, by counting the patient back by age; by 'bridging' (see discussion in Chapter 5); by asking the patient to 'scan' either chronologically or randomly for past positive experiences, and so on. Phillips and Frederick (1995, p. 58) ask patients which personal qualities they would like to have at their fingertips before making more challenging journeys into the unknown or traumatic past. The positive experiences (for example, confidence or courage) can then be 'anchored' by having the patient rub the tips of his or her fingers together. In addition to bringing the thumb and forefinger together, there are many other ways to 'anchor' experiences; for example, saying a word or phrase ('relax'; 'I'm feeling relaxed and confident') or touching a 'magic' object such as a small stone, ring or coin.

The following script to recapture positive feelings is commonly used in hypnotherapy.

Script 14 – A favourite outdoor place (or a private safe place)

Allow yourself to float gently and effortlessly to your favourite outdoor place (*if the therapist knows where this is then he or she can be more specific; otherwise keep it vague*) . . . a place where you felt relaxed, happy and safe . . . and notice what you can see as you look around . . . and I really don't know what you will find most interesting in your favourite place . . . maybe the shapes and colours, other people . . . listening to the sounds . . . being aware of the temperature of your hands and face . . . and feeling joyful and happy . . . allowing those positive feelings to flow around your body massaging away all the residual tension in every cell . . . and I wonder whether you have already noticed that your mind and body are becoming more relaxed, comfortable and peaceful . . . knowing that you are doing this for yourself quite effortlessly, no place to go right now except to enjoy that pleasant experience. When you are feeling really good you can put your thumb and forefinger together so that in the future, and when you are awake, you can do this as a private way of accessing those positive feelings. (*It could also be suggested to the patient that he or she say a word, such as 'relax' or 'peace', to him- or herself.*) You can remain in this special place of yours for just as long as is appropriate for you to feel totally calm and relaxed. And you can visit your favourite place at any time that is convenient by sitting in a quiet place, closing your eyes and allowing yourself to effortlessly float there. And when you are ready to leave your special place, then open your eyes and return to this room. You can continue to feel just as good as you do now, completely relaxed and peaceful, ready to do whatever needs to be done.

Hawkins (1990) working with a bulimic patient found that regression to past events when the patient experienced feelings of control, hope and expectation was very effective.

Script 15 – Scanning positive experiences

Imagine that you have a television monitor in front of you with a number of controls for the various channels, volume and picture quality. On Channel 1 you can watch all those positive experiences in your life going all the way back to when you were very young (*other channels, or video tapes, can be established that are appropriate to the patient; for example, eating experiences, experiences relating to phobias, sexual experiences, the future, etc.*). And as you watch yourself on the screen just enjoy the pleasant experiences, allowing yourself to feel good and relaxed . . . and there may be experiences that you would like to return to later, perhaps in a dream tonight, or when you do this for yourself at home during the week. In a moment, when you come back into this room, you can allow the channel to continue playing at the back of your mind so that you will go on feeling all those good feelings of those times and places in your life, and allowing them to pervade your whole being and everything that you do.

This approach introduces the patient to the idea that it is possible to review past experiences and to feel the emotions and sensations associated with these positive events. As many people have the idea that regression necessarily leads to a recall of negative memories and feelings, introducing patients to the idea that it can also be positive is an effective way of teaching them that the process provides valuable learning experiences that can be utilised in resolving their problems. Later on in the context of psychodynamic approaches and trauma work, the therapist can then introduce the idea of regressing to (possible) traumatic memories without too many problems, as much of the preparatory work has already been done.

Hypnotic age regression is a rich source of recalled, revivified, positive, nurturing ego-strengthening experiences in childhood. However, good and enjoyable experiences are often 'mixed up', and associated, with negative traumatic experiences. It is always a possibility that when a patient recalls good nurturing experiences, negative experiences will be dialectically 'pulled up' out of the abyss. In fact, this may be a good 'paradoxical' method for helping the patient bring the traumatic material closer to the surface (i.e. the conscious) for working 'dynamically' in psychotherapy. The clinician should not be surprised, therefore, if occasionally negative experiences and associated catharsis occur during ego-strengthening work. If spontaneous negative regressions and abreactions occur during initial ego-strengthening work, it is best not to develop them at this stage. Phillips and Frederick (1995) suggest that the patient: 'Ask their unconscious mind to create a safe place or container that can store all the experiences from the session until a time when they, along with the therapist, decide to open it up' (p. 59). Indeed, one patient of mine gave me the key to the locked box so that she could only unlock it during a therapy session!

As well as the 'learned positive experiences' that can be called upon from the past to help a patient become stronger, so enabling him or her to do the necessary psychotherapeutic work required for psychosomatic change, it is also possible for the patient to call upon his or her 'inner strengths and resources' (McNeal & Frederick, 1993).

Script 16 – Finding inner strengths and resources

> When you're ready, just allow your eyes to close and go inside your mind and find your inner resources . . . your inner strengths . . . that part of your mind that is at the centre of your very being . . . those strengths and resources that are available to you at an unconscious level for helping you to deal with those times in your life when you are under stress. . . . And with every breath that you take, allowing those positive strengths to flow around your body . . . nothing you need do to make that happen . . . and as those strengths massage away all the stress and tension, knowing that you are already feeling more positive about yourself, and that you have the potential to deal effectively with issues in your life that are making you feel (un)comfortable . . . and when you feel really strong, then put your thumb and forefinger together . . . and as you rub them together you may notice how those positive feelings can become even stronger. . . . And when, in the future, you need to get in touch with this inner strength, then all you need do is to put your thumb and forefinger together . . . and now with every breath that you take, allowing your body to become lighter, spreading from your feet up through your legs into your abdomen . . . into your chest . . . and face . . . into your eyes . . . as they gently flutter open . . . feeling yourself in contact with the chair, your feet on the ground, listening to the sound of my voice . . . and knowing that your inner strength will continue to flow through your body even whilst you are asleep later today.

Another approach to finding inner strengths and resources, which can be valuable at the beginning of treatment, is the 'inner-guide', or 'friendly animal', technique (Jaffe & Bresler, 1980, pp. 45–59). The inner guide is a process that allows the patient to tap into his or her rich inner resources of healing and strength. The first major school of psychology to work with the inner guide as part of a therapeutic process was Jungian psychoanalysis, and similar approaches were later developed by Assagioli (1965/1975) in a method called 'psychosynthesis', and by Progoff (1977, 1982) in his 'intensive journal'. For many people, the inner guide takes the form of a respected authority figure, such as a teacher or parent, or some other respected symbolic figure, such as a wise old man, with whom the patient is able to carry on an internal conversation, asking questions and hearing answers. Jaffe and Bresler developed similar approaches, but used light-hearted and humorous fantasy creatures (e.g. 'Freddy the Frog') and animals as inner guides.

Script 17 – The friendly animal (inner-guide technique)

The patient is first invited to go to his or her favourite place (refer to Script 14).

> And you notice an inviting path leading into the distance. At the end of this path you notice a very friendly, bluish-green light that is gently moving towards you . . . as it gets closer it gradually changes into a friendly animal, your inner guide or therapist, who can help you with any problem that you may have. Please introduce yourself to your friend and tell them what your problem is . . . your friend listens very carefully and then replies . . . listen carefully to them, acknowledging that you may not understand the communication completely at this moment in time, that the full significance of the communication may be appreciated much later, perhaps in the form of a dream later on today or next week, sooner or later. And now say goodbye to your friend, knowing that you can meet them at any time by visiting your favourite place and calling their name . . . you can share with them any concerns that you have, knowing that they will listen and understand.

This approach was used successfully by Hawkins (1990) in the treatment of a bulimic patient (see Chapter 8), and can also be particularly useful for pain management and decision making.

Future orientations

Many of the ego-strengthening approaches described above contain a directed future orientation. However, the projective/evocative ego-strengthening technique of age progression has its roots in Erickson's interest in experimenting with the utilisation of time perception during trance to help his patients discover and achieve their attainable goals (Erickson, 1954; Erickson & Rossi, 1989; Hammond, 1990a, pp. 543–5). Erickson had patients in deep trance visualise the steps involved in achieving their goals within a series of hallucinated crystal balls. He concealed the nature of these goals from his patients by producing a profound amnesia, thus protecting the unconscious goals discerned in trance from contamination by the conscious mind (Erickson, 1966). He also insisted that his patients be dissociated from their surroundings during trance. However, it is not deemed essential that the patient is dissociated or amnesic to the future-oriented solutions (Phillips & Frederick, 1995). What seems to be the case is that positive age progressions are extremely valuable in that they can help patients counteract some of the past and present feelings of hopelessness. Frederick and Phillips (1992) express this as follows:

> We became aware, initially, of the self-soothing capacities of hypnotic age progressions in our work with psychosomatic disorders; we found that hypnotic age progressions could calm panic in our acutely distressed patients, thus allowing them to use their problem-solving and other ego faculties to better advantage. (p. 93)

Nevertheless, the clinician must ensure that the patient is able to construct positive future goals, otherwise any feelings of hopelessness and despair may be exacerbated.

Eventually, this interest in future goals contributed to the development of solution-focused therapy (De Shazer, 1985, 1988).

Script 18 – Climbing a mountain

Imagine that it is a beautiful, sunny spring day . . . the warm sun is shining down on you . . . making you feel comfortable and relaxed yet full of enthusiasm for the journey ahead. As you look up towards the summit of the mountain, you know that your goal is to reach the top to discover a personal secret. Imagine the path now, gradually ascending this gentle slope. At the beginning the walk is very easy as you pass by gently flowing streams. As you climb higher and higher the path becomes narrower and the ground rougher. Take a rest for a moment, and notice a soft cool breeze blowing on your skin and on your hair. You are quite high up the mountain and you have a wonderful view below . . . you can see for miles and miles around. Here and there you may come across a rabbit or a few mountain sheep or goats. They live peacefully up here along with the birds and butterflies. As you go higher, so the mountain becomes a little steeper and, in places, the path becomes even narrower. Gorse bushes border your path in places, and mountain flowers peep out to greet you. You can see another mountain, which looks so close that you almost feel you could walk over to it; but in reality you know it's much too far away. As you climb higher and higher, ascending up the mountain, you eventually reach a plateau where you stop to rest. Just pause there, rest a while, relax and take in the beautiful view. Looking down the mountain you can see how far you've come. You've come a very long way, up a mountain path that was, at times, difficult, at other times easy, but you continued. And you can continue now until you reach the summit. Go closer now towards your goal. (*The therapist could now suggest to the patient that at the summit he or she can meet a significant person in the individual's life who may provide an answer to an important existential issue.*)

The two-mirror approach

In an approach described by Bandler and Grinder (1979), the patient is 'hypnotised' and then asked to imagine the problem situation (e.g. phobic situation), and then to switch to an image depicting a successful outcome to the problem. The patient then opens his of her eyes. The process is then repeated: 'eyes closed – imagine problem situation – imagine successful resolution of the problem – open eyes'. Before opening the eyes, the good feelings associated with the successful outcome can be anchored; for example, by asking the patient to put his of her thumb and forefinger together, in this way pairing the two responses. If this is carried out a number of times, putting the thumb and forefinger together should involuntarily produce the good feelings.

Sometimes a similar approach is used where patients imagine two mirrors, one behind them (the past) and one in front (the future). The patients look into the mirror behind and experience themselves with the problem; they then turn and look into the mirror in front and see themselves without the problem. Appropriate suggestions are made by the therapist to help the patient build up strong images with respect to each condition. An example of this is provided in Case Study 6 in Chapter 8.

These approaches, which connect past events with current and future events, are often referred to as 'time line' approaches.

Script 19 – Goal-directed ego-strengthening

> Imagine a line stretching from the time you were born, or even before that, to a time in the future when you complete your physical life on this earth, just as the river of life starts as a spring high in the mountains and ends as a large, mature river merging with the sea to become at one with it . . . and place yourself somewhere on your time line . . . a place where you are at this moment in time. Now look at (an imaginary) mirror in front of you. . . . Imagine yourself as you would like to be, feeling good and happy about that. See this reflection . . . brighter, clearer, more colourful, and walk towards it, and become that person. You know that this is already happening, even though you may not fully appreciate it yet.

Ericksonian Approaches

Metaphors and stories can be presented as a way of helping a patient develop a greater sense of self-esteem and confidence by communicating this to his or her unconscious mind (Erickson & Rossi, 1979; Zeig, 1980; Lankton, 1980; Yapko, 1990b; Kopp, 1995). Lankton and Lankton (1986) define a therapeutic metaphor as: 'A story with dramatic devices that captures attention and provides an altered framework through which the client(s) can entertain novel experience'. (p. 154)

Metaphors usually contain embedded ideas and messages that 'seed' various healing possibilities. Many hypnotherapists have emphasised the use of metaphors for 'seeding' the ability to achieve goals related to mastery and redecision, flexibility, stress management and the accomplishment of somatic healing (Lankton & Lankton, 1983, 1987; Yapko, 1990b; Hammond, 1990a). Stories that reflect hopefulness about healing and that result in positive resolution of struggles similar to the patient's can stimulate a more optimistic view.

One of the main advantages of metaphor and storytelling is that they can be offered to the patient in a non-threatening manner that facilitates rapport, deepens internal communication and allows the individual to respond comfortably, privately, and at his or her own pace. This method will bypass any conscious resistances that the patient has to accepting these positive validations. Hammond (1990a) points out that a metaphor can be used to gradually 'seed' an idea that may be threatening or challenging, followed by an associational 'bridge' that is more directly related to the patient's problem and offers the possibility of resolution, and then reinforced with more direct communication. Elements in the story can be indirectly accented for the patient through embedded suggestions that are organised by shifts in the therapist's voice, speech rhythm, breathing rate, eye gaze or changes in posture.

Construction of metaphors

Stories have often been constructed around the following themes: the life of an oak tree (see Script 20) or tomato plant, the changing seasons of the year, the metamorphosis of a caterpillar into a butterfly, or the course of a river from its source to the sea (Script 21). There are, of course, countless more scenarios that can be used in working with patients, and these should be selected (or made up) according to the assessment of the therapeutic situation. While the material for metaphors can be chosen from any source, it should bear some relationship to the patient's own life and interests. Indeed, the patient will usually inform the clinician as to what metaphor should be used. What is important is the way in which the therapist creatively uses images and words that appropriately match the patient's interests, experiences and aspirations, as well as the presenting symptomatology. Often it will be possible to take well-known stories from literature – e.g. *The Ugly Duckling*; *The Very Hungry Caterpillar* (Carle, 1974); *Jonathan Livingston Seagull* (Bach, 1970); *The Wonderful Wizard of Oz* (Baum, 1900) – which are related to positive transformation and thus convey a sense of hope and optimism.

Script 20 – The life of an oak tree (a therapeutic metaphor)

Whilst the patient is in trance, the following story is told. It can be adapted to reflect the clinical content (e.g. the age of the patient, presenting symptomatology, etc.).

Are you sitting comfortably? Then I'll begin. Once upon a time there was a very small oak tree . . . with a very slender trunk that moved to and fro in the wind . . . and this little tree noticed all the large and wise oak trees in the forest and wished that he/she (*depending on sex of patient*) could be just like them . . . perhaps even the biggest and tallest and wisest tree in the whole forest . . . but then its beautiful green leaves started to change colour . . . to orange and brown . . . and then gradually one by one the wind blew them way . . . and the little tree felt very sad and lonely . . . and stayed feeling depressed and alone all through the cold winter . . . but then when the spring rains came, and the first of the summer sun, the energy rose up from its roots and flowed up into the branches so that the flowers blossomed beautiful colours and the little buds once more began to open into attractive green leaves . . . and the little tree was very happy all through the spring and summer time . . . until once again the leaves changed colour and were blown away by the autumn winds. But soon the little tree came to realise that during the winter whilst he/she felt cold and sad without his/her leaves, something was going on beneath the soil . . . its roots were still alive . . . changing and growing so that when spring came again the roots were able to send healing energies up to the whole of the tree, into all the branches and leaves . . . and this happened all by itself, quite naturally . . . just as the seasons change from autumn into winter into spring and into summer . . . quite imperceptibly and timelessly until the little tree grew up to be the biggest, most handsome, most confident and wisest tree in the whole forest . . . its roots reaching deep into the ground, anchoring the tree so that it could stand proud even in the strongest winds. Its branches reached high into the sky and offered sanctuary to many birds and small animals.

Script 21 – The life of a river

And as you look into the still quiet and peaceful waters of the river as it is now at this time of its life (*this description should be related to the patient's present life, as indeed should the remainder of the intervention*) you know that at the very beginning the water from the rain and snow that fell on the mountains and hills percolated into the earth and eventually emerged as a crystal-clear spring . . . full of exuberant energy as it gushed forthwith . . . sparkling in the sunshine and contemplating its journey ahead to the far distant ocean. And as it flowed forth it was joined by other small rivulets who were embarking on their own exciting journeys to the ocean . . . the stream becoming wider as it rushed forever onwards . . . through the mountains and the forests

... tumbling playfully and excitedly forward, full of hope and expectation. And as time went on the stream slowed and enjoyed the green meadows and the trees and flowers ... and as it moved closer to the ocean it began to slow down even more and to meander through the countryside in a more leisurely fashion ... and when obstacles got in the way of its progress it followed the path of least resistance ... just flowing in its own path until it reached and fused with the ocean ... knowing that it had followed its own path of destiny and had reached its ultimate goal as it merged with the ocean.

Similar metaphors suggesting growth and renewal include the rosebush (see Script 40 in Chapter 6) and the cycle of wheat (Assagioli, 1965/1975, p. 216). Further examples of therapeutic metaphors will be provided later on as part of a detailed presentation of case histories.

Stanton's Five-Step Approach

Stanton (1989, 1991) presents a five-step approach to ego-enhancement involving hypnotic induction, trance deepening, positive suggestion and imagery. His five steps are:

- physical relaxation induced by asking the patient to focus on his or her breathing and to develop a dissociated, detached attitude;
- mental calmness encouraged through imagining the mind as a pond, the surface of which has a glass-like stillness; the patient is encouraged to drop beautiful stones of calmness, relaxation and confidence into the pond, which sink 'deeper and deeper';
- disposing of 'rubbish' by having the patient imagine 'dumping' his or her fears, worries, doubts and guilt down a chute;
- having the patient destroy a barrier that represents everything that is negative in his or her life by the use of imagination;
- enjoyment of a special place where the patient feels content, tranquil and still, filling his or her mind with thought of success and happiness. The patient also thinks about the past day, with respect to things that have gone well, followed by things that have not gone as well. Each day is made successful through the creation of positive images.

In a small-scale study using the above method, Stanton (1991) reported that subjects showed significantly reduced stress levels following treatment.

Further Clinical Issues

Adequate time should be given over to ego-strengthening with the patient at the beginning of the treatment, as this enables the individual to develop a positive attitude about him- or herself and the future. I use this general approach at the beginning and end of every session. This positive process helps the patient to reverse the feelings of despair and helplessness that accompany many stress-related problems. It also assists the patient in dealing with formative stressful experiences by creating a strong anchor so that the processes of catharsis, 'working-through' and re-evaluation can take place. This issue will be discussed in greater detail in the next chapter.

As well as using the approaches described above, the clinician should also help to create a feeling of self-worth in the patient by validating the individual as a human being. This acceptance allows confidence and self-esteem to rise, and when this happens the patient becomes more relaxed and better at problem solving. For example, there may be occasions when a patient claims that he or she has no inner resources, or is reluctant to engage in any inner exploration for fear of what he or she might find. In this situation, the therapist could 'cooperate' in the following way: 'I am really glad you are being honest with me about your fears. Your honesty about your beliefs and what you need will make sure that we don't go too soon or too deeply into your inner experiences until you feel safer or more ready to do so' (Phillips & Frederick, 1995, p. 96).

Ego-strengthening tapes

There is some controversy as to whether it is useful to provide patients with audiotapes. In my view, it can certainly do no harm to make an individual tape for a patient, perhaps a recording of his or her hypnosis session, with respect to positive aspects such as relaxation, ego-strengthening and goal setting. This can be a very good way of helping the patient cope with stress. By playing the tape everyday, the patient reinforces and consolidates the ego-strengthening that occurred in the session. Wolberg (1980) lists the following benefits of using 'supportive' audiotapes:

- the tape is material evidence that something palpable and tangible is being done for the patient;
- the relationship with the therapist becomes more intensified;
- therapeutic leverage is maintained between sessions;
- tensions and anxieties become alleviated through relaxing and reassuring suggestions;
- a more constructive self-image is encouraged through positive persuasive suggestions neutralising negative suggestions, which the patient has habitually preoccupied;
- termination is more easily achieved because separation anxiety is ameliorated;
- after therapy, the patient has a resource that he or she can utilise if need be;
- supportive and re-educative suggestions add to a hypnoanalytic approach.

Wolberg claims that over a 15-year period, he did not encounter a single patient who became dependent on the tape, or in whom dependency increased. However, I must admit that a former patient of mine recently telephoned me to ask for another tape since the old one had worn out. Further inquiry revealed that I had provided her with the tape approximately 15 years ago! Examples of ego-strengthening tapes to help patients increase their self-esteem are provided by Helen Watkins (1990a).

A Speleological Reflection

As a one-time geologist and speleologist, I know how important it is to prepare adequately before descending into a cave. Firstly, it is essential to gain as much information as possible about the cave – the entrances and exits, the tunnels and waterways – but always bearing in mind that many caverns are not mapped accurately. In this context, it is usually appropriate to cave with someone who has more experience. Secondly, the speleologist requires some essential training, not only in caving, but also in basic survival techniques. Thirdly, the speleologist needs appropriate clothing and equipment, such as a torch, to illuminate his or her path. And lastly, it is also useful to be connected to the surface with a rope or at least some form of communication – just in case something untoward happens.

Chapter 5
Hypnoanalytic Approaches

Two monks were trekking through the mountains when they came to a river that was swollen by the torrential rains. The bridge had been washed away and the only way across was to wade in the deep and swiftly flowing water. A young woman needed to cross to the other side to visit her ill mother, but she was afraid to cross alone on foot. One of the monks offered to carry her across on his back and she readily agreed. Although the crossing was hazardous, they crossed safely. When they reached the other side, the young woman went her own way and the two monks continued their journey in silence. Later that day, the monk who had watched his companion carry the young woman across the river commented that it was not permissible for monks to have anything to do with females, and that he had behaved in a dangerous manner, and he wanted to know why he had done so. The monk replied that he had left the girl at the river during the morning and wondered why his companion was still carrying her!

Psychodynamic Psychotherapy

Hypnoanalytic approaches are essentially developed from the psychodynamic psychotherapies. These are systems of understanding, explanation and practice based on the broad principles of psychoanalytic theory, and the therapy is often short term and time limited (Wolberg, 1980; Strupp & Binder, 1984; Budman & Gurman, 1988). This type of therapy is designed to uncover and illuminate the origins of the symptomatology, linking the present to the past and behaviour to motivation. Psychopathology is understood as a product of repression and dissociation, and therapy is designed to uncover the repressed dynamics and allow the patient to gain insight into the formative (causative) events as experienced at physiological, affective and cognitive levels. For a valuable recent comprehensive discussion of dissociation and its implication for clinical practice, refer to Holmes et al. (2005), available online at www. sciencedirect.com.

Psychoanalytic perspectives refer specifically to Freudian principles and techniques, and therapy is generally long term. It may be noted here that the evidence Freud had provided for his theories was rather tenuously based on patients in clinical settings, interwoven with theoretical inferences. Recently, however, the field of neuropsychoanalysis has gained momentum (Solms, 2004). Solms presents a controversial argument that recent developments in neurology allow for a scientific understanding of the major tenets of psychodynamic practice. Indeed, contemporary neurosciences research can offer much towards our understanding of stress and brain functioning and the implications of this for treatments that integrate psychotherapy, psychiatry and medicine (Damasio, 1994; Solms, 2004; Panksepp, 2004).

Many therapists employ short-term dynamic therapies that have been substantially influenced by developments in humanistic, phenomenological, transactional and behavioural approaches (e.g. Alexander & French, 1946; Malan, 1963; Balint, 1968; Davanloo, 1978, 1980; Sifneos, 1979). Nevertheless, all of these therapies stay remarkably close, in terms of their central propositions, to the theory propounded by Breuer and Freud (1895/1955), as discussed in Chapter 2. The most important dynamic concepts include:

- the influence of the individual's past on his or her current functioning;
- the importance of the unconscious mind in determining how a person functions psychosomatically;
- the repression of traumatic 'experiences';
- the somatisation (hysterical conversion) of repressed negative affect;
- the unconscious dynamic;
- resistance;
- the development of ego defence mechanisms and other coping strategies to deal with the repressed 'dynamic'.

The practice of brief psychodynamic psychotherapy has increased rapidly over the past few decades. The many approaches that have developed can still be referred to as dynamic even though the range of techniques used come from many theoretical systems. Brief psychodynamic therapists are often pragmatic and eclectic, and integrative in both method and technique. In general, brief dynamic therapists pay attention to all the psychological domains of human functioning – cognitive, behavioural and affective – as well as the interpersonal dimensions of human interaction (Levenson & Butler, 1994; Hawkins, 1997a).

The psychodynamic approach encourages the patient to 'find' the origin of the conflict or problem. This 'insight' into a traumatic event or experience will often lead the patient into experiencing associated distressed feelings, such as sadness, anger, guilt, and so on, even when appropriate dissociative techniques (e.g. ego-strengthening) have been used. It should be emphasised that such abreactions indicate the reassociation and release of affective, somatic, cognitive, visual and sensory aspects of a past or present experience. The therapist can encourage the patient to express the feelings either motorically (Nichols & Zax, 1977; Pierce, Nichols & DuBrin, 1983; Hawkins, 1995) or cognitively, as 'silent abreaction', an approach often used in hypnoanalysis (H. Watkins, 1990b). Of course, abreaction can occur with respect to any emotionally laden experience, whether this is in the past, is current or is an imaginary experience relating to the future. Patients, and sometimes also clinicians, are often surprised and sometimes distressed by these signs of arousal because they are usually associated with stress and discomfort. Many clinicians believe that abreaction enables therapy to progress more rapidly (Hammond, 1990a), whilst others view it as a way of providing relief to the patient and of resolving hysterical and other psychogenic symptoms related to a traumatic event (Watkins, 1992). Rossi (1990) has further hypothesised that the arousal and relaxation phases of cathartic psychotherapy are time linked to the release of adrenal corticotrophic hormone (ACTH) and endorphins over a 20–30-minute period.

Hypnoanalysis

In hypnoanalysis, the clinician uses hypnosis to assist patients in uncovering the origins of their problems in their unconscious, and to help them deal with the behavioural, emotional, cognitive and somatic consequences of this. Several approaches have been developed to facilitate this process. However, before exploring these, some further consideration will be given to the handling of catharsis, as this often occurs when engaging in hypnoanalytic work, and it is important that therapists appreciate its significance.

Catharsis

When patients access and experience painful states, varying degrees of catharsis sometimes occur that may involve emotions, imagery, intuitions and sensations in ways that cannot be easily verbalised. In fact, as was discussed earlier, this process can be understood as an important curative factor common to all psychotherapeutic approaches. The therapist may notice that the patient shows outward signs of emotional catharsis, that is, shaking, sweating, trembling, tearing, rapid or shallow breathing, and so on. When this happens, therapists can encourage patients to vent their feeling motorically; for example, by hitting a cushion. If the clinician is appropriately trained, he or she might also use techniques drawn from emotionally oriented approaches such as Gestalt therapy (Perls, 1969), bioenergetics (Lowen, 1975), psychodrama (Moreno, 1946) and primal therapy (Janov, 1973).

Sometimes during an intense spontaneous regressive experience, the patient can temporarily lose contact with his or her immediate surroundings along with the ability to communicate verbally. This may be because the patient has entered a state of revivification (Kroger, 1977), a full regression with an actual reliving of an early experience. The therapist should attempt to avoid this situation, as nothing is gained by reliving a traumatic experience. Generally speaking, if the patient has been adequately prepared in the early stages of therapy – for example, appropriate ego-strengthening, structured positive regression, establishment of positive anchors, as well as the development of a good therapeutic alliance – then the likelihood of spontaneous abreactions is minimised. Hearing the therapist's voice along with a reassuring touch reminds the patient that he or she is in the therapy room. Paradoxically, by using these positive approaches, the patient is also being encouraged to explore the dialectical tensions; for example, negative experiences, feelings of low self-worth, and so on.

If spontaneous regressions and abreactions do occur, the therapist must be adequately trained and have the confidence to deal with the situation. In these situations the best policy is to encourage the patient to stay with the experience, whilst giving him or her full support and providing indications of the present time. Essentially, the therapist's task is to help the patient express his or her feelings as fully as possible in a way that leads to insight, the liberation of intentionality and behaviour change. In general the therapist pursues this goal by:

• continuing to work effectively against defences as feeling expression unfolds;
• being in intimate contact with the patient;
• choosing appropriate methods;
• not being afraid or upset by strong feelings.

Script 22 – Encouraging catharsis

That's right . . . just allowing those feelings to flow . . . letting all of those feelings out, just like a pent-up mountain stream . . . that's fine . . . keep it going as you continue to breathe from deep within your body . . . and with every exhalation allowing those unexpressed feelings to well up and flow out, and to dissolve into thin air. And, if it's appropriate, you can put some actions to the feelings, allowing your body to move in any way that feels natural . . . that's fine, just letting those natural movements occur . . . and maybe you could put some words to the movements . . . letting go of all those deep feelings so that you can learn from those experiences in order that they no longer trouble you. And you may be surprised that you can find unconscious learnings from reviewing this experience in such an emotional and somatic way, and you may be wondering how and when you will know this. Will it be now or later, consciously or unconsciously, or in a dream later tonight, or before or after next weekend?

Watkins (1995) writes:

> It is our contention that, when a patient is overwhelmed by the material
> released there is often insufficient attention to the following points: ego-
> strengthening; preparation of therapist; experience situation with the patient;
> follow-up with interpretation and reintegration, in order to undo past destruc-
> tive learning; repeat the abreactive experience until the painful affect has been
> released and subsides. . . . because the therapist attempted only to initiate the
> experience rather than actually to share it with the patient. (By 'coexperience'
> or 'resonance' we mean that the therapist does not merely observe the patient's
> obvious pain but rather that the therapist truly experiences the pain, fear or
> horror alongside the patient, albeit at a lesser level. When that 'coexperience'
> is the essence of the abreactive experience, the patient does not feel alone and
> can generally handle a far greater load of confrontation.)
>
> There will be times, however, when it may be advisable to attenuate and mit-
> igate the abreaction. These are situations in which the clinician should employ
> the slow release (or 'slow burn') approach described by Kluft (1988) or a 'silent
> abreaction' (H. Watkins, 1980, 1990b). These will occur when the therapeutic
> self of the clinician does not feel that 'we' (the patient and therapist together)
> can tolerate the raw affect that is expected to be released. (p. 6)

As an alternative to expressive motoric catharsis, silent abreactive methods
can be used. In these approaches the therapist suggests, for example, that the
patient imagines being angry with the protagonist. Alternatively, 'metaphorical' and guided imagination approaches may be used; for example, the
patient is asked to imagine hitting a large rock with a stick in order to clear
a pathway (as illustrated in Script 23). In imagining this scene it may be suggested to the patient that the rock 'changes into a person'. As the patient continues to hit the 'person', he or she 'silently' abreacts any repressed anger and
rage towards that person – an action that is often profoundly 'de-stressing'.

Another silent abreaction (distancing) approach is to ask patients to watch
themselves, or someone else, engaging in the abreactive experience on a television screen. I had an occasion to use this approach when a patient became
enraged and 'violent', and probably would have caused some damage to
himself or other members of the group. I suggested to the patient that he
watched himself continuing with the emotional behaviour on a television
screen. Such silent abreaction techniques provide useful approaches for
dealing with anger and rage (H. Watkins, 1980, 1990b). If resolution cannot
be accomplished in one session then the patient can be asked to imagine the
experience on videotape, which is then stopped, to be continued at the next
session.

Script 23 – Guided imagination for catharsis

And as you continue to follow the path along the river of life, beginning in
the mountains and ending where the river meets and merges imperceptibly

with the universal ocean . . . you come to a place where your path is blocked by a large fallen rock, leaving the way ahead impassable . . . there is no way around or over and the only way forward is to move the rock, but it is so large and heavy. Fortunately, you notice a big stick nearby and you have the idea to hit the rock with the stick so as to break it into smaller pieces . . . you pick up the stick and begin to hit the rock, noticing how you are feeling as you do that . . . noticing any images . . . thoughts . . . sensations . . . that you may experience . . . , and so on.

Script 24 – Managing catharsis

You can continue to experience those feelings that you had in the past, but knowing that it is not for real . . . that all this happened a long time ago . . . although you can eventually learn from these experiences . . . knowing that I am here with you in this room in the clinic on (*date*) . . . and you may prefer to watch and hear yourself on the television as you begin to feel more comfortable and relaxed just observing that experience . . . knowing that you can return to that time in your life to learn more in the future when it is more appropriate and you are able to utilise the experience in a more effective manner . . . and being aware of the sound of my voice . . . and the touch of my hand on your shoulder. And as you continue to breathe effortlessly in and out, then the next time you breathe in you may just allow your eyes to open . . . and being fully aware of where you are . . . the time of day . . . what is good in your life right now . . . how old you are . . . , and so on.

It is a matter of personal therapeutic style, theoretical framework, related training and experience and contextual appropriateness, as to whether the therapist encourages motoric or silent abreaction at any particular time in therapy.

Frequently, patients will need to continue to review or 'work through' formative experiences in successive sessions. Such cathartic 'working through' includes both cathartic uncovering and encouragement of behaviour change and goal-oriented work. It is important to ask their unconscious minds whether there are any other experiences they need to know about before they can go into the future without the problem. In any event it is important that the therapist supports this inner accessing so that patients do not foreclose prematurely before the problem solving and symptom resolution has a chance to take place.

Rossi (1995b) suggests using 'basic accessing questions' in order to facilitate a safe locus of control within the patient during this arousal phase. He provides the following examples of key questions (p. 9):

• Can you let yourself continue that for another moment or two in a private manner – only long enough to experience what it leads to next?

- Good, can you stay with that only long enough to learn what it is all about?
- Will it be okay to allow yourself to continue experiencing that privately for a while, difficult though it may be, so that you can learn what you need for healing (problem solving or whatever)?
- And will it be all right to keep most of that a secret that you don't have to share with anyone?

Rossi believes that patients have learned to shut off their natural ultradian problem-solving process to the point where they need a therapist to help them to relearn how to experience the normal tension of sympathetic system arousal in problem solving in everyday life. The following therapeutically reframing questions can help to facilitate the relearning (p. 9):

- Yes, breathing like that often means your mind and body are getting ready to deal with important issues. Can you allow it to continue for another moment or two until you recognise what it is?
- Can you actually enjoy your experience of energy (sweat, shaking, nervousness, trembling, confusion, uncertainty or whatever) coming up for a moment or two as a sign that you are on the way to dealing with whatever you need to?
- Have you ever let yourself have a good shake-up (or whatever) like this before, so you could really reorganise yourself?

Age regression

As well as effectively managing catharsis, therapists need to be able to manage regression appropriately. Age regression will probably occur when using hypnoanalytical approaches, as this is the essence of the various clinical approaches. Experiences that have been repressed since childhood, or even before, may become available in the trance state, and may contain a richness of imagery not usually associated with the waking state (Phillips & Frederick, 1995). It is important to ensure that the patient can deal with the recovered memories and to retain some attention outside of these powerful and often painful experiences. In order to assist the patient in maintaining an appropriate degree of dissociation, the clinician might offer the following suggestions:

> Wherever you are right now and whatever you are experiencing, it's important to know that there is an adult part of you who can hear my voice and respond to what I am saying. I would like that part of you to give me some kind of signal that it is present. . . . Good. Now your unconscious mind has given you a powerful experience and we certainly want to explore it in a way and at a time that will be fully useful to you. Since out goal today is to access positive experiences, I am going to ask your unconscious mind to use its creative resources to create a safe place or container that can store all of this

experience until a time that we both decide we're ready to open it up. I'd like the adult part of you to make sure that this is happening and, when the process is complete, let me know by moving a finger, or nodding your head. (Phillips & Frederick, 1995, p. 59)

Even though your conscious mind may not know what is happening, your unconscious can help find the source of your current stress and symptoms. . . . That's right, you can have the courage right now to continue receiving all those feelings of distress that tell the real story of your troubling symptoms. . . . That's right, as one part of you really feels that fully, another part of you can watch comfortably and calmly from the sidelines, so you can give an accurate report about the source of your problems. . . . When your unconscious mind knows it can continue this healing work all by itself, whenever it's entirely appropriate [*pause*], and when your conscious mind knows it can cooperate by helping you recognise these moments throughout the day when it is right to take a breather [*pause*], will you find yourself awakening feeling refreshed, alert, and as aware as you need to be of the meaning of this experience here today? (Rossi, 2002, p. 87)

Ideodynamic approaches in hypnoanalysis and stress management

That the mind can signal answers or responses that were apparently outside the control of consciousness has always been a mystery. Approaches to healing that utilised this phenomenon go far back in history, and have included visions, 'speaking in tongues', spirit writing, mystical rituals and dance. More recently, the work of Chevreul formed the basis of the clinical investigations of Braid and Bernheim, who recognised that the essential nature of trance and suggestion could be explained as ideomotor and ideosensory action (Weitzenhoffer, 1957). Although ideomotor movements were intensively investigated because of their importance to the basic theories of behaviour and hypnosis, ideomotor signalling in the context of clinical work is relatively recent (LeCron, 1954).

Dynamic theories of psychotherapy argue that there is usually amnesia for the source of the psychological problems and neurosis and, further, that it is necessary to gain insight into this repressed dynamic. Ideomotor signalling can be used as a procedure for uncovering unconscious material in a much shorter time than the traditional psychoanalytical approaches. It is also an excellent approach to introduce early on in the treatment process because it literally puts the 'control' in the hands of the patient.

The major goals of this form of combined exploration and therapy are as follows:

- To reveal unconscious resistance factors early in the course of treatment.
- To involve patients as active co-workers in the therapeutic process.
- To diminish the chance of forcing the patient to relive traumatic experiences that reinforce the original maladjustment patterns of behaviour. A

distant view in a partial regression using the patient's adult knowledge, perspective and mature understandings offers the optimum circumstances for productive, rapid therapy.

- To use a retrograde approach, going back in segments of time, which is best for the beginner in hypnoanalysis as it avoids chances of troublesome abreactions.
- To diminish the risk of an abreaction, which can be achieved by the therapist stating in advance of the search that the patient does not have to relive a troublesome event, that they may look at it as though the event is happening to someone else.
- To get unconscious permission before attempting to have the patient report a very stressful experience at a verbal level of communication. Problems can often be viewed at sub-verbal levels of awareness without the need for conscious recognition or verbal communication. The patient is best equipped to decide on this matter.

Ideodynamic signalling

Ideodynamic signalling is a utilisation approach that is particularly useful for uncovering repressed traumatic events, and their associated distressed feelings, related to current psychological and psychosomatic problems (Cheek & LeCron, 1968; Erickson & Rossi, 1979, 1981; Rossi & Cheek, 1988; Hawkins, 1994c, 1997a; Rossi, 1995a, 1996). By using ideodynamic approaches, the therapist, in collaboration with the patient, can 'control' the level of dissociation, and consequently the degree of emotional distancing and associated catharsis. In this way the 'cathartic process' can be managed very effectively. Ideodynamic finger signalling rapidly accesses state-bound information that may not be available to the patient's conscious verbal levels of functioning and, consequently, allows patients to reframe their problems unconsciously and psychosomatically. Rossi and Cheek (1988) state: 'Ideodynamic approaches appear to be most suitable for the rapid accessing and reframing of the psychological encoding of traumatic and stress-related problems, particularly when they are already in the process of becoming reactivated because of current stress' (p. 382).

Because the therapist and patient can therapeutically manage the levels of dissociation and emotional distancing collaboratively, the possibility of negative iatrogenic reactions is minimised considerably. It is also recognised that the repetitive, recursive and sequential reviewing of the original experience is often necessary in order to break through the traumatic amnesia (Scheff, 1979). Rossi and Cheek (1988) suggest that:

The permissive, exploratory, and ideodynamic approaches to therapeutic hypnosis pioneered by Milton Erickson eliminates the type of emotional pressures that encourages patients to fabricate (p. 12). . . . The induction and maintenance of a trance serve to provide a special psychological state in which patients can reassociate and reorganise their inner psychological complexities and utilise their own capacities in a manner in accord with their own experiential life. (p. 14)

Nevertheless, therapists need to be constantly vigilant regarding the validity of the information accessed through ideodynamic signalling. Rossi & Cheek suggest that there is a definite three-stage sequence involved in the valid recall of meaningful material. They argue that before a designated finger lifts changes in respiration, pulse rate and emotional reactions occur that demonstrate an inner orientation to the time of an important experience. Ideodynamic signals usually occur a few seconds after the appearance of this physiological memory. Verbal reporting of the experience may follow (if appropriate) these physiological and ideodynamic indications of the inner accessing of significant material.

A basic framework for using the ideodynamic finger-signalling methods for resolving psychological and psychosomatic problems is presented below (Figures 5.1–5.3), along with an indication of some of the potential problems. However, therapists are reminded that this is only a guide to possible interventions, and that they must creatively adapt the suggestions to meet their patients' requirements as well as their own. Cheek sums up the ideodynamic approach very aptly in the following statement: 'It proceeds best in an open and supportive atmosphere of positive therapeutic expectations and engages a sense of curiosity and wonder in both the therapist and patient' (Rossi & Cheek, 1988, p 21).

The approach recommended here is one that has been 'tried and tested' by the author with numerous patients over a number of years and with considerable success. Case studies illustrating the approach are provided in later chapters. It should be noted that the approach suggested here does differ in some respects to the model advocated by Rossi and Cheek. For example, no effort is made to have the signals on the same hand although some therapists (e.g. Braun, 1984; Putman, 1989) have advocated this strategy.

In order for patients to engage in these ideodynamic processes, they must focus their attention in ways that are trance inducing and, consequently, no other induction is required. For those with whom formal hypnotic inductions are used first, ideomotor and ideosensory signalling are excellent ways of deepening the hypnotic trance experience in such a way that the patient feels safe and in control.

Establishing finger signals

The ideodynamic 'yes' signals can be established in the context of ego-strengthening (Script 26), although the patient can simply be asked to say the word 'yes'.

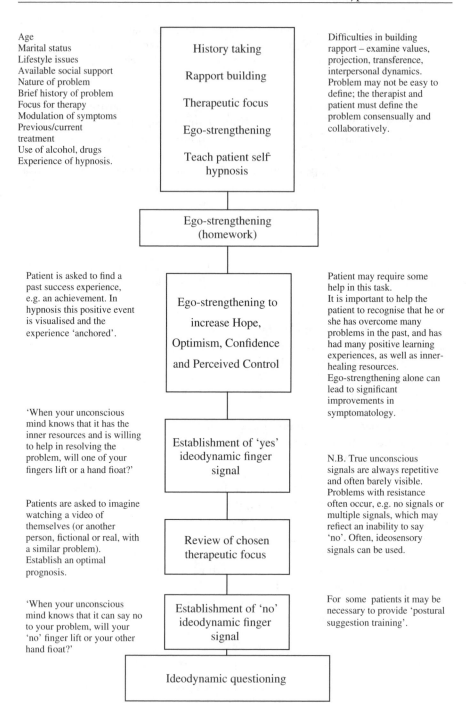

Figure 5.1:   Initiating the ideodynamic approach.

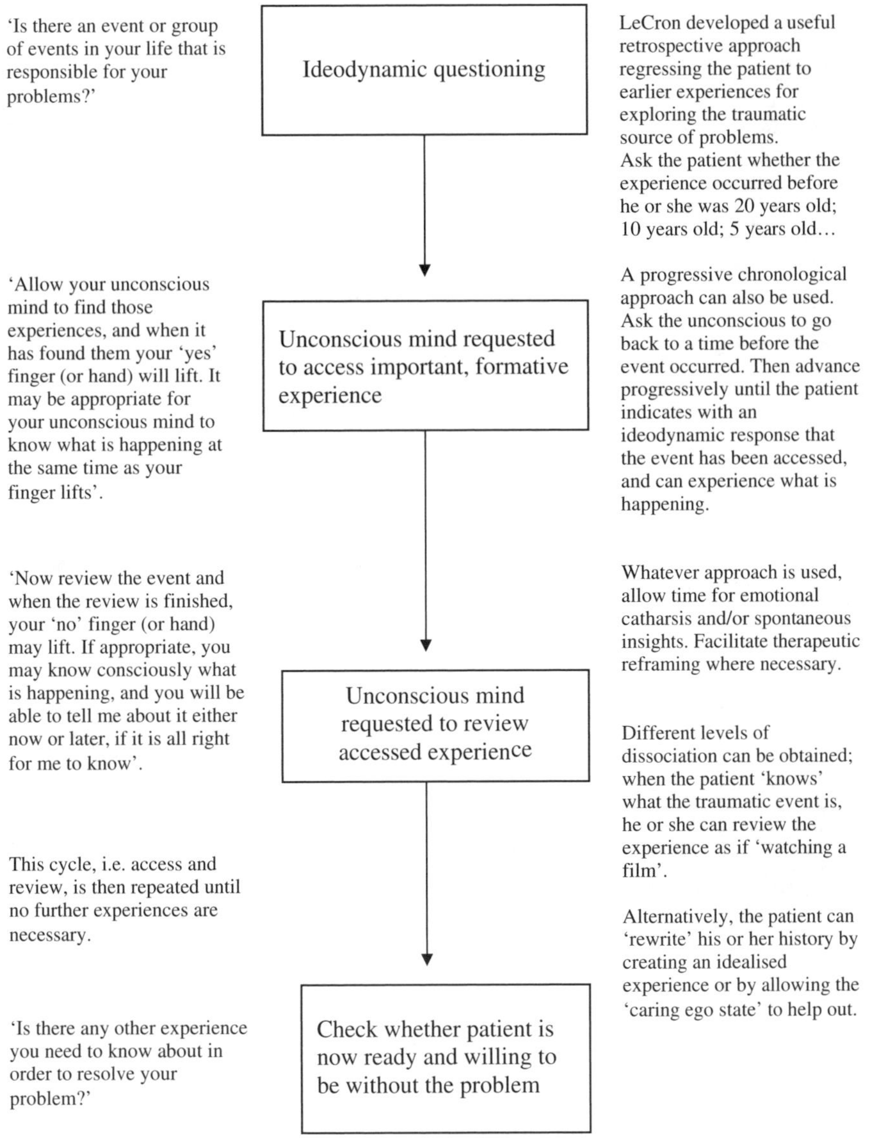

'Is there an event or group of events in your life that is responsible for your problems?'

Ideodynamic questioning

LeCron developed a useful retrospective approach regressing the patient to earlier experiences for exploring the traumatic source of problems.
Ask the patient whether the experience occurred before he or she was 20 years old; 10 years old; 5 years old...

'Allow your unconscious mind to find those experiences, and when it has found them your 'yes' finger (or hand) will lift. It may be appropriate for your unconscious mind to know what is happening at the same time as your finger lifts'.

Unconscious mind requested to access important, formative experience

A progressive chronological approach can also be used. Ask the unconscious to go back to a time before the event occurred. Then advance progressively until the patient indicates with an ideodynamic response that the event has been accessed, and can experience what is happening.

'Now review the event and when the review is finished, your 'no' finger (or hand) may lift. If appropriate, you may know consciously what is happening, and you will be able to tell me about it either now or later, if it is all right for me to know'.

Unconscious mind requested to review accessed experience

Whatever approach is used, allow time for emotional catharsis and/or spontaneous insights. Facilitate therapeutic reframing where necessary.

Different levels of dissociation can be obtained; when the patient 'knows' what the traumatic event is, he or she can review the experience as if 'watching a film'.

This cycle, i.e. access and review, is then repeated until no further experiences are necessary.

'Is there any other experience you need to know about in order to resolve your problem?'

Check whether patient is now ready and willing to be without the problem

Alternatively, the patient can 'rewrite' his or her history by creating an idealised experience or by allowing the 'caring ego state' to help out.

Figure 5.2: Ideodynamic accessing and review.

Script 25 – Setting up the 'yes' finger signal

Keep saying to yourself the word 'yes', feeling 'yes' in your body as well as thinking and imagining 'yes' in your mind . . . and when your unconscious mind can identify which is the 'yes' finger . . . just allow any changes in your hand to occur quite naturally, and you might notice that you can allow a

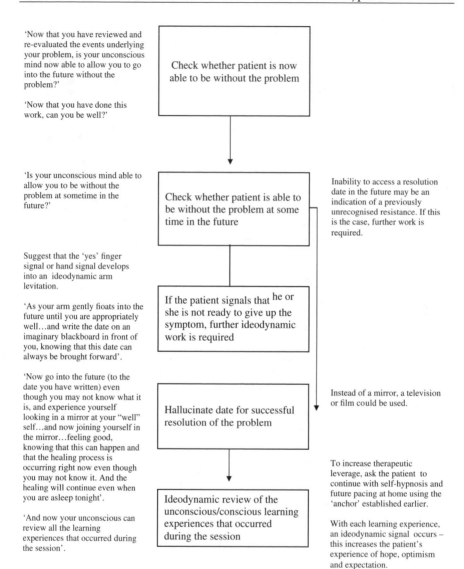

'Now that you have reviewed and re-evaluated the events underlying your problem, is your unconscious mind now able to allow you to go into the future without the problem?'

'Now that you have done this work, can you be well?'

Check whether patient is now able to be without the problem

'Is your unconscious mind able to allow you to be without the problem at sometime in the future?'

Check whether patient is able to be without the problem at some time in the future

Inability to access a resolution date in the future may be an indication of a previously unrecognised resistance. If this is the case, further work is required.

Suggest that the 'yes' finger signal or hand signal develops into an ideodynamic arm levitation.

'As your arm gently floats into the future until you are appropriately well...and write the date on an imaginary blackboard in front of you, knowing that this date can always be brought forward'.

If the patient signals that he or she is not ready to give up the symptom, further ideodynamic work is required

'Now go into the future (to the date you have written) even though you may not know what it is, and experience yourself looking in a mirror at your "well" self...and now joining yourself in the mirror...feeling good, knowing that this can happen and that the healing process is occurring right now even though you may not know it. And the healing will continue even when you are asleep tonight'.

Hallucinate date for successful resolution of the problem

Instead of a mirror, a television or film could be used.

'And now your unconscious can review all the learning experiences that occurred during the session'.

Ideodynamic review of the unconscious/conscious learning experiences that occurred during the session

To increase therapeutic leverage, ask the patient to continue with self-hypnosis and future pacing at home using the 'anchor' established earlier.

With each learning experience, an ideodynamic signal occurs – this increases the patient's experience of hope, optimism and expectation.

Figure 5.3:   Future pacing and reframing.

sensation to develop in one of your fingers that may change into a movement . . . , and so on.

The same approach can be used for the development of the 'no' finger. Also, the therapist can use ideosensory responses or sensations by asking the patient to verbalise whether a 'yes' or 'no' response has been experienced internally (and is therefore not observable to the therapist). The patient could also be asked to intentionally move a finger contingent upon an ideosensory experience (Script 26).

Script 26 – Setting up the 'yes' finger signal with ego-strengthening

> Just go inside your mind and find a time in the past when you were successful in decreasing the severity of your problem, when you felt in control . . . when you were more confident . . . and if you like you can experience yourself in that situation on a television screen . . . and when your unconscious mind knows that it has the resources to solve problems just as it did then, will it move one of your fingers? . . . you may notice it first as a sensation or a different kind of feeling . . . maybe a tingling, or a warmth, or even a twitch . . . just waiting for that to happen . . . and allowing that finger to gently move all by itself. (*The therapist can even suggest that the patient assists the finger to move.*) And when you're aware of those sensations in your 'yes' finger, then just lift it consciously so that I can know too.

It is also important to note that patients may demonstrate some considerable resistance to cooperating in the ideodynamic investigative process. Sometimes patients cannot, or will not, develop finger signals. Cheek suggests that this often occurs with patients who have experienced failure with other modes of treatment. An approach used by the author with patients who do not readily produce ideodynamic signals is to suggest the following:

> And in a moment, but not just yet, open your eyes and look at one hand, you already know which one to look at, and as you do, then will a finger lift, all by itself?, . . . and you may already know which finger that will be, . . . just waiting to see what happens . . . wondering what might happen when you open your eyes now.

Once the signals are established, the following questions can be asked of the patient's unconscious:

- Does your unconscious mind know that you can get totally well?
- Is your unconscious mind willing to help you do that?
- Would it be alright for you to go back to earlier events in your life and review all those relevant memories and experiences so that you can understand and resolve your problems?

If the answers to these three questions are negative, further investigation is necessary.

Managing dissociation

Ego-strengthening is a very important procedure prior to the engagement of the patient in uncovering (recovering) past events that are aetiologically important in the development of the presenting symptomatology. In the context of hypnoanalytical approaches, regressing to positive experiences when the patient has overcome problems and difficulties introduces the patient to the process of regression and is often the preferred method of treatment. One method of facilitating this process is to ask the patient to imagine that he or she is viewing a videotape of his or her life, or is tuned into a particular channel on the television. It can be postulated that an unconscious search for resources and solutions to the problem are initiated.

Anchoring positive resources

When patients are experiencing a positive event, which will be readily demonstrated to the therapist in a profound physiological way, they can be asked to 'anchor' the positive feeling by, for example, putting their thumb and forefinger together. Later on in the session, when they are accessing and reviewing negative experiences, they can use the 'anchor' in order to distance (partially dissociate) themselves from that experience. Utilising 'paradoxical' techniques such as relaxation, self-hypnosis and ego-strengthening will often lead to a dialectical 'pulling up' of the underlying and, often unconscious, negative memories and feelings and, consequently, make them more available to the patient at a therapeutically appropriate time in the future.

Balance of attention

It should also be emphasised that helping patients recover and build up their strengths and resources will enable them to access and work through negative and traumatic experiences in a more effective manner without negative iatrogenic reactions, including the risk of retraumatisation and the contamination and distortion of memories. This is particularly important in the context of the current debate concerning 'false memories'. Such an approach essentially reinforces the 'adult self' that is functioning on a rational basis in the 'here and now'. This enhancement of the 'ego split' between the 'hurt child' and the rationally functioning adult is an important element in allowing the patient to re-evaluate the (earlier) critically formative experiences from a 'distance'. Scheff (1979) argues that when patients are optimally distanced from their feelings (referred to as an 'aesthetic distance', or a 'balance of attention'), they can be both participants in, and observers of, their experience.

Greenson (1967) speaks of an 'experiencing ego' and an 'observing ego', and states that the successful patient is one who can move back and forth between these two types of experiencing. If the patient is purely the observing ego, then little emotional abreaction will occur, and the experience will be primarily a cognitive one, which in the psychodynamic context is not particularly useful. On the other hand, if the patient is an experiencing ego, this could result in negative iatrogenic reactions since dissociation is minimised. Ideally, the patient should experience historical (or current) traumatic/

conflictual events whilst observing them and, at the same time, remaining partially dissociated from them. In this way the patient can re-evaluate the experiences that dynamically maintain the symptomatology, either immediately post-catharsis or later on. An optimal balance of attention can be developed by careful preparation of the patient with respect to the enhancement of his or her rational adult functioning and critical awareness (i.e. sense of present-time reality).

However, regardless of the consideration devoted to the preparation of the patient, a premature dissolution of the dissociation may sometimes occur, although this may not involve an immediate and full revivification. On one occasion during a demonstration, the patient started to shake uncontrollably. When asked 'what's happening right now?' she replied that she was visualising a line of vertical black bars that made her feel very afraid. I asked her unconscious mind whether it was appropriate to know more about this and an affirmative ideomotor finger movement occurred. The following dialogue then took place.

Therapist: You're feeling very afraid. How old are you?

Patient: I'm four years old

Therapist: You're four years old and where are you and what is happening?

Patient: My father has just sexually abused me and is holding me by my ankles over the stairwell, and all I can see are the stair rods (*the black bars referred to earlier*)

Therapist: You know that this is not happening for real right now since I am here and you can hear my voice. Is there anything else you want to say about this experience?

Patient: My father is saying, 'If you tell your mother then I will drop you'.

At this point the patient started to sob and I encouraged this emotional behaviour by hugging her and applying a light fingertip pressure to her back. Further sessions were required in order for her to fully resolve this issue and the related problems.

Although appropriate levels of dissociation are probably managed effectively by the utilisation of ego-strengthening methods, other methods are also available (Script 27).

Script 27 – Managing dissociation

Imagine the (past) event on a television set where you can control the clarity of the image, the intensity of the sound, the intensity of the feelings by separate controls . . . just allowing yourself to experience what you can see, hear, feel . . . the intensity and clarity of your experiencing being appropriate to what you can effectively deal with right now . . . and you may be surprised to know that you can come to know later on something (more) about these experiences when it is more appropriate . . . and this may come as a thought, an image, a feeling or maybe in a dream . . . sooner or later.

The patient should be encouraged to keep a diary of these occurrences (i.e. dreams, feelings, thoughts), which can then be taken to the subsequent therapy sessions where further explorations can be made.

The 'bubble' technique described by Alden (1995) also allows for the management of dissociation. The patient can observe, from the safety of the 'bubble', the traumatic effects of the past without the danger of being retraumatised with consequent overloading of effect. Briere (1992) argues that getting in touch with the feelings associated with the past significant events whilst avoiding being sucked in facilitates a powerful psychosomatic reframing that is often an important component of therapeutic interventions with survivors of child sexual abuse.

Future pacing

With recursive accessing and reviewing of experiences, both at cognitive and affective levels, patients (usually) arrive at a point in time when they indicate ideodynamically by lifting the 'yes' finger that their unconscious mind is able to allow them to be without their problem(s) at sometime in the future. The patient can then be asked to try for a hallucinated date in the future when they are free of the problem and no longer afraid of it coming back. Be very careful how the request is worded. Your patient may have been told that he or she will 'just have to learn to live with your (problem)'. For this reason a simple request for a future commitment on a time when there will be no problem may subconsciously be interpreted as a death sentence. The alternative to having the problem means death if the problem is no longer present. To hallucinate a cure date means that a patient has relinquished immediate sources of resistance. It also means that a seed of hope has been planted and the unconscious mind may find ways of reaching a goal if the idea of a constructive aim has been accepted.

Script 28 – Future pacing

Your unconscious mind has indicated that it is now able to allow you to go into the future without your problem . . . and when you really know that this is happening will your arm float into the future to the time that your problem has been resolved? . . . knowing that healing is happening right now even though you are not aware of this . . . and will your hand write the date by which you will be totally well? (automatic writing), but knowing that you may become totally well before this time . . . and will you choose to forget to remember this date?

I have worked this way with many patients and follow up suggests that they usually do solve their problem(s) on or before the hallucinated date. However, it should be emphasised that no definitive research data are available to confirm this subjective finding. Nevertheless, this method sets up very powerful expectancies for change to occur. A ratification of the learnings that have occurred during the session can be carried out as this provides valuable feedback to both the patient and the therapist.

Script 29 – Ratification (1)

Go back to the time when you first started the therapy session and allow your unconscious mind to experience all the learning events that occurred . . . and each time that this happens then your 'yes' finger will lift as an indication that something positive is happening, even though you may not be aware of anything consciously . . . and when that review has finished will your arm float to the date by which your problem will be satisfactorily resolved?

Script 30 – Ratification (2)

Just experience yourself now (*current date*) . . . and now as time passes you already know that your unconscious mind is healing your mind and body, utilising all those learnings and experiences that have occurred during this session(s) . . . allowing those positive changes to get stronger and stronger until by (*the date the patient has indicated*) you are totally well . . . experiencing those changes . . . knowing that they are occurring with the help of your other (unconscious) mind. And experience yourself clearly in a manner that feels comfortable and appropriate.

As well as the ideodynamic signalling approach discussed above, there are a number of other standard uncovering techniques available, including Watkins' affect bridge (Watkins, 1971), ego-state therapy (Watkins & Watkins, 1979, 1990, 1993), the theatre visualisation technique (Wolberg, 1964), regression techniques, jigsaw and dream analysis (Wolberg, 1980; Rossi, 2000).

The affect bridge/somatic bridge

The patient is first provided with appropriate ego-strengthening techniques. He or she is then requested to experience the situation in which the negative feelings associated with the problem occur; for example, fear, anger, sadness. The clinician then asks:

Can you allow that feeling to grow stronger and stronger?

A number of different approaches can then be used to create the 'bridge' to the earliest time at which the feelings occurred. For example, when the patient is fully experiencing the negative emotions, whilst retaining an 'anchor' to his or her positive resources, he or she can be asked:

> When was the first time you felt like that? . . . First thought. How old are you now? . . . Where are you? . . . What's happening? . . . Who else is there? Who's not there?

Of course, the exact nature of the interventions, including the questions asked, will be contingent upon the patient's verbal and non-verbal behaviour. Other methods of effecting a regression to an earlier event associated with the elicited feelings include the use of appropriate imagery, such as following a road over a bridge, counting backwards from the patient's current age, as well as the use of ideomotor responses. It is also possible to use a 'somatic bridge' for somatic problems. A patient with psychogenic pain could be asked to:

> Focus on the pain and allow it to intensify (perhaps to a level of 7 or 8 on a 10-point visual analogue scale (VAS)) . . . when was the first experience associated with this sensation?

At all times it is important that the therapist manages the levels of dissociation related to the prototypical events in order to control for any iatrogenic reactions. As well as 'bridging' back in time to negative experiences, it is possible to 'bridge' back to positive events and experiences.

Ego-state therapy

Helen Watkins (1993) defines ego-state therapy as follows:

> Ego-state therapy is a psychodynamic approach in which techniques of group and family therapy are employed to resolve conflicts between various 'ego states' that constitute a 'family of self' within a single individual. Although covert ego-states do not normally become overt except in true multiple personality, they are hypnotically activated and made accessible for contact and communication with the therapist. Any of the behavioural, cognitive, analytic, or humanistic techniques may then be employed in a kind of internal diplomacy. Some 20 years experience with this approach has demonstrated that complex psychodynamic problems can often be resolved in a relatively short time compared with more analytic therapies. (p. 232)

Although the concept of segmentation of personality has been mentioned in the literature for many years (e.g. Janet, 1907; Freud, 1923; Assagioli, 1965/1975; Jung, 1969), the specific theory of ego-state therapy is attributable to John G. Watkins (Watkins, 1978; Watkins & Watkins, 1979, 1986, 1997; Watkins & Johnson, 1982). Watkins expanded the concept of ego-states developed by Federn (1952) and Weiss (1960), as well as Berne (1961) in transactional analysis. Phillips and Frederick (1995) state that:

> Ego states can be understood as 'energies' within the greater personality. They are not real people who are simply smaller or younger than the greater personality but rather aspects or energies of the individual. Ego states are adaptational. They always come to help. (p. 63)

Watkins contends that through hypnosis it is possible to focus on one segment of personality and temporarily ablate or dissociate away other parts. Ego states do not generally appear spontaneously and overtly, but can be activated through hypnosis.

In the early stages of therapy, the focus of ego-state exploration is primarily in the context of ego-strengthening, that is, in identifying and working with positive ego states, such as those responsible for nurturing, protection, survival, confidence, relaxation and inner healing. However, it should be emphasised that ego-state work should not be attempted until a good therapeutic alliance has been established, nor until the patients can trust in their own internal processes (Phillips & Frederick, 1995, p. 57).

There are many ways to begin ego-state therapy. A simple method is to hypnotise the patient, either with a formal induction, progressive relaxation or imagery. The therapist can then say to the patient:

> I'd like to talk to the part that is upset by what is going on, but if there is no such separate part, that's all right (H. Watkins, 1993).

Or, more specifically,

> I'd like to talk to that part of your mind that doesn't want to sleep (*or is alcoholic, or bulimic or a drug addict*) and maybe that part would like to step forward or make its presence known in some way, but if there is no separate part then that's all right.

The latter admonition is to prevent the creation of an artefact. The content is determined by the information received from the waking patient. Although one should strive at all times not to suggest the creation of a state by the therapist, it is unlikely that with normal precautions anything of significance will be initiated. Nevertheless, according to Watkins, highly hypnotisable individuals are capable of producing what they believe the therapist may want. Watkins adds:

> Even artefacts tend to be very transitory and disappear, because they represent no truly meaningful experience, past or present, to the patient, and with continuous, many-session therapy, fiction tends to get 'weeded out' from fact.

I often use a hallucinated room in which the hypnotised patient sits on a couch while I sit on a chair and then have the patient watch the door to see if 'anyone' comes in. There is an implicit suggestion that 'someone' may come in, but there is no demand to do so. An even less suggestive way is to ask the hypnotised patient, 'I wonder why Mary (name of the patient) has been having those headaches lately?' Or to probe further, 'I wonder if anyone can tell me about the headaches (or any other symptom)'. An ego state will often make itself known.

Sometimes an ego state will express itself only through a symptom in the body. For example, a headache may represent a communication from a particular ego state. The capability of the brain to develop patterns to protect itself seems limitless. (p. 238)

Gibson and Heap (1991) describe a procedure for helping patients resolve traumatic and disturbing childhood memories using the concept of ego states as follows:

The patient is regressed to any such incident and any abreaction is allowed to take place; the therapist then takes the patient through a kind of psychodrama in fantasy in which it is suggested that the patient's adult ego state, possessed of all the resources, knowledge and learning accumulated since that incident, goes back in time and provides the child ego state with all the reassurance, comfort and resources with which to cope with and resolve that memory so that it no longer causes problems for the patient. (p. 87)

Phillips and Frederick (1995) use both traditional and Ericksonian approaches. The treatment process involves uncovering the trauma(s) that are presumed to have caused the dissociative symptoms and strengthening the personality sufficiently to establish mastery over, and integrate, the uncovered material. They describe their basic working rationale as follows:

Hypnosis is of unparalleled assistance in this process because it enables the patient to enter the psychological and biochemical state in which state-dependent learning originally occurred and permits activation of individual ego states for therapeutic work. We endeavour to help personality parts tolerate uncovering and abreaction without retraumatisation, to master, renegotiate, and integrate the recollected experiences, to become strengthened, and to mature to such an extent that inner harmony is restored. The balance between ego-strengthening in the present and uncovering of experiences from the past is critical. We emphasise utilising the patient's own internal resources and assist the patient in learning to direct those resources into mind/body discovery, correction, reorganisation and integration. (p. 19)

Degun-Mather (2003) describes the treatment of a woman with a diagnosis of binge-eating disorder and a history of bingeing and periods of starvation throughout adolescence and adulthood. Ego-state therapy with hypnosis helped her to understand the cause of her compulsive bingeing. This was followed by the use of the affect bridge, which enabled her to access another child part of herself concerned with a fear of starvation and abandonment, and wanting to remain 'solid' but not 'fat'. By accessing the ego states, she was able to start an inner communication, and make cognitive and emotional changes. This was reinforced later with cognitive therapy, from which she had not gained much benefit previously.

Theatre visualisation technique (Wolberg, 1964)

In this approach the patient is requested to imagine that he or she is visiting a theatre to see a play. The therapist 'guides' the patient through the play (which is related to the problem) whilst allowing the patient the space for his or her own personal material (thoughts, feelings, sensations) to emerge spontaneously during the session. The play can be organised by the therapist into 'acts and scenes' depending on the information already provided by the patient – for example, Act One, Scene 1: The birth of the baby; Scene 2: The first year; Act Two, Scene 1: Six years later, and so on. Of course, this approach can also 'progress' into the future as well as 'regress' into the past.

A patient of mine presented with difficulties in relating to her father, who was terminally ill in hospital. She was unable to 'get close' to him either psychologically or physically, although she wanted to do so. In the 'theatre technique' she uncovered early material concerning sexual abuse by her father, and although she at first denied this, she gradually came to accept it. After four therapy sessions she was able to forgive her father and visited him in hospital to tell him this. He died soon afterwards.

Age regression

In the initial stages of treatment, age regression should be used primarily for ego-strengthening. Phillips and Frederick (1995) write: 'If the patient cannot experience positive age regression . . . this procedure should be postponed until the individual demonstrates more ego strength and has had more experiences of mastery during the other types of hypnotic experiences' (p. 58).

Positive age regression is achieved by suggesting that the patient go back in time to review positive experiences related to success, solving problems, passing examinations, feeling relaxed and confident, being physically and psychologically well (i.e. without his or her current stress-related problems), and so on, in order to discover (recover) stress coping abilities and resources that have been forgotten or are not currently in use. When the patient experiences these 'forgotten memories' psychosomatically, he or she can be asked to 'put their thumb and forefinger together'. As discussed earlier, this creates a positive anchor and can be used as such when the patient is accessing and reviewing negative scenarios later on in therapy. The 'positive anchor' can also be invaluable to the patient between sessions as a way of accessing positive feelings and sensations as a way of coping with stress.

An earlier discussion of catharsis in hypnotherapy has stressed the importance of partial regressions, where part of the patient feels the regressed age
whilst another part retains an adult perspective, with a consequent enabling
of a constructive reframing after an appropriate abreaction. In a complete
regression, or revivification, the patient 'relives' earlier experiences, often
with considerable abreaction, without the apparent presence of adult learnings, experience and rationality. In my view, a full 'conscious' regression is of
little therapeutic value, although some therapists advocate it in some clinical
situations (e.g. Greenleaf, 1969, 1990). Several psychotherapists claim that it
is possible to regress patients to birth and prenatal experiences (e.g. Janov,
1973; Grof, 1976, 1988; Lake, 1981; Verny, 1982). In my own experience, hypnosis can be very helpful in assisting this process. The experiences encountered may be positive or negative.

Methods of facilitating age regression

The hypnoanalytic approaches already discussed in this chapter all facilitate
age regression. Other approaches include both direct and indirect methods.
It should be remembered that it is important to ask for the patient's unconscious permission to access and review important aetiological experiences,
which may be traumatic, before proceeding with age regression and potentially abreactive approaches.

A simple direct method is to count the patient back chronologically from
his or her current age, noticing the patient's non-verbal behaviour throughout. This 'scanning' technique, or 'possibilia mapping', can initially be carried
out fairly rapidly as this usually prevents the patient from accessing state-
bound memories at a conscious level, although ideomotor and ideosensory
behaviours will often occur. During the regression, these can be noted and
verified during the age progression (i.e. counting forward to the patient's
current age). If it is judged to be clinically appropriate, the therapist can work
with the patient at any age during the regression or progression using whatever techniques the therapist has in his or her armamentarium.

Patients could also be asked to imagine themselves getting younger (Script
31).

Script 31 – Age regression

And you see in front of you a television monitor and a video machine. Beside
it there is a videotape with your name on it, on which your life is recorded
(*specific reference could be made to experiences related to the patient's problem,
e.g. sex, food, relationships, etc.*). Perhaps you would like to insert the tape into
the machine and play it in reverse, starting with the good things in your life
now in 2005 . . . and as you see and hear yourself in situations be aware of
how you are feeling . . . and if at any time the feeling becomes too uncom-

fortable then you can adjust the television set by turning down the sound control or the feeling control . . . and conversely you can turn up the controls when you're feeling really confident and happy . . . and when you are ready to unconsciously explore and re-evaluate all the relevant memories and experiences that occur whilst you're reviewing your life story, will a hand float naturally away from your leg?

A similar approach could have the patient imagine a television monitor with different channels for the patient's life, the patient in therapy, the patient in the future, for example. An analogous approach, the photograph album (Script 13) was presented in Chapter 3 as an ego-strengthening method. These methods all create a partial dissociation in that the patient is distanced from complete emotional experiencing. The patient is also presented with an opportunity to control the amount of dissociation by regulating the sounds, images and feelings. Remember that, in the early stages of therapy, it is important to facilitate significant dissociation, particularly where trauma is implicated.

Metaphors can also be used to facilitate the process of reframing stressful experiences. Hammond refers to these as 'trauma metaphors' (Hammond, 1990a, p. 535). These metaphors can include reference to the patient's own recovery from an illness or injury, or can refer to people in general. The oak tree metaphor presented earlier as an ego-strengthening method (Script 20, Chapter 4) could be suitably adapted as a trauma metaphor.

Jigsaw

The 'jigsaw' is designed to set off a process of visualisation, which may lead the patient into an awareness of any unresolved issues.

Script 32 – Jigsaw puzzle

Imagine yourself sitting in a chair and picture a small table in front of you. On that table are several different coloured and different shaped containers; there are red, blue, yellow and green; some containers are square, box like, some cylindrical. Inside each one of these containers is a separate set of jigsaw puzzles. Nod your head when you can see yourself, sitting at the table, with the different coloured containers. That's fine! Now I want you to choose just one of these containers – any colour and shape that you prefer – and take out the pieces of the jigsaw puzzle and put them on the table. Notice how there is no picture on the lid of the container, so I have no idea what the picture will eventually be – neither have you at this stage. But it will be a picture of a scene or an incident that is closely connected to your present problem.

Your unconscious mind knows exactly which pieces it is looking for, and will help you to fit those pieces together so that you can see what the picture is. So start now, putting the jigsaw together – a piece here – a piece there – and you can do it so much quicker in this relaxed state – much quicker than you would normally do – and when you wake up in a few moments you will be able to tell me exactly what you saw in the picture as it began to build up.

(*Ask patients to describe what they saw, providing as much detail as possible. Find out what was going on in the picture or what people are thinking about. Most people should have been able to visualise something that will describe their inner-mental state – whether in actual or symbolic form. Sometimes there are pieces still missing or the revelation may cause surprise or even abreaction – if the patient becomes upset then you can ask him or her to break up the jigsaw and put the pieces back into the box until they're ready to re-examine them.*)

A patient of mine added pieces to the jigsaw every session until there was only one more piece to find. She told me that she would complete the jigsaw at our meeting the following week. Unfortunately, she died unexpectedly the day before the session was due.

Dream work

Dreams are an enablement of a person's inner life, and both Freud and Jung utilised dreams as a means of understanding unconscious processes (Freud, 1900/1976; Jung, 1943/1966, 1954; Singer, 1973). A controversial aspect of psychoanalysis was its assertion that dreams not only provided information about the unconscious, that is, that they had a meaning, but that they were also a means of healing. However, there were essential differences between the theoretical views and techniques of Freud and Jung.

Jung's constructive method

Importantly, Jung was dissatisfied with the emphasis Freud placed on wish fulfilment and the sexual aspect of the unconscious. Jung was more interested in exploring the context of the dream itself, rather than trying to find its origin. Singer (1973) states it succinctly, as follows:

> This is based on the principle that the dream really means what it says. The unconscious presents a point of view, which enlarges, completes, or compensates the conscious attitude. Through the dream it supplies the missing elements of which the ego is unaware, thus exercising its function of striving towards wholeness.
>
> To discover what is missing from the conscious viewpoint, it is helpful to *amplify* the *associations* to specific elements of the dream itself. (p. 309)

This is unlike the Freudian approach of unilateral interpretation by the analyst, and a consequent imposition of ideas on to the patient. In contrast, Jung stated:

The analyst who wishes to rule out conscious suggestions must therefore consider every dream interpretation invalid until such a time as a formula is found which wins the patient's assent. (1954, p. 241)

I had first come to the fundamental realisation that analysis, in so far as it is reduction and nothing more, must necessarily be followed by synthesis, and that certain kinds of psychic material mean next to nothing if simply broken down, but display a wealth of meaning if, instead of being broken down, that meaning is reinforced and extended by all means at our disposal – by the so-called method of amplification. The images or symbols of the collective unconscious yield their distinctive values when subjected to a synthetic mode of treatment. Just as analysis breaks down the symbolical fantasy-material into its components, so the synthetic procedure integrates it into a general and intelligible statement. (1943/1966, p. 81)

Jung ultimately advocated a technique called 'active imagination', which required the patient to redream a dream in the therapy session, and to re-experience it. Sometimes the patient would regress back to a childhood experience, often with considerable emotional ventilation. Singer (1973) likens this to: 'a copious bowel movement after a long period of constipation' (p. 313).

A second aspect of Jung's constructive or synthetic method is the 'finalistic' standpoint, that is, what is the meaning of the dream for the future? It should be noted that dreams do not generally occur as isolated events, but as emerging evidence of ongoing unconscious processes often represented as a thematic series (Rossi, 1997). In an anecdotal report of a personal dream series, Rossi (2003b) describes how he replayed dreams in active imagination throughout the day in order to aid recovery from a stroke. He reports how he became preoccupied with certain numinous experiences in dreams and active imagination during his rehabilitation, which he regards as the 'royal road to mind–body healing, and rehabilitation'. In essence, Jung's constructive approach is a natural process that brings together conscious and unconscious in a synthetic manner, that is, in a dream. Rossi (2002) writes:

Sensitive but highly focused consciousness facilitates inner rehearsal and creative dialogue with the emergent, novel, and numinous images of our dreams and fantasies that Jung called 'active imagination'. Active imagination is a dramatic and numinous experience of arousing, engaging, and facilitating the psychobiological processes of healing and individuation. (p. 133)

The healing dream

As dreams can be easily induced and/or utilised in the psychotherapeutic process, the dream may be conceived as the 'healer within us' (De Benedittis, 1999). Although interpreting dreams may be useful for the hypnotherapeutic process, it is the induction and manipulation of hypnotic and nocturnal dreams that are most therapeutic for patients.

Erickson (1952a) frequently used the 'rehearsal technique' in working with dreams hypnotically. In this technique, the patient replays the dream and, with each replay, changes the characters as well as the setting of the dream. This approach allows patients to derive their own conclusions with respect to optimal problem solving. Edgette and Edgette (1995) liken the technique to a 'flower beginning to bloom, with the petals becoming more and more open with each dream' (p. 166).

In the context of hypnotherapy, asking patients to replay their dreams in the therapy session as well as between sessions would seem apposite. It would also make sense to provide post-hypnotic suggestions concerning dreaming, for example:

And later today, when you are asleep, will you find healing answers in your dreams? . . . or will you discover new learnings about the stress in your life and the inner resources that you have available to deal with it?

In 1972, Rossi proposed the dream-protein hypothesis, which is now substantiated by considerable research evidence. Rossi (2002) presents evidence that the immediate early gene-zif-268 is expressed during dreaming, which generates new protein synthesis, neurogenesis and stem-cell differentiation into new tissues (Ribeiro, Goyal, Mello & Pavlides, 1999; Hall, 2001). Rossi hypothesises that just as negative states of emotional arousal can initiate the psychogenomic network to initiate gene expression with resultant overproduction of stress proteins and illness, so can positive psychological experiences (e.g. ego-strengthening) initiate the novelty–numinosum–neurogenesis effect to facilitate gene expression, neurogenesis, problem solving and healing.

Case Study 1 – Hypnoanalysis: An Integrative Approach

The case study below illustrates the use of an integrative hypnoanalytical approach as well as a number of representative techniques. The 'patient' in this session was a 22-year-old female student (Ana) with a problem concerning anxiety and irritability, specifically in her relationships with people closest to her. She volunteered to take part in a demonstration given in a hypnosis and stress management course. The session was recorded and, afterwards, the therapist and patient added their comments. It should be noted that this presentation is not an analysis of the whole session, but of key selected segments.

The task of the therapist was to facilitate the process of unconscious healing in the patient using ideodynamic approaches. As discussed earlier, ideodynamic exploration can provide a systematic way to access, review and transform past experiences in a safe and creative way. Because this approach works at the level of unconscious integration and psychosomatic problem resolution, there is less chance of reopening traumatic wounds. Painful events can be restructured using available adult resources to re-experience the trauma from a different perspective, while developing a general sense of mastery over the past.

Initial interview

The therapist carried out an initial interview, which covered the following areas:

- The patient's suggestibility was assessed by using an adaptation of Spiegel's hypnotic induction profile (Spiegel & Spiegel, 1978 – refer to Script 1 in Chapter 3). This indicated that the patient could produce good ideodynamic finger responses and arm levitation.
- It was explained that the therapy was a collaborative process in which the therapist was there to assist Ana in finding her inner resources and the solutions to her stress-related problem. Questions were asked concerning the modulation of the problem; for example, Is the problem sometimes worse/better? Who is responsible for that, you or me?
- Questions were asked about the past, particularly with respect to Ana's approximate age when the problem began, and whether she had her own 'story' concerning an explanation.
- Expectations were set up in the patient at both conscious and unconscious levels by describing what kinds of things were about to happen (i.e. what the therapist will do and what the patient can be expected to do).
- Ana was asked to rate the problem on a scale of 0 to 10. By using the VAS, Ana learned that her problematic behaviours modulate, and that she could affect this process both consciously and unconsciously. Her unconscious mind was also requested to allow her arm to float to the time when the problem was non-existent or less severe.On a scale of 0 to 10, where 10 is the most severe, what is the intensity of your problem currently? . . . the worst it has ever been? . . . the most comfortable it has been? . . . Who is responsible for these changes? . . . and when your unconscious mind has found a time in your life when the problem was much better, will your arm float to that time? (*Ana's right arm floats*) . . . that's fine! . . . and when you know that you still have these resources to deal with your problem, will your arm drift back downwards towards your leg?

This is another example of Rossi's basic accessing question, where the implied directive is turned into a question (Rossi, 1995).

Establishing ideodynamic signals

No formal induction was used. However, the initial interview had included many suggestions that helped to initiate the trance. It should also be noted that Ana had already seen a number of 'pantomime' demonstrations.

Establishing the 'yes' signal

The ideodynamic 'yes' finger/arm signal was set up by utilising what Ana had already achieved, that is, to find a time in her life when she did not have the problem or when the problem was less severe:

> Allow your unconscious mind to find a time in your life when you did not have the problem . . . or when the problem was not bothering you, when you utilised the resources to stay healthy; allow your unconscious to do this without any interference from your conscious mind . . . it can happen all by itself as it did just a short while ago (*remember that Ana's right arm lifted during the implementation of the VAS*) . . . a finger may move first on your right hand, and you may be wondering which finger will move first . . . and you may be surprised when this happens . . . sooner or later, or your hand and arm may become lighter and float effortlessly away from your leg (*Ana's right arm floats again*).

Establishing the 'no' signal

The 'no' finger signal was established by asking the unconscious to signal with a finger when it knows that it can say 'no' to the problem:

> See yourself on a television screen with your problem. If you want you can turn the sound down and have the picture in black and white . . . and when you know that you can say no to the problem, then will a finger move on your other hand? And you may notice it first as a sensation in one of your fingers, which can change into movement, or your left arm may float . . . and when it does I wonder how surprised you will be (*a finger on Ana's left hand lifted and then her arm floated*).

The suggestion to Ana that she watch herself on a television screen created a dissociation that ostensibly decreased the possibility of an abreaction. The level of dissociation could be increased by suggesting to her that the picture could be black and white or even 'blurred', or by adjusting the sound.

Internal review

After the ideodynamic signals were established, Ana was requested to focus on her problem, and her unconscious mind was then asked the following:

> When your unconscious mind knows that it is appropriate to work with this issue in your life, will your 'yes' arm float? . . . Or, if it is not appropriate for you to do this work right now, will your 'no' arm float?

Ana's right arm lifted, indicating that her unconscious was ready to cooperate in the therapeutic work. The session continued:

When you know that you have the inner resources, will your unconscious mind indicate this (*her right arm began to lift*), . . . and when you are ready to access all those memories, experiences, emotions and sensations related to your problem, will your hand continue to float upwards? (*Ana's hand floated higher*) . . . and there is nothing you really need to know consciously unless it is appropriate for you to know right now . . . and you may learn more, if it is appropriate for you to know, from a dream when you are asleep tonight, or maybe tomorrow or the next day . . . and you may be wondering when this will happen.

During this experience, Ana showed signs of distress. When patients engage in an internal review, a spontaneous state of emotional arousal often occurs – for example, changes in respiration and muscular tone – as state-bound memories are released (Rossi, 1996).

I asked her:

As you're experiencing that feeling, how old are you?

Ana replied that she was eight years old. After the session she made the following comment:

I was almost certain that it (*the problem*) came into existence when I was 15, but as I was about to say that, my mouth opened and 'somebody' said 8. I found this not only surprising, but frightening too. The entire conversation that followed also went almost without my knowledge, as if I was not the one speaking. I could only sit there, observe, think what is going to be said next and try to make some sense of it!

I continued:

You're eight years old . . . what's happening in your life right now? Just staying with whatever comes into your mind knowing that you only need to allow those memories that are appropriate to come into your conscious mind . . . and all other memories, emotional, somatic and cognitive can stay in your unconscious. . . . Complete the sentence, 'I'm eight years old and I'm feeling . . .'. Say that again allowing the feelings to grow stronger and stronger . . . and stay with the feelings.

The techniques used (e.g. finish the sentence, repetition, say it louder or paradoxically, say it softer, stay with the feelings) encourage the patient to access and strengthen the feelings associated with the experience.

Ana found the experience too painful and discovered a 'natural' way of dissociating by consciously reminding herself of the fact that she was 22 years old and sitting in a classroom in Finland. The therapist should always make sure that an appropriate level of dissociation is maintained although, as in this example, sometimes the dissociation can partially collapse. A thorough preparation of the patient using ego-strengthening and present-time approaches, which build up the 'rational adult' and facilitate the patient's inner resources, is a necessary initial procedure. I noticed that Ana's breathing had become very shallow, so I requested that she breathe more deeply and indicate to me where she was experiencing any tension in her body. Ana indicated that she was experiencing tension in her chest, and I applied fingertip pressure to the area as she exhaled. Permission to touch her for therapeutic purposes, if appropriate, was sought earlier in the session.

> A little more sound as you exhale . . . just letting that happen quite naturally . . . bringing those sounds or words up from your chest as you continue to breathe more deeply and effortlessly. . . . What are you feeling right now? And maybe you can find some important conscious or unconscious learnings from this experience that you can utilise in the future to solve the current problems as well as others . . . knowing that you have the healing resources to allow that to happen. . . . And as I count forwards from 8, you can allow yourself to progress from that age until you are 22 years old . . . and when you are 22 years old will your eyes open so that you can come back into this room knowing that some important internal changes and learnings are taking place?

Appropriate touching of patients when they are in a 'regressed and emotional state' also provides them with an important positive communication about the 'here and now'. For example, in Ana's case that she is not really eight years old, even though part of her may be experiencing the memories of being younger. The patient is essentially 'split', with part of her being 8 (child) and another part being 22 (adult), thus facilitating the process of re-evaluation. Further ideodynamic questioning, including accessing and reviewing experiences related to the problem, was carried out until Ana indicated ideodynamically that she was able to go into the future without the problem(s).

Verification and progression

The experience was then verified and consolidated in the following way:

> And when your eyes close, will your unconscious mind review all of the learning experiences that you have had during the session? . . . and when you unconsciously review all of these experiences, will a finger on your right hand move all by itself when each of these learnings is recognised? . . . and when you have finished reviewing all of these experiences, then will your arm float up in recognition that the process is complete and you are ready to go into the future, sooner or later, without the problem? (*Ana's right arm floated*) That's fine . . . and your arm can float to the date by which the problem will have been completely resolved and you can write this date with your uncon-

scious mind . . . and you may choose to forget to remember this date . . . and when you know that your unconscious can continue with this inner healing, will you find your feet moving first or will your arms stretch first as you awaken to discuss whatever is necessary?

Verifying the therapeutic learning experiences is valuable both for the therapist and the client. Ana was given feedback concerning the observed finger movements, arm levitation and automatic date-writing. She was told that this was a positive indication of the success of the therapeutic session, and that any negative experiences can have positive effects in the longer term.

Homework

The following homework was then suggested:

When it is convenient you can find a relaxing place and just look at your right hand and allow it to float up, just closing your eyes as this happens, and go to the time when your problem(s) have been resolved . . . experience yourself clearly at this time in the future and, when you feel good and confident that your inner work can allow this to happen, then rub your thumb and forefinger together, and open your eyes. You can do this now.

Ana has learnt a powerful self-hypnosis approach, which she can use in a positive and goal-directed way (Alman & Lambrou, 1997), not only to improve her relationships, but for other problems also.

Positive regression

At the end of the session a positive regression was carried out:

Go inside your mind and go back to the time when you were eight years old or even younger, and find some very positive experiences . . . and when you have found those positive experiences, just allowing the feelings to flow through your whole body . . . getting stronger and stronger with every breath that you take . . . that's right, you are experiencing something a little different now? . . . those positive feelings are really showing in your face now . . . and when they are really strong then rub your finger and thumb together. . . . so that in the future, when you wish to access those positive feelings, all you need do is to rub the thumb and finger together just as you are doing now . . . and now as I count from 5 to 22, finding positive experiences with every age that you pass through . . . and when you reach 22 will your eyes open in anticipation that you are now actively using all of your healing resources to solve your problems, and that something within you knows it can continue this creative healing entirely on its own, nothing you need do . . . at appropriate times throughout the day when you need to take a break?

Present-time reorientation

This was part of the preparation for completing the session and returning to everyday life. A number of present-time techniques were used to ensure that Ana had reoriented to the present. These included asking her to:

- describe the room;
- describe how she would go home after the session;
- keep her present positive orientation and let go of all the negative images that possibly come to mind
- look forward to later in the day;
- describe her homework.

Eight months later, Ana reported that her hypnosis session had helped her cope with her relationships as well as other issues in her life.

Summary

It is important to note that the therapist had a 'working map' relating to the hypnotherapy session, although it should be emphasised that this was regarded only as a general and approximate guide, with creativity and uti- lisation being important aspects of the therapy. An integrative approach was adopted, incorporating cognitive-behavioural as well as generic dynamic strategies (Hawkins, in press). The broad approach was humanistic and phe- nomenological with no interpretation or diagnosis.

The therapist helped to facilitate the process of 'unconscious search' both for the 'inner healer' and for the underlying repressed dynamic that was main- taining the symptom and preventing solutions. The clinical approach adopted was democratic and collaborative, involving choice and self-determination, where patient and therapist worked together in finding solutions. This view promulgates the idea that the patient has the conscious and unconscious resources available, but requires assistance from a caring facilitator. It also implies that individuals participate in their own illness, and thus their own health, through a combination of mental, physical and emotional factors.

The overall hypnotherapeutic approach was considerably influenced by the work of Erickson and Rossi, although the theories, practice and research drawn from generic psychotherapy also made a significant contribution; for example, the importance of developing a trusting relationship and instilling a sense of hope and optimism.

In the next three chapters, the clinical techniques and approaches consid- ered hitherto will be applied to working with a number of specific stress- related problems.

Chapter 6
Treatment of Specific Problems (1)

In the recent film, *Motorcycle Diaries*, Ernesto Che Guevara's journey through Latin America on an old motorcycle is vividly captured. The roads were in a very bad condition and full of potholes and ruts, and so it was inevitable that parts of the motorcycle kept falling off because of the continuous vibrations. When this happened, Che initially repaired his machine by fixing the replacement parts with screws or nuts and bolts. But his repairs didn't last long because the repair was so rigid and quickly broke again. After mending his motorcycle in this way on a number of occasions, he decided on a different strategy. Instead of a rigid repair with screws and bolts, he used pieces of old chicken wire. When the motorcycle hit a rut, the replacement parts just flexed, without breaking!

Introduction

Many dysfunctions are often associated with, or exacerbated by, psychosocial stress. There are many psychosocial situations that might give rise to acute anxiety, such as surgical and dental interventions, gynaecological examinations, as well as adverse family and work situations. There is increasing evidence that hypnosis can be useful in the treatment of a wide range of stress-related problems, including:

- anxiety (Barnier et al., 1999);
- addictions (Green, 1999; Medd, 2001);
- obesity and eating disorders (Erickson, 1960; Hammond, 1990a; Young, 1995; Degun-Mather, 1995, 2003; Evans, Coman & Burrows, 1997);
- cardiovascular problems and hypertension (Crasilneck & Hall, 1985; Milne, 1985);

- the immune system and cancer (Spiegel, Bloom, Kramer & Gottheil, 1989; Walker, 1992, 1998; Walker, Johnson & Eremin, 1993; Walker et al., 1999; Walker & Eremin, 1995);
- dermatological problems (Price, Mottahedin & Mayo, 1991; Ewin, 1992);
- gastrointestinal problems (Whorwell, Prior & Faragher, 1984; Harvey, Hinton, Gunary & Barry, 1989; Whorwell, 1991; Gonsalkorale, Houghton & Whorwell, 2002; Gonsalkorale, Miller, Afzal & Whorwell, 2003; Simren, Ringstrom, Bjornsson & Abrahamsson, 2004);
- sexual dysfunction (Bakich, 1995; Hawkins, 1996, 1997b);
- sleeping disorders (Hearne, 1993; Kingsbury, 1993; Hawkins & Polemikos, 2002);
- respiratory problems (Wilkinson, 1988);
- chronic pain (Hilgard & Hilgard, 1994; Jack, 1999; Williamson, 2002);
- headaches (Alladin, 1988);
- tinnitus (Karle, 1988).

Good reviews with respect to specific medical, dental and psychological problems are provided by Hammond (1990a), Heap and Aravind (2001) and Barabasz and Watkins (2005). In this chapter, a number of specific problems will be examined with respect to hypnosis treatment. It is not intended to provide a comprehensive review, but that sufficient information is given to enable the clinician to develop appropriate therapeutic interventions for stress-related medical, psychological and behavioural problems. It should be remembered that it is extremely important that, prior to carrying out hypnosis interventions with a patient, all relevant examinations have been carried out by the appropriate professional; for example, if treating a patient for persistent headaches, all relevant neurological examinations should have been performed and the results evaluated. It goes without saying that appropriate contact with other significant professionals is made.

For the treatment of all problems, it is recommended that ego-strengthening is carried out in the first few therapy sessions, and at the beginning and end of a session. Ego-strengthening interventions could be generic (for example, see scripts in Chapter 4), or constructed for the patient's specific problem. All problems can be approached, at least initially, by assisting the patient to find his or her inner resources, as well as with Rossi's generic hypnotherapy approach.

Script 33 – Finding inner resources

Just close your eyes . . . and go inside your mind and find all those inner healing resources that you can utilise to solve your problem . . . and you already know that you have the solutions to your problem(s) and that a conscious and unconscious understanding of the experiences related to the problem can assist you in finding and utilising those resources now and in the future . . . and when your unconscious mind knows that you have those resources I wonder whether you will notice this as a sensation or a move-ment in one of your fingers or a hand? . . . and when you do can you allow those resources to flow to that part of your mind and body . . . healing that part of you to optimal functioning? . . . knowing that this healing process will continue long after you have left here and into the future . . . even whilst you are asleep . . . and when you really know that this is happening all by itself, will your eyes open, finding yourself awakening, feeling refreshed and alert?

Occasionally there are patients who say that they 'cannot find any inner resources' even when asked to signal ideodynamically with their finger. In these instances it is important for the therapist to provide an indication that the resources will be available later on.

Script 34 – Finding inner resources: seeding

Although the resources may not be available to you right now, you can allow your unconscious mind to continue to search for those inner resources that you have within you . . . even though you may not realise that right at this moment . . . knowing that sooner or later you will find those resources . . . and that this searching process will continue at the back of your mind long after you've left here today even though you're not aware that this is hap-pening . . . and you may learn about your inner resources when you are asleep, perhaps later today as you dream . . . this may happen tonight or tomorrow night and I would be surprised if you didn't learn something before the weekend . . . just waiting for that to happen, nothing you need do right now except trust in your unconscious mind to continue with the process of natural healing . . . wondering when you will notice your inner resources for dealing with your stress problems.

Script 35 – General hypnosis intervention for medical problems

Close your eyes and go inside your mind and find your healing resources . . . allowing the healing energy to flow around your body deep into every cell . . . healing and restoring every cell to optimal functioning . . . gently flowing through your body quite effortlessly . . . as it will continue to do so long after you have left here and into the future . . . and there may be a part of your body that would like to receive this special loving, healing energy right now . . . allowing that healing energy to flow to that part of your body . . . massaging away all the discomfort . . . and restoring those cells to optimal functioning . . . allowing this process to continue long after you have left here . . . even in your sleep later tonight.

The above approach is also very useful as an adjunctive procedure with patients receiving conventional medical treatment such as chemotherapy or dialysis.

Script 36 – A complete hypnotherapeutic session using the basic accessing question (adapted from Rossi, 1996, p. 194)

The patient starts the session with his or her hands outstretched and palms facing one another.

When your inner mind is ready to solve your problem, will those hands move together all by themselves to signal yes? . . . or will they move apart indicating that your unconscious mind is not yet ready to work with this particular problem but maybe another problem? . . . when your inner mind is able to know all those memories, sensations, emotions and experiences related to the chosen problem, will one of your hands float down towards your leg all by itself? . . . and when that hand touches your leg, will your other hand drift down when your unconscious mind is able to utilise all those options for solving the problem now and in the future? . . . and when your unconscious knows that it can continue this inner healing into the future, even whilst you are asleep, will you find yourself becoming more alert as you find yourself back in this room?

Autogenic Training

Although autogenic training is not strictly a hypnosis approach, it is similar in some respects, and is included here due to its usefulness in many stress-related situations. A detailed examination of the methods commonly used can be found in Schultz and Luthe (1969, p. 73). The script below combines a number of the standard exercises described by Schultz and Luthe.

Script 37 – Modified autogenic training for generic stress management

Be aware of your breathing, following the passage of air up through your nose and back out again . . . and the next time you breathe in just roll up your eyes under your closed eyelids if they are already closed, allowing your eyelids to relax and close to a point where you feel they just will not work . . . and allow that feeling of relaxation and peace to flow right down to the tips of your toes . . . and say to yourself, 'my right foot is warm and heavy' (repeat several times) . . . just noticing how warm and heavy your right foot is becoming . . . and now say to yourself 'my left foot is warm and heavy (repeat several times) . . . noticing how both your feet are becoming warm and heavy . . . and say to yourself, 'both my feet are warm and heavy' . . . allowing that warmth and heaviness to spread up into your legs, massaging away all the residual stress and tension as your legs become warm and heavy, and say to yourself, 'my legs are warm and heavy' (repeat several times) . . . allowing the warmth and heaviness to spread effortlessly to your abdomen and say to yourself, 'my abdomen is warm and heavy' (*N.B. not to be suggested for women who are pregnant*). (*Similar suggestions can now be made progressively for the whole body, that is, chest, shoulders, arms and hands, neck and face).* Your body is now warm, heavy and relaxed . . . and say to yourself, 'my body is warm, heavy and relaxed' . . . allowing your forehead to become cool and comfortable, and say to yourself, 'warm heavy body, cool relaxed forehead on a warm summer's day, I am at peace' . . . and you can remain in this peaceful state as long as it is appropriate. And this is something you can do for yourself when it is suitable for you to do so.

Once again, it should be emphasised that the above script is very abbreviated and should be adapted by the clinician to meet the requirements of the particular situation.

A number of specific problem areas, often related to stress, are presented in detail below. Although individual patients will, of course, be treated differently depending on many factors – for example, nature of the problem, available social support, degree of chronicity, previous treatment, and so on – the cases discussed below provide some clinical templates for working with patients 'in general'.

Anxiety

It is likely that most patients who are stressed feel anxious. People are more likely to experience high states of anxiety or panic attacks when their general stress levels are higher (Hollander, Simeon & Gorman, 1994). This can occur with respect to many situations, such as performance anxiety in relation to work, sexual behaviour and academic examinations, stressful medical procedures such as gynaecological examinations, surgery, injections and childbirth, relationships, interviews, specific situations (e.g. dental phobia), and so on. Anxiety has increased in contemporary society due to the growing number of decision-making choices available (Schwartz, 2005), as well as the pressure of time and finances to achieve well-balanced and healthy lifestyles (Script 38). The influence of advertising and the media have also augmented stress and anxiety by increasing peoples' expectations with respect to the acquisition of material wealth, the realisation of glamorous lifestyles and the attainment of an ideal body shape. This focus on consumerism and 'the cult of the celebrity' is endemic in Western society and contributes to the increasing problem of stress and unhappiness. As a consequence, counselling and psychotherapy have often become the 'prescribed medicine' for problems of living.

In working hypnotherapeutically with anxiety, a combination of relaxation, ego-strengthening, goal setting, time management and action planning using some of the approaches already presented in previous chapters is often sufficient. This can be complemented by the integrative use of hypnoanalytic approaches. Many of the ego-strengthening approaches described in Chapter 4 are useful for anxiety/stress management, as well as other general scripts presented in the book, such as breathing relaxation (Script 45), the ball of light (Script 47), magic shower (Script 48) and magic flower (Script 49).

Script 38 – Time management/work–life balance

When you are ready to review the way you spend your time, just allow your eyes to close . . . and will one of your arms float as your unconscious mind reviews the way in which you spend your time with respect to important aspects of your life . . . your work . . . your personal relationships . . . your leisure time . . . experiencing all those sensations, emotions, thoughts, images and memories . . . related to how you live your life? . . . and when you know that you can utilise all those learnings, will your other arm float all by itself? . . . that's fine! . . . utilising those learnings to find solutions to any issues in your life right now. And, when you know that changes are happening in you right now, with respect to the prioritisation of goals and activities, will your arms float back down to rest comfortably on your legs so that your eyes can gently open? And often changes occur quite imperceptibly just as ice gradually changes into water, and water can get warmer and warmer without there being any changes apart from temperature, and it is only when the water reaches 100 degrees that it changes into another form, steam. . . . And you wonder whether you will have an important dream later today that may tell you something significant about the way you lead your life and positive changes that are being made deep within you right now without you even noticing until they happen.

There are many approaches to facilitate decision-making processes with individual patients. One that I have used on a number of occasions is the 'inner guide', or 'friendly animal' (refer to Script 17 in Chapter 4). The patient meets his or her friendly animal and allows it to make the decision. One of my patients could not decide whether to leave her partner, which was causing her considerable stress and anxiety. Both partners had attended counselling, but this approach was considered to be unsuccessful. In the hypnosis session her 'friendly cat' informed her to leave and she felt very confident that this decision was the right one. She left her partner within days of the session and a one-year follow-up revealed that she did not regret making this decision. Another approach utilising an ideodynamic approach is presented below.

Script 39 – Decision making

First, 'yes' and 'no' signals are established and the patient is then asked to acknowledge whether or not he or she is ready to make a decision (refer to Chapter 5 for more information regarding ideodynamic signalling). If a 'yes' signal is provided, the therapist can proceed as follows:

Focus your mind on leaving your partner, allowing your unconscious mind to process all those experiences, memories, motivations and feelings related to this possibility . . . and you don't need to know anything consciously just yet . . . and when this is happening so that you can learn from this experience, will one of your hands float all by itself? . . . That's fine! . . . And now focus on the possibility of staying with your partner . . . allowing your unconscious mind to process all those experiences, memories, hopes and aspirations related to this possibility . . . and when you know that you can utilise these experiences and learnings, will your other hand float? (*The patient now has a way of representing the two courses of action*) And maybe you can allow your unconscious mind to make a decision with respect to your problem . . . perhaps now or maybe later in a dream . . . or in some other way . . . or if it's appropriate right now, will one of your hands lift by itself in recognition that a decision has been made? . . . That's fine! . . . your unconscious mind has indicated that . . . , and so on.

If there are no ideodynamic movements, this could indicate that either the patient is not ready to make the decision, or that there are other solutions apart from the two being proposed.

And your unconscious mind can continue to review all the experiences related to this issue in your life, trusting that you can learn from this inner healing process . . . and when you are ready to utilise those learnings, then you may know in a dream or in some other way what you may need to do with respect to the relationships in your life . . . and you may be surprised when this happens . . . sooner or later . . . maybe tonight or perhaps before or after this weekend or next . . . so that when we meet for our next session, will you have something important to tell me?

The two cases described below present an integration of strategic and dynamic approaches, and illustrate a number of hypnotherapy techniques for dealing with general interpersonal and social phobias as well as specific phobias (e.g. lifts, heights, animals).

Case Study 2 – Lift Phobia

The patient was a 22-year-old Portuguese female psychology student (Sonia) who volunteered to be a patient in a hypnosis course that she was attending in Finland. She had no experience of hypnosis apart from involvement in group hypnosis sessions earlier in the course. She had also watched a number of demonstrations. A short interview elicited the following information: that she was afraid to use the lift as far back as she could remember, and that this posed considerable inconvenience for her. She always used the stairs even when this involved a large number of flights. On a few occasions when Sonia had been forced to take the lift, she experienced considerable emotion, including intense fear and crying, which lasted for some time after the event. She had received no previous treatment for the problem. It was explained to her that she had the resources to solve this problem and that, by the end of the session, she would be able to take the lift to the ground floor of the building. The therapist also mentioned that he had successfully treated another Portuguese student from the same university with a similar problem, and that Sonia could achieve the same success.

Ideodynamic exploration

It was decided to use an ideodynamic exploration along with goal setting and ego-strengthening, as outlined in Chapter 4. First, the 'yes' and 'no' finger signals were established and Sonia was asked to imagine herself with the problem on a television screen (in order to increase the dissociation so that any negative reactions could be avoided):

> Experience yourself with the problem on a television screen and let me know by nodding your head that this is happening . . . you may experience some sensations, feelings and thoughts when doing this but these will be minimal and won't disturb you too much . . . and when you know that you have the resources to solve this issue in your life, will your unconscious mind move one of your fingers?

A finger moved, and was designated the 'yes' finger. The therapist continued:

> Experience yourself once more with the problem on the television screen, and when you know that you can say no to this problem, will another finger move?

A finger moved, and this was designated the 'no' finger.

> Experience yourself once more with the problem on the television screen, and I would like to ask your unconscious mind whether there is an experience that you need to know about in order to solve the problem?

The 'yes' finger moved, indicating that this was the case.

> Allow your unconscious mind to find an experience in your life that is connected to the problem, and when it is found will your unconscious mind move your yes finger? . . . even though you may not know what that experience is consciously.

The 'yes' finger lifted again, indicating that the experience had been found.

> And now allow your unconscious mind to go through that experience from the beginning to the end and, when this has been completed, your 'no' finger will lift.

The 'no' finger lifted.

Experience yourself once more on the television screen. Is there any other experience you need to know about either consciously or unconsciously in order for you to go into the future without the problem?

After a little while the 'yes' finger lifted.

Recursive finger questioning and progression

The procedure detailed above, involving access and review of a causative event, was then repeated. The next time that Sonia was asked whether there were any other events that she needed to know about, a 'no' finger response occurred. She was then requested to go into the future with the unconscious solutions that she had discovered and to see herself on the television screen entering a lift whilst feeling calm and comfortable. This she did without any difficulty. Whilst she was engaged in this, the therapist related to the group details of a similar case involving a young female patient from the same university. They were told that immediately after the session the student went to the lift outside the classroom and travelled up and down a few times without any problems. These comments were not directed specifically at Sonia, but, inevitably, she will have listened to the story (this approach is similar to Erickson's 'My Friend John' technique described in Chapter 3).

Reality testing

The therapist then accompanied Sonia to the lift outside the classroom and she was able to enter it and travel up and down without any major problems. There was, of course, some initial apprehension, but this was soon followed by surprise that the session had been so effective. She was asked to write some comments sharing her impression of the session, and these are reproduced below:

> Before the hypnotherapy session I had tried many times during the past two years to go in the lift, but without success. I don't know why I have this problem, although my personal explanation is that as a child I used to watch horror movies, and this might have something to do with it! I never use the lift, even if I am on the twelfth floor of a building. I will always use the stairs. Obviously this is often very inconvenient, but I feel that I have no choice. Since coming to Finland as an international student I have tried on a couple of occasions to use the lift with a friend. On both occasions my body was shaking and I was in a panic. When I attended the hypnosis course at the university I was looking forward to learning something about hypnosis, but I never thought I would try it. The curious thing is that this very week I was thinking about contacting a psychologist to help me with the problem. The first lecture on hypnosis created a very favourable impression. The next day a student with a spider phobia volunteered to work with her problem in front

of the whole class. Her therapy seemed to work very well and she produced some excellent ideodynamic behaviours, and was able to experience herself in the future without her problem. At this point I felt that I could do the same, so I volunteered to be next. During my hypnotherapy I became quite emotional and had tears in my eyes. I was happy to be 'cured', but I didn't really believe that it could happen. At the end of the session I felt really good and the therapist invited me to take the lift, which was close by. I was still apprehensive, but I did it. I have now been using the university lift for over two weeks without any problems, and yesterday I used a lift in a large shop. I expect that I will not experience any further problems.

Follow-up

A three-month follow-up revealed that Sonia continued to use lifts without too much stress, although she preferred to be accompanied by friends. She wrote a personal report on her experience and her final words were: 'Now I have no more phobias and I am free to do whatever I want in my life because nothing bad is going to happen!' Further follow-ups, at 6 and 12 months, revealed that Sonia, because of her job situation, was using lifts everyday without problem.

Case Study 3 – One-Session Treatment for Dental Phobia

During the initial phase, it was important to establish rapport and a warm trusting relationship. Other tasks, which have already been discussed in Chapter 3, included the following:

* taking the history;
* defining the problem;
* defining the therapeutic focus, which had to be realistic and pragmatic for the patient;
* promoting a sense of hope for the future via the use of positive and optimistic language.

It was established that the patient (Cristina) had a phobia for the dental clinic. Whenever she thought about visiting the dentist, and in particular the dental chair, she experienced a strong feeling of anxiety with concomitant physiological changes. Additionally, Cristina had a fear that the local analgesia would not be sufficient to deal with the pain, and that extra analgesic would be required. The therapeutic goal was negotiated and it was agreed that a realistic aim was for Cristina to be able to go to the dentist without experiencing strong negative feelings.

Hypnosis demonstration

Preparation for the main treatment session was primarily a demonstration of hypnosis and the setting up of ideodynamic finger responses. Cristina was informed about the hypnotic procedure and given the opportunity to ask questions. This procedure helped to overcome resistance to the hypnotic experience and also reinforced the development of the therapeutic alliance.

> Be aware of your breathing, just imagining that, as you breathe out, you are breathing away all of the residual distress in your body . . . and the next time that you breathe in take an extra deep breath . . . hold it . . . and as you breathe out just allowing your body to become totally limp and relaxed . . . just like a rag doll . . . no place to go right now except to just relax and enjoy those peaceful feelings and sensations . . . just letting your body and mind float . . . and as you continue to enjoy those floating sensations you may notice how you can allow one hand to become lighter . . . and lighter . . . floating into the air as the sensations gradually melt away, allowing your hand to eventually become totally numb . . . and when it is appropriately numb then a finger on your other (left) hand will lift on its own . . . nothing you need do . . . just allowing it to happen.

A finger on Cristina's left hand moved gently upwards, indicating that her right hand was now numb. She was then requested to allow her hand and arm to float gently down to rest on her leg, and to open her eyes to look at it, but keeping the sensations just as they were. Cristina was then told that if she could make her hand go numb she could do the same with her mouth when relaxing in the dental chair.

> And in a moment when I count from one to six, will the normal sensations return to your hand and arm? . . . knowing that you have the ability and inner resources to allow your arm to become lighter and lose its sensations . . . an ability that you can make use of to deal with the problems that you have concerning the dentist . . . but only utilising this resource when it is safe and appropriate to do so and for your own health and well-being.

A short discussion with respect to the hypnosis session followed. Cristina was then asked to look at her hand and notice what happened. Cristina's hand started to float into the air as she looked on with some surprise! She also allowed it to become numb, demonstrating that she had complete control over this phenomenon. She counted herself out from one to six, at which point the normal sensations returned.

Further hypnosis was induced as follows:

> Close your eyes and go back to the experience that you were enjoying just a moment ago, just letting that happen . . . nothing you need do to make it

happen . . . you have a memory in your unconscious mind and body of everything that happened. . . . And now allow your mind to float back to a time in
your life when you were feeling positive and confident about yourself . . . and
to allow the associated feeling to become stronger and stronger . . . knowing
at one level or another that you can utilise these positive resources to deal
with current and future issues in your life.

Ideodynamic signalling

This ego-strengthening procedure was linked to the development of ideodynamic finger signals.

And when your unconscious mind knows that it has the resources to allow
you to feel like you're feeling now whenever you wish, even when you are
sitting in the dentist's chair, then your unconscious mind will move one of
your fingers . . . it may be on your right hand . . . it may be on your left hand
. . . just waiting to experience which one will lift first. You may be wondering which finger will move first all by itself . . . nothing you need do to make
it happen . . . You may notice it first as a sensation in the tip of the finger or
across the back of your hand . . . a way of preparing that finger to move . . .
sooner or later (*after a short while a finger lifted*). And that finger can be your
'yes' finger, so that your unconscious mind can communicate a 'yes' by
moving that finger when it is appropriate later on in this session.

Having established the 'yes' finger signal, a 'no' finger signal was then established in the following manner:

And now, Cristina, I would like you to imagine that you have in front of you
a television set that has all the usual controls for sound and brightness, as
well as another control for feelings. You can turn this feelings control up or
down to increase or decrease the feelings that you are experiencing. There is
a videotape on the table labelled, 'My visit to the dentist'. . . . I want you to
watch that tape, but before you do, allowing yourself to become even more
relaxed, calm and peaceful . . . and now watching the tape staying calm,
peaceful and relaxed knowing that you can feel like this in the future . . . and
when your unconscious mind knows that it can say no to the problem that
you are here for, then it will move another finger, maybe on the same hand,
maybe on the other hand . . . just waiting for that to happen . . . that's right!

The therapist waited until another finger moved and designated it as the 'no'
finger.

Hallucinating a 'cure' date

Ideodynamic signals were thus established within the context of ego-
strengthening. These were then utilised for ideodynamic questioning so as to

allow the patient to access the experiences that were dynamically related to the dental phobia. These experiences were accessed and reviewed 'unconsciously' and recursively until a 'no' signal was given, at which point the patient was asked the following question:

> Is there any other event that you need to know about in order that your unconscious mind can allow you to go into the future without the problem?

When a 'yes' signal was confirmed the therapist continued:

> Just allowing that 'yes' finger to continue lifting, taking with it your left hand and lower arm . . . allowing your hand to float up into the future, and when your hand touches your shoulder you can be in the dentist's chair at sometime in the future, knowing that you can, now that you know the underlying reasons, experience that event feeling calm, relaxed and comfortable . . . and just allowing that hand to write the date when you can do this on the imaginary writing pad in front of you. And now just letting your hand drop back down to your leg, just as slowly as that takes, knowing that you already have the solution to the problems that you brought with you today.

Cristina was then brought out of the hypnosis by counting from one to six. In hallucinating a 'cure date', Cristina indicated that she had relinquished immediate sources of resistance. The possibility that the unconscious mind may find ways of reaching the therapeutic goal had also been achieved, thus continuing the 'optimistic language' used throughout the therapeutic procedure.

Future pacing

Cristina was asked to close her eyes again and to:

> Go inside your mind and find the good feelings that you were experiencing just a moment ago. It can help if you just put your thumb and forefinger together, allowing those good feelings to fill your whole body, and flowing into your mouth and gums . . . and floating into the dentist's chair at some time in the future . . . knowing that you can allow the analgesic injection to work optimally and effectively . . . as the dentist works inside your mouth you are aware of mild, but not unpleasant sensations . . . and when the dentist has finished the work you can rinse your mouth out, just dissolving away all of the numbness, leaving your mouth fresh and comfortable.

Homework

Cristina was told that it was essential to continue with the therapy in the comfort of her own home. She was given the following suggestions:

Just look at your hand and notice what happens (*Cristina's hand began to float away from her leg*) . . . and as it floats allow yourself to gently float into the dentist's chair the next time that you go in the future taking with you all of those positive and comfortable feelings . . . and allowing the dentist to do what needs to be done whilst you experience that in the most comfortable way possible . . . knowing that you have the resources to do that now. And it can help if you just put your thumb and forefinger together, and gently rub them together knowing that you will be able to access those comfortable feelings at any appropriate time in the future when you do that. And now counting yourself out from one to six . . . feeling lighter and lighter as you do that and when you reach six your eyelids can just float open . . . feeling calm and relaxed . . . knowing that you have learned a valuable skill in making your life more comfortable, but that you will only use this when it is appropriate and safe to do so. And you can do this for yourself in the comfort of your own home or any other appropriate place.

Cristina then successfully repeated the exercise on her own.

A six-month follow-up revealed that Cristina had made two successful visits to the dentist without experiencing any profound problems, either before the visit or during the course of treatment.

Summary

The approach used with Cristina demonstrates clearly a number of the key aspects of the integrative hypnotherapeutic approach. First, a positive and collaborative relationship was established during the initial phase. A brief demonstration and explanation of hypnosis was given, with the opportunity to ask questions, which dealt effectively with any residual resistance to the hypnotic process. Ideodynamic finger signals were then established by using visualisation and ego-strengthening methods, followed by recursive ideodynamic finger questioning. The patient was encouraged to access and review events that were aetiologically related to the defined problem whilst maintaining appropriate levels of dissociation. When the unconscious mind indicated that the patient was able to go into the future without the problem, a progression occurred (arm levitation) with a hallucination of the date of problem resolution signalled ideomotorically (automatic writing). The patient was later able to induce a state of 'self-hypnosis' and imagine visiting the dentist whilst remaining calm and comfortable. Throughout the procedure the therapist and patient worked collaboratively utilising Cristina's own past experiences and healing resources.

Smoking Cessation

Research suggests a link between stress and smoking behaviour in terms of smoking initiation, relapse and the amount smoked (Wills, 1985;

Lichtenstein, Weiss & Hitchcock, 1986; Carey, Kalra, Carey, Halperin & Richard, 1993). Paradoxically, research also shows that increased smoking may be effective at reducing stress (Perkins, Grobe, Stiller, Fonte & Goettler, 1992). Smoking is a powerful addiction and a difficult habit to quit. Individuals start to smoke for various reasons, often when they are adolescent. However, smokers often assert that a cigarette reduces stress, although physiologically it acts as a stressor on the body. The relationship between stress and addiction (Gottheil, 1987), and stress, smoking and gene expression are now well documented (Siegfried, Bourdeau, Davis, Luketich & Shriver, 2000). Despite the addictive nature of smoking and the risk of some weight gain during attempts to quit, there are now a number of studies that suggest that hypnosis is an effective method of achieving smoking cessation (Pederson, Scrimjeour & Lefcoe, 1975; Spiegel & Spiegel, 1978/2004; Cornwell, Burrows & McMurray, 1981; Frank, Umlauf, Wonderlich & Ashkanazi, 1986; Williams & Hall, 1988; Green, 1996; Bayot & Capafons, 1997).

Smoking-cessation programme (Lynn, Neufeld, Rhue & Matorin, 1994)

Lynn et al. found that abstinence rates secured through the use of hypnosis ranged from 14 to 61%. This wide range is not surprising given that the hypnotic protocols used vary widely among clinicians. The efficacy of hypnosis approaches does not appear to be any better or worse than other treatments. Lynn et al. designed a multidimensional smoking-cessation programme focusing on cognitive-behavioural skills and the use of hypnosis. Green (1999, pp. 253–64) presents a clear account of smoking-cessation treatment with a 34-year-old man using this particular protocol. This demonstrates how hypnosis can be used as a secondary strategy within a primary cognitive-behavioural framework. The approach included the following aspects:

(i)   Education about the dangers of smoking: the health risks were explained along with the presentation of a few health statistics. It was also explained how people learn their smoking habits through the positive reinforcing effects of nicotine; for example, decreased anxiety and increased arousal. In this context the patient was also asked about his first smoking experience.

(ii) Stressing the importance of motivation and social support: past studies have shown that high motivation is an important factor in successful treatment (Perry & Mullin, 1975; Perry, Gelfand & Marcovitch, 1979). The patient was asked to record his level of motivation on a five-point scale. He was instructed to inform his family, friends and work colleagues of his commitment to quit. A behavioural contract reflecting his commitment was signed in front of 'a significant other'. He was also encouraged to write down his motivations on cards that he could keep on his person, as well as placing them throughout his home, workplace and car. The patient was asked to visualise a 'high road' where he could see himself as a non-smoker:

> Think for a moment about what it would mean to you to be a non-smoker. . . .
> Now visualise two roads: a high road where you imagine your future if you quit successfully . . . think of the social rewards, and the health rewards. Now imagine a low road where you see your future if you are not truly motivated to quit . . . the choice is yours. Which road will you walk down? Do you think or fear that you may not be able to quit?
>
> If I were to promise you a million dollars if you could remain abstinent for a year, do you think you could do it? But the question I would like to ask you is whether your health is worth a million dollars. Close your eyes now and tell yourself all the reasons why you have to quit, and see yourself walking down the road of health and well-being as a non-smoker (Lynn et al., 1994, p. 562).

The man was also asked to identify the 'triggers' for the problem behaviour, as well as devising coping strategies to cope with smoking urges. He was encouraged to restructure his attitudes towards smoking to resist urges by repeating positive coping statements, such as 'I am aware of the urge to smoke, but I do not have to smoke; I am a non-smoker'.

(iii) Using self-monitoring, self-management and self-reinforcement: the patient monitored the number of cigarettes he smoked between sessions, which focused attention on the problem behaviour and broadened the awareness of triggers.

(iv) Attempting to minimise weight gain as a side-effect of treatment: the patient was encouraged to engage in regular physical exercise as this is incompatible with smoking (Marlatt & Gordon, 1985), as well as reducing physiological and psychological stress. Exercise, combined with eating balanced meals, are simple yet quite effective methods to minimise any associated weight gain.

(v) Integration of hypnosis: the patient was instructed that he must use his imagination and visualisation skills and be open to the suggestions in order to maximise treatment effects. Hypnosis was presented as a powerful tool that could promote positive change in self-image and assist in achieving the goal of smoking cessation. The first part of the hypnosis script was taken from Gorassini and Spanos' hypnotisability-modification programme (1999), and included the following:

- closing of the eyes and imagining standing at the top of a spiral staircase;
- slowly walking down the staircase and going deeper and deeper into hypnosis, leading to a state of relaxation, serenity and confidence;
- suggestions relating to increased receptivity of ideas and openness to images;

- an invitation to anchor positive feelings by repeating a keyword or phrase as well as rubbing the thumb and forefinger together;
- using this cue-controlled relaxation tactic whenever the urge to smoke occurred, or when feeling stressed, to visualise being a non-smoker;
- practising self-hypnosis, visualisation and cue-controlled relaxation so that such strategies become automatic.

The second hypnotic session was modified from Lynn et al.'s smoking-cessation protocol (pp. 565–70). This involved a short, progressive muscle-relaxation exercise followed by deepening. The patient was then informed that, at the very 'deepest level' of his being, he could redefine himself as a non-smoker. He visualised writing on a chalkboard all of the advantages of not smoking, which would allow his body to become resistant to illness, and heal itself from years of smoking. It was suggested to the patient that his conscious and unconscious minds were now collaborating to assist him in becoming a non-smoker. When he felt confident that this was happening, he was asked to anchor these feelings, and to visualise himself reaching his goal. He agreed to practise self-hypnosis at least twice daily. In response to both 6- and 12-month follow-up questionnaires, the patient reported complete abstinence from smoking.

Cognitive strategies

Spiegel and Spiegel (1978/2004) taught patients a cognitive strategy that alters their perspective on the smoking behaviour (i.e. 'restructuring'), reinforced by hypnosis. The principle of restructuring within hypnosis is to help the patients develop a strategy for change that affirms the experience, rather than struggling with it. Instead of focusing on stopping smoking per se, patients focus on a broader commitment to assist their bodies in staying healthy by concentrating on three critical points during hypnosis:

> The first point is: for your body, smoking is a poison. You are composed of a number of components, the most important of which is your body. Smoking is not so much a poison for you as it is for your body specifically.
>
> The second point is: you cannot live without your body. Your body is a precious physical plant through which you experience life.
>
> The third point is: to the extent that you want to live, you owe your body respect and protection.
>
> This is your way of acknowledging the fragile, precious nature of your body and, at the same time, your way of seeing yourself as your body's keeper. You are, in truth, your body's keeper. When you make this commitment to respect your body, you have within you the power to have smoked your last cigarette ... as a consequence of your commitment, it becomes natural for you to protect your body against the poison of further smoking ... notice that when you make this commitment to respect your body, you incorporate with it a view towards eating and drinking that reflects the respect

for your body. . . . You can, if you wish, use this same exercise to maintain your ideal weight while protecting your body against the poison of further smoking. . . . The exercise is as follows: you sit or lie down, and to yourself you count to three . . . at one, look up towards your eyebrows; at two, close your eyelids and take a deep breath; and at three, exhale, let your eyes relax and let your body float. As you feel yourself floating, you permit one hand or the other to feel like a buoyant balloon and let it float upwards as your hand is now. When it reaches this upright position, it becomes the signal for you to enter a state of meditation. In this state of meditation you concentrate on these three critical points:

(i)   for your body, not for you, smoking is a poison;
(ii)   you need your body to live;
(iii) you owe your body this respect and attention.

Reflect on what this means to you in a private sense, then bring yourself out of this state of concentration, called 'self-hypnosis', by counting backwards in this manner. Now, three, get ready. Two, with your eyelids closed, roll up your eyes . . . and one, let your eyelids open slowly. Then when your eyes are back in focus, slowly make a fist with the hand that is up and as you open the fist slowly, your normal sensation and control returns. Let your hand float downward. That is the end of the exercise, but you retain a sense of floating. (p. 212)

Spiegel and Spiegel suggest that a similar restructuring strategy can be applied to other problems as well, such as overeating and pain management. Indeed, the author has successfully used this approach with a bulimic patient (see Case Study 6, Session 1, in Chapter 8).

A case presented by Rossi (2002)

Rossi presents a case of a highly stressed schoolteacher who wanted to quit smoking. First, the Spiegel hypnosis induction profile (Spiegel & Spiegel, 1978/2004) was administered, with the patient scoring in the highly hypnotisable zone. In his first session, he appeared to experience a deep trance that was ratified by arm levitation, amnesia and other behavioural cues. Direct suggestions that utilised his desire to be a healthy role model for his child were enough to motivate him to stop smoking in one session. In the next session he reported that he had not smoked, but craved for a cigarette. This yearning for a cigarette was accompanied by yawning and tearing eyes, along with a statement that, 'I have a lot of stress and need to smoke'.

These behaviours were recognised by Rossi as an opportunity to convert an 'ultradian stress syndrome' into an 'ultradian healing response' (Rossi & Nimmons, 1991). From a psychobiological perspective, his yawning suggested that he was beginning to experience 'the common everyday trance' (Erickson, Rossi & Rossi, 1976; Erickson & Rossi, 1979). Rossi proceeded to facilitate a permissive naturalistic trance induction with the following words:

That's okay, just let yourself take a comfortable break right now. That's right, just allow yourself to sit back and be with the craving and enjoy not having to do anything right now about your stress. When your inner mind is ready to let the relaxation deepen so that it can relieve the stress and craving while you rest, will you notice your eyes closing naturally all by themselves?

After about 12 minutes of inner focus, Rossi continued:

When your conscious and unconscious minds know that they can continue to allow you to enjoy periods of rest and comfort like this several times a day so that you don't have to experience stress and smoking, will you find yourself awakening refreshed and alert?

When the patient opened his eyes, he reported visualising himself holding his baby and feeling proud that he did not smoke. He stated that his craving for smoking had gone. He was encouraged to take these 'ultradian healing rests' whenever he felt a craving. He developed the habit of taking these during the lunch break, which helped him to avoid overeating and consequent weight gain. By reframing his need to smoke into a need to do an ultradian healing response, he was able to reduce stress and give up his smoking addiction.

The above discussion demonstrates that there are many ways of using hypnosis within a treatment programme. In many of the examples, hypnosis is clearly being used as a secondary and facilitating strategy to primary approaches (e.g. diet, cognitive behavioural, education).

Sexual Problems

Before working with sexual problems, the clinician should be familiar with the physiological and medical aspects of normal and abnormal sexual functioning, bearing in mind that there are also important social and cultural aspects to be considered when attempting any definition of 'normal' and 'abnormal' with respect to sexuality. Sexual dysfunctions occur when there are disruptions of any of the four stages of sexual response (i.e. desire, excitement, orgasmic, resolution) because of anatomical, physiological or psychological factors. Sexual dysfunctions may be life long or develop after a period of normal sexual functioning. They may also be present in all sexual activities or may be situational; for example, a man who has an erection during masturbation, but not during sexual interaction with a partner.

Psychosexual problems

There are a number of common psychosexual problems (*Diagnostic and Statistical Manual of Mental Disorders: DSM-IV*: American Psychiatric Association, 1994; Watson & Davies, 1997). They can be defined as an inability to derive pleasure and satisfaction from sexual activity and include:

- inhibited sexual desire (deficient sexual fantasies and desire for sexual activity);
- sexual aversion disorder (extreme aversion to, and avoidance of, all genital contact with a partner);
- male erectile disorder (inability to attain or maintain an erection conducive to sexual activity);
- female sexual arousal disorder (inability to attain or maintain an adequate lubrication-swelling response of sexual excitement until completion of sexual activity);
- female orgasmic disorder (delay in, or absence of, orgasm following a normal excitement phase);
- male orgasmic disorder (delay in, or absence of, orgasm following a normal excitement phase during normal sexual activity);
- premature ejaculation (ejaculation with minimal sexual stimulation before, upon, or shortly after penetration and before the person wishes);
- dyspareunia (recurrent and persistent genital pain in either male or female);
- vaginismus (involuntary spasm of the musculature of the vagina which interferes with sexual intercourse).

It should be noted that for a diagnosis to be made, the above dysfunctions need to be persistent and recurrent. The possibility of there being an organic basis for the dysfunction should be excluded before assuming a psychological causation.

Kaplan (1974) argues for a multicausal theory of sexual dysfunctions on several levels – intrapsychic, interpersonal and behavioural – and lists four factors as playing a role in the development of these disorders:

- misinformation or ignorance regarding sexual and social interaction;
- unconscious guilt and anxiety concerning sex;
- performance anxiety, as the most common cause of erectile and orgasmic dysfunctions;
- partners' failure to communicate with each other their sexual feelings and those behaviours in which they want to engage.

One of the main barriers to successful performance and enjoyment is stress and anxiety. Worrying about performance can cause impotence or premature ejaculation, and repeated failure during intercourse leads to anxiety and frustration. In women, unconscious conflicts concerning sexual activity may be responsible for vaginismus, an involuntary reflexive spasm of the vaginal muscles and perineum that prevents penetration from taking place. Cognitions (thoughts) and moods (emotions) shape each person's experience of sexual arousal and behaviour. Attentional processes are also important: in the common experience of spectatoring, people focus on their own performance, often expecting failure, rather than on the sensuality of lovemaking. Pain, ruminations and worries divert attention. Intense negative emotions tend to reduce sexual activity and performance, but the association is not close. In depression, sexual enjoyment is often diminished, but occasionally increased; the preferred erotic behaviour may alter, often becoming more passive; and antidepressant drugs may adversely affect sexual response.

One of the most common sexual problems is inhibited sexual desire, which affects more women than men. Low libido is something that one in three women experiences at some point in her life, often with a concomitant feeling of inadequacy and abnormality. The usual response of a sex therapist is to design a programme to restore or enhance the woman's libido, whereas a more appropriate intervention might be one of reassurance. Pertot (2005) contends that the male model of sexual appetite has duped both women and professional sex therapists. She argues that women are now beginning to challenge the male model of sexual needs, which as a result may cause considerable discord between couples. This is another case that clearly demonstrates how behaviours and consequent medical and psychotherapeutic interventions are essentially politically and culturally defined. In a similar vein, it has recently been postulated that variations in female orgasmic functioning may be a result of genetic influences rather than sociocultural ones (Dunn, Cherkas & Spector, 2005). The results showed a significant genetic influence with an estimated heritability for difficulty reaching orgasm during intercourse of 34%, and 45% for orgasm during masturbation.

Philips and Frederick (1995) have suggested that sexual dysfunction may be related to interpersonal traumatic re-enactment. There is extensive evidence of impaired sexual functioning among victims of childhood sexual abuse, rape, domestic violence and combat (e.g. Becker, Skinner, Abel & Cichon, 1986). Issues may include fear of sex, arousal dysfunction and decreased sexual satisfaction. Specific issues to be explored by the therapist include: frequency of sexual contact; degree of satisfaction; arousal level; nature of sexual interactions; thoughts, feelings and fantasies that accompany arousal; and any concerns that patients may have about their sexual functioning. One of the major hypnotherapeutic methods used to deal with this type of problem is ego-state therapy, although other hypnoanalytical methods reviewed earlier may also be utilised (Watkins & Johnson, 1982; Phillips & Frederick, 1995).

Good accounts of human sexual functioning can be found in standard textbooks (e.g. Kaplan, 1974, 1979, 1988, 1995; Masters, Johnson & Kolodny, 1995; Charlton & Yalom, 1997; Leiblum & Rosen, 2000; Wincze & Carey, 2001; Kleinplatz, 2001; also refer to www.sexology.cjb.net).

Hypnosis and sexual problems

Hypnosis has been used in the treatment of sexual disorders for many years. Erickson and Kubie (1941) presented the earliest known case of the successful treatment of inhibited sexual desire with hypnosis. Hypnotic interventions with sexual dysfunctions seem to hold considerable promise in sex therapy (Araoz, 2005), although the literature consists almost exclusively of case studies and outcome reports (Erickson, 1953; Cheek and LeCron, 1968; Erickson, 1973; Crasilneck, 1979, 1982; Beigel, 1980; Araoz, 1980, 1982, 1985; Degun & Degun, 1982; Hammond, 1984, 1985; Zilbergelt & Hammond, 1988; Bakich, 1995; see also www.hypnosis-research.org). Sexual problems can often be dealt with by self-hypnosis, which helps the individual relax. Hypnosis can also be used to assist with issues relating to poor body image, guilt, fear of sex and fear of sexual encounters.

Often, there is an overemphasis on the individual patient with the neglect of important relationship factors. Hypnosis can be helpful in fostering healthier interactions with partners and families, and healthier perceptions of relationships. If the relationship between partners is bad, this is not conducive to sexual desire and, consequently, sexual problems may be manifested. In the context of the treatment of sexual problems, it should be recognised that hypnosis is often a secondary or facilitating strategy that increases the effectiveness of a range of adjunctive psychotherapeutic approaches; for example, insight-oriented psychotherapy, rational emotive cognitive restructuring, desensitisation, and so on.

Hammond (1990a, pp. 350–2) presents some of the advantages of using hypnosis in sex therapy:

- May be used in the treatment of the individual patient without a partner (the largest and most extensive follow-up reports on the use of hypnosis with sexual dysfunction have been on individual patients with erectile dysfunction – Crasilneck, 1979, 1982).
- Allows rapid exploration and identification of underlying conflicts, unresolved feelings about past events and factors beyond conscious awareness. Such repressed experiences, and associated feelings, can be accessed and 'worked through' at unconscious levels (by using ideodynamic finger signalling, for example), thus minimising any of the often occurring problems in using 'uncovering' approaches in conventional psychodynamic therapy.
- Learning self-hypnosis may provide the patient with a sense of self-control and a technique for stress management. This can provide them with a tool for anxiety reduction and decompression, as well as for the arousal of sexual passion through sexual imagery prior to sexual involvement.
- Increases expectation to promote personal change. Hypnosis may be used to provide hope, increased feelings for self-efficacy, and confidence that change can occur. 'Trance ratification procedures can convince patients of the power of their own mind to do things unconsciously, and without them willing or trying', for example, when the patient's arm floats up involuntarily, they are often convinced that hypnosis may be capable of helping them with other problems; when a needle is painlessly put through a fold

of skin on the back of the patient's 'glove anaesthetised' hand, they are convinced that they have more potentials than they realised and that perhaps their mind is powerful enough to stir sexual desire, facilitate orgasm or create erections.

- Allows the use of a variety of techniques for altering problematic emotions and increasing desired emotional states. Symbolic imagery techniques often allow patients to release 'bottled up' feelings such as anger and resentment.
- Ego-strengthening can increase the patient's feelings of control and self-esteem. Hypnotic age-regression may revivify memories that help rekindle and recapture positive sexual and affectional feelings.
- Hypnosis and self-hypnosis can help to focus attention and increase sensory awareness, thereby facilitating increased arousal and pleasure.
- Can aid in elucidating internal (cognitive, imagery) processes that are impossible to observe and difficult to explicate through discussion alone.
- Can provide an evaluation of both negative and positive sexual experiences encountered during therapy (i.e. whilst engaged in assigned tasks, such as sensate focus).

Hypnosis approaches

Hypnoanalysis

The aims of hypnoanalysis in sex therapy are:

- to uncover unconscious conflict;
- to release fears that inhibit sexual arousal;
- to restructure associations and orientation to sex objects;
- to dispel inhibiting identifications;
- to provide ego-building.

There are a number of reports of the use of hypnoanalytical approaches in dealing with sexual problems, including: hypnotic age-regression (Wijesinghe, 1977); dream analysis (Degun & Degun, 1988); ventilation of repressed negative feelings (Levit, 1971). Rossi and Cheek (1988) suggest that a 'combination of light hypnosis with use of unconscious, symbol movements or ideomotor responses allows rapid access to significant information and rapid, productive rehearsal with problems of sexual dysfunction in the time limitations of three office visits, comprising two hours' (p. 346).

Direct symptom removal

Several studies involving direct symptom removal have been reported, for example:

- visualisation of sexual encounters with suggestions of improved sexual performance (Schneck, 1970);
- hypnotic recall of previous positive sexual experiences coupled with hypnotic time distortion to prolong pleasure (Mirowitz, 1966);
- positive imagery of having successful sexual intercourse combined with positive self-statements (Cheek, 1976);
- suggestion of catalepsy (see Case Study 4, Session 3).

Indirect approaches

Hammond (1990a) describes a number of metaphors and guided imagery approaches that could be used as a basis for working with sexual problems, for example:

- 'The master control room technique' (for inhibited sexual desire, ejaculatory inhibition, orgasmic dysfunction, erectile dysfunction and sexual addictions).
- 'Pee shyness' (a brief metaphor illustrating the fact that sexual responses are automatic and unconscious).
- 'Going out for dinner' (facilitating salivation and lubrication); moistening and lubrication could also be achieved by facilitating ideosensory responses.
- 'Perspiring on a warm day' (useful for women who have problems with sexual arousal and, specifically, in becoming lubricated).
- Guided imagery and erotic fantasy, where the patient is engaged in spectatoring (see Case Study 4, Session 4).
- Induced erotic dreams (see Case Study 4, Session 5).

I have used guided imagery successfully for orgasmic dysfunction and vaginismus. The following rosebush metaphor is a good example.

Script 40 – The rosebush metaphor (adapted from Assagioli, 1965/1975, p. 214)

Imagine that you are looking at a rosebush, and in particular one stem with green leaves and a rosebud. The bud appears green because the sepals are closed, but at the very top a rose-coloured point can be seen. Now, as you focus on the rose-coloured point, the green sepals begin to separate, to gradually open, revealing the delicate rose-hued petals within. The sepals continue to open until you can see the whole of the tender bud. The petals follow suit and slowly separate, until a perfect, fully open rose appears. Now take a deep breath and smell the perfume of this delicate rose, inhaling its characteristic and unmistakable scent; so delicate, sweet and delicious. Continue to breathe in the healing fragrance as it delights and massages all of your senses in every part of your body. Imagine the life force that arises from the roots to the flower and originates the process of opening.

It is obvious that the symbol of the rosebud can also be used for general ego-strengthening (i.e. inner 'flowering').

Hypnosis as an adjunct in behaviour therapy

Hypnosis facilitates relaxation and vivid imagery in order that graded hierarchies of sexual scenes and situations can be presented in the hypnotic state (systematic desensitisation). This may contain elements of sexual foreplay and scenes of progressive social and physical involvement (Fabbri, 1976; Beigel & Johnson, 1980; Degun & Degun, 1982). Araoz (1982, 1985) described a number of approaches in systematic desensitisation with hypnosis:

- hypnosis with ego-strengthening;
- video hypno-sensitisation – whilst hypnotised patients watch a series of videotape scenes of normal sexual relationships;
- hypno-conditioning with slides – whilst hypnotised patients watch a graded series of slides of sexual situations;
- hypnotic recall – under hypnosis patients imagine past successful sexual experiences. The conditioning process is reinforced by post-hypnotic suggestion, deep relaxation, visual imagery and the recall of past experiences. Self-hypnosis is used to reinforce post hypnotic suggestion.

Cognitive and experiential approaches

Negative self-statements and sexual imagery may create and perpetuate symptoms, which happens particularly after sexual failure has been experienced. This is covert self-reinforcement and acts as a turn-off. Hypnosis is used to recreate negative moods and the rehearsal of negative statements, dramatising the adverse effects of the process. It is then employed to elicit counter-positive statements and imagery. Finally, self-hypnosis is taught to reinforce cognitive restructuring (Burte & Araoz, 1994).

Case Study 4 – An Integrative Hypnotherapeutic Approach for the Treatment of Male Erectile Disorder (Hawkins, 1996)

The case study that follows demonstrates how an integrative hypnotherapeutic approach can be used for the treatment of an erectile problem. Each session is briefly described, paying attention only to the main interventions.

Session 1

As well as asking the normal questions that would be expected in taking the case history, it is important to ask questions that are relevant to clinical hypnosis strategies in the treatment of sexual problems. As already explained, the initial interview is critical in establishing rapport and building the therapeutic alliance. It is also useful to obtain information regarding the euphemistic and vernacular vocabulary that the patient uses to describe sexual organs, as well as his or her knowledge of sexual anatomy and sexual functioning. Once John's case history had been taken (during which it was established that he had been examined by a urologist), he was taught how to increase sensory awareness by accessing the times early on in his marriage when he was able to become aroused quickly and achieve a good erection followed (appropriately) by orgasm. He was asked to:

> Look at your hand and allow it to become lighter and lighter and float into the air . . . just allowing your mind to go back to the time when you were first married and enjoyed having sex with your wife . . . an activity that you both enjoyed . . . be aware of the sensations all over your body. You can feel the same sensations and pleasure, and function just as you did then . . . just allowing that to happen . . . knowing that you have the resources to allow that to occur when it is appropriate in the future, maybe even later today or tomorrow or sometime soon. Just allowing those sensations in your body to increase in intensity and enjoying those feelings as they flow into your penis . . . noticing how enjoyable that is. Just as it happened, then so it can happen again now . . . nothing has changed. The only important thing is the sensations you experience. Experience the texture, temperature, pressure and movement. Immersed in feeling and sensation . . . nothing to do but to feel and experience the pleasure.
>
> You can feel the same feelings, experience the same sensations and pleasure, and function just as you did then. Everything can be just as it was when you first married.

This technique accessed John's positive psychosomatic memories and allowed him to become more confident, expectant and optimistic. The approach is an effective method of stress management and can be expected to lower feelings of anxiety and despair.

The level of experiencing of sensations can also be 'controlled' by the patient with an imaginary dial (master control room technique), so that he or she can turn the level of felt sensations up and down (reported by Hammond, 1990b).

It was also important that John set realistic goals early on in the treatment process.

> Now that these sensations are very strong, take them into the future . . . experiencing yourself making love with your wife . . . engaging in foreplay that is satisfying for both of you . . . achieving a good erection and inserting your penis into her vagina . . . both enjoying this and then reaching an orgasm. Be aware of how you are now feeling . . . knowing that this can happen if you

and your wife allow this to occur . . . feeling more confident and excited about this prospect and wondering whether this will happen later today or tomorrow . . . but knowing that this is a goal that you can aspire to and reach at some time in the future if it is appropriate for you and your partner to do that. And this is something that you can practise at home between now and the next session. All you need do is look at your right hand and, as it floats, allow your eyes to close, trusting in your unconscious mind to find an appropriate level of trance for accessing those early positive sexual experiences . . . and experience yourself at some time in the future utilising those sexual resources for a mutually satisfying sexual relationship with your wife.

Session 2

As discussed earlier, ideodynamic signalling is a utilisation approach that is particularly useful for uncovering repressed traumatic events, and their associated distressed feelings, related to current psychological and psychosomatic problems. First, 'yes' and 'no' finger signals were established, and John then accessed prototypical experiences that were related to his sexual problem. Some conscious awareness of these events occurred; for example, his early relationship with his mother, and a later homosexual experience. These events were reviewed with minimal emotional abreaction. In this instance, no interpretations were made by the therapist, nor were any interventions made that actively encouraged the emotional ventilation, although this could have been a viable option.

After three 'cycles' of ideodynamic questioning, John gave an unconscious 'yes' signal that he was able to go into the future (sometime) without the problem. He hallucinated a date when this could happen at approximately four weeks from the date of the session. He was progressed to this date and experienced intensive positive responses. In hypnosis he was told that:

> You have the resources to allow this to happen and you already know that you can change your bodily responses in an appropriate way to allow you to respond sexually when you are with your wife . . . and your unconscious mind is utilising the learnings that you have experienced here today concerning the origins of the problem to help you find solutions by the date that you have experienced or even earlier if it is appropriate for you . . . and you may experience these pleasant sensations and experiences when you are dreaming later tonight . . . and wake to find that you have a strong erection . . . and you may be wondering when and whether this can really happen . . . maybe tonight or will it be some other time . . . although part of you knows that it really can.

Session 3

In this session, John was hypnotised and arm rigidity suggested in order to demonstrate the control that he has over his own somatic functioning, and also that he has the (unconscious) resources to allow his arm to become rigid and hard without doing anything to make that happen.

> Just as you have complete control over your hand and arm, that you can make your arm go rigid, so you have the resources to control any part of your body in the same way, including your penis . . . and you can keep the rigidity for as long as is appropriate for both you and your partner to enjoy a sexual relationship together. You have complete control over every part of your body, including your penis. Your fears and anxieties will be less and, as time progresses, you may gain some understanding of your problem if this is appropriate for you.

The utilisation of hypnotic phenomena in psychotherapy has recently been comprehensively discussed by Edgette and Edgette (1995).

Session 4

It is useful to encourage impotent patients to talk about their innermost sexual fantasies and to replay them in trance. It might be useful to engage the partner in these sessions. Patients can also be taken on a guided sexual fantasy:

> Perhaps you will picture yourself at a sexual orgy, watching as people undress and seductively explore one another, and experience the excitement flow through your own body and into your genitals . . . perhaps encouraging your own real memories of fun and pleasure . . . and I don't know whether you will be able to use these important sexual memories tonight, or tomorrow, or after the weekend . . . and you can wonder when your unconscious mind will allow you to enjoy a sexual experience with your partner . . . and when it does you may find it particularly surprising to discover how aroused you can become.

Session 5

John entered hypnosis (using a self-hypnosis method taught earlier) and was given a gardening metaphor that included references to green shoots, development beneath the soil, the seasons of the year, and so on. This is similar to the 'life of an oak tree' metaphor (Script 20, Chapter 4). The session concluded by utilising creative dreaming as a way of involving unconscious search processes in problem resolution:

> You already know how to experience stimulating dreams. And it's perfectly natural, following the kind of work we're doing, to have some pleasurable dreams. And your unconscious mind can work to increase your sexual desire towards your wife . . . and you may find that your dreams can be very

creative and enjoyable . . . and you may be already wondering what you can dream later tonight. . . . And because your goal is to increase your sexual desire, in all probability, you will have an interesting experience tonight, or it may be tomorrow night or even the night after . . . and you may be surprised when it actually happens, but I would be surprised if you have to wait until the weekend. And those desires will be carried with you into your day, where they will appropriately influence your thoughts and behaviour. And even though you won't remember all your erotic and sexy dreams, in the morning, you can still sense and know that something is different, even if you can't quite put your finger on precisely what it is. And even if you don't believe that this can really happen, you will be even more surprised when it does, knowing that you have this resource to allow you to find solutions even whilst you are asleep.

John reported that on the night following the session he had a very erotic dream in which he awoke and 'discovered' that he had an erection. He was extremely pleased with this 'discovery' and the fact that he still had this ability. John was requested to replay his dream in trance and to indicate ideodynamically that appropriate physiological changes occurred. In this final session, emphasis was placed on further ego-strengthening and goal setting.

Session 6

This was a conjoint session involving both the patient and his wife. They were both regressed to a positive sexual experience early on in their marriage. Afterwards they were encouraged to describe their experiences to each other, including the sensations and feelings they experienced in their bodies. Both partners were then progressed (in hypnosis) to some time in the future when these experiences could be actualised, *knowing that your unconscious minds are already searching for the solutions even though you are not aware that this is happening*. In this session the emphasis was on the development of hope and optimism, of personal control and positive feelings of mastery.

Follow-up

A follow-up six months later revealed that the couple were functioning sexually in ways that were appropriate for both of them. They were no longer concerned about the struggle to have 'good sex' and consequently a major stressor in their lives had been removed.

Sex addiction

Sex addiction is a way some people cope with their stresses to the degree that their sexual behaviour becomes their major coping mechanism. This can be cynically expressed as 'an orgasm a day keeps distress at bay'. Heron (1998a)

– available at www.human-inquiry.com/homebase.htm – presents an 'authentic sex-negative theory' in which he states:

- A person in whom the cathartic function is denied, and distress emotions repressed, is likely to undergo a distortion of the sexual function. The repressed distress displaces into compulsive sexuality. Nor is the displacement difficult to understand: the purely somatic release of orgasm temporarily diverts attention from the ache of buried distress, but without reducing or unloading that distress – hence the need to have another orgasm soon. The result is a compulsive, repetitive use of sexual release as a maladaptive anodyne.

- The corollary, of course, is that the level of sexual tension and arousal may be falsely inflated by the displacement of repressed feeling into the sexual function, so that the person is seeking and obtaining sexual release to a degree that has no relation to her real physical needs, but bears blind witness to early interrupted personal needs and the distress that surrounds them.

- The compulsive sexual behaviour itself will show symbolic maladjustment: the person blindly acts out in the present unfinished emotional business from the past. Thus the petty or emotional rapist blindly acts out against a succession of women, his repressed anger against his mother and the frustrated longing she imposed upon him. An older woman has a series of disruptive affairs with younger men as she blindly acts out the grief and anger and interrupted love at the death of her eight-year-old son. And so on. The sexual longing is but the leading edge of an unidentified distress and frozen need that give the longing its direction and much of its motive power.

- The underlying distress may be early repressed personal distress due to the negation of sexuality in childhood: the child's need to share love and joy playfully through the whole of its body including the genitals, may have been grossly interrupted by parents or siblings. Hence a hidden incest compulsion: the interrupted need for love, together with grief and anger at its interruption, genitally fixated and oriented to a member of the family – this whole constellation being repressed and denied, while at the same time being repetitively projected in a blind manner, and with disastrous results, into the adult social world. (p. 42)

The most common type of excessive sexual behaviours can be classified within the DSM category, paraphilia (Schneider & Irons, 1998). Although the sex addict expends much time and energy in connection with his or her behaviours and associated distressing life consequences, he or she is unable to stop. When experiencing increased levels of stress, the addictive behaviour (e.g. masturbation) often increases in both frequency and intensity and can lead to physical injury. Carnes (1991) discerned 10 patterns of behaviour associated with addictive sexual disorders:

- fantasy sex: obsession with a sexual fantasy life;
- seductive sex role: seduction and conquest are the key – for example, multiple relationships, affairs and/or unsuccessful serial relationships;
- anonymous sex: engaging in sex with anonymous partners, or having one-night stands;
- paying for sex: paying for prostitutes or for sexually explicit phone calls;
- trading sex: receiving money or drugs for sex or using sex as a business;
- voyeuristic sex: use of pornography in books, videos and Internet. Highly correlated with masturbation, even to point of injury;
- exhibitionist sex: self-exposure (Epstein & Deyoub, 1983);
- intrusive sex: touching others without permission/use of positions of power to sexually exploit another person;
- pain exchange: causing or receiving pain to enhance sexual pleasure;
- exploitative sex: use of force on vulnerable partner to gain sexual access or sex with children. (pp. 42–4)

For many sex addicts, pornography combined with masturbation, sometimes physically risky, is the cornerstone of their addictive activities. In the later stages of sex addiction, the addict prefers the fantasy world and fantasy sex with themselves or others instead of relational sex with a partner. Internet sex addiction is becoming an increasingly important issue for clinicians (Cooper, 2002).

Addictive sexual disorders often coexist with substance-abuse disorders and are frequently an unrecognised cause of relapse. Sex addicts were often sexually abused as children (Carnes, 1991, p. 35), and because they have distorted ideas about sex, they frequently lack information about healthy sexuality. Hypnotherapy for sex addicts can address some of the issues that relate to the role of stress in the maintenance of compulsive sexual behaviours. Strategies may include ego-strengthening, hypnoanalysis and teaching the patient self-hypnosis. Hypnosis may also be integrated into both relationship counselling and group therapy. Shame is the cornerstone of sex-addiction treatment, and this is often best addressed through group therapy. A more detailed discussion of diagnosis and treatment issues is provided by Irons and Schneider (1997). It is clear from the discussion above that, in order to work successfully with sex addicts, a thorough training in the specialism is absolutely necessary.

Sleeping Problems

Stress often affects a person's sleep in ways that leave him or her tired, and even more stressed. The sleeping problems often associated with stress include difficulties in getting to sleep, waking up during the night and remaining awake and waking up early. Insomnia is probably the most common disorder of sleep and may be related to situational stress and anxiety, although there are many other possible causes (e.g. sleep apnoea syndrome and other respiratory difficulties, worry about not sleeping, pain, excessive caffeine intake and depression). When the individual is awake, he or she is often consumed with thoughts relating to events in his or her life. The field of sleep medicine has expanded rapidly in the past three decades and the various disorders identified require specific evaluations and interventions. Neylan, Reynolds and Kupfer (1994) provide a succinct nosology. It should be reiterated that psychotherapists must work in collaboration with physicians, which may include referral to a sleep clinic, in order to provide a comprehensive and integrated treatment for patients. The psychotherapeutic approach, which might include hypnosis, may cover both symptom management (e.g. organisation of a routine in conjunction with keeping a diary), cognitive-behavioural therapy and hypnoanalytic approaches, depending on the clinical assessment.

Spiegel and Spiegel (1978/2004) suggest that patients can become 'traffic directors' for their thoughts, projecting them on to a screen, and thereby dissociating from the evoked physical response. They conclude that such approaches can be helpful in conjunction with standard sleep-laboratory approaches, which include keeping the bedroom as a place where work and other anxiety-arousing activities do not occur, and avoiding constantly looking at the clock when awake.

Rossi and Cheek (1988,) discuss a number of ideodynamic approaches to sleep problems. For example:

> The most satisfying and restful method of dealing with occasional insomnia is to get out of bed and use self-hypnosis with any induction method before asking for an ideodynamic answer to the question, would it be all right for me to go to sleep when I get back to bed, and to sleep with pleasant dreams and pleasant thoughts until I awaken at __ o'clock in the morning? The usual answer is a yes. Now ask your yes finger to lift when you know you will keep that promise. (p. 383)

The following example is representative of a more dynamically oriented approach.

Script 41 – Facilitating a good night's sleep

When your unconscious mind is ready to collaborate in a healing process to understand and solve your sleeping problem, will one of your fingers lift? . . . perhaps you can discern that movement firstly as a sensation in your finger. . . . That's fine! . . . and you can be pleased that your unconscious mind has agreed to participate in this voyage of discovery. Allow your unconscious mind to go back and find the first experience in your life when something happened to make sleeping important in some way . . . and you may be curious to discover whether this is related to current sleeping experiences. . . . And if it is, will your finger lift? . . . That's fine! . . . Understand what you could have done to have prevented that experience from troubling your sleep . . . and now that you know about that, is there any other reason for the event interfering with your sleep at the present time? . . . Now go back to some time when you slept very well and got up the next morning feeling really well. . . . As you are falling asleep that night, your yes finger will lift . . . and I think you are going to enjoy a deeply healing sleep . . . and you may be fascinated to experience that healing sleep as your unconscious mind reviews everything that happens including those periods when you dream answers that are important to you. . . . Will it be all right now for you to sleep deeply and restfully at night and awaken in the morning feeling rested and relaxed? When you know you will keep that promise to yourself and to the people who will be pleased when you are sleeping well, will your yes finger lift? . . . and your eyes open?

Rossi (2002) reports the following approach with a patient suffering from insomnia:

> When your eyes close all by themselves in a moment or two, will it be a signal that your inner mind is ready to help you solve your sleep problem? I wonder if you can recall a time when you slept very well? And will your unconscious help you go comfortably to sleep before you even realise it? When you feel like waking up and stretching, will it be a signal that your inner mind has learned something useful to help you find comfort and healing when you lay down to rest? (p. 77)

Rossi told the patient to enjoy an ultradian healing response whenever she felt the need for one, and that her mind and body could use this time to solve 'their own problems in their own way'. He emphasised that problems with marriage and family could often be sorted out in ways that were surprising, or even unknown, to the conscious mind. She was encouraged to discuss whatever relevant fantasies and ideas were going on during her ultradian rest-rejuvenation periods.

I have found the following general approach useful in working with patients with sleeping difficulties.

Script 42 – Difficulties in sleeping

> Close your eyes and go inside your mind and find all those psychosomatic memories of sleeping well in the past . . . allowing those resources to flow around your body and mind . . . relaxing every part of your body and mind . . . and when you really know that you can utilise these natural healing resources to engage in a peaceful, restorative sleep, will your finger lift? . . . That's good! . . . just letting that happen all by itself, no place to go right now except to know that later today when it is appropriate to use these learnings

to sleep peacefully for as long as your unconscious mind wants. Experience yourself now preparing for bed . . . and I wonder whether you will get into bed from the left side or from the right side . . . or maybe from the bottom of the bed . . . or perhaps you will just float into bed . . . laying your head on the pillow and allowing those sleeping resources to flow around your body and mind . . . feeling warm and comfortable . . . as you drift into a peaceful restorative sleep . . . and will there be times when you dream healing experiences? . . . waking in the morning feeling relaxed and refreshed and ready to deal with issues in your life that need attending to. I don't know whether you will experience a good restorative sleep tonight or will it be tomorrow night or the night after, but before the weekend?

A detailed account of the use of self-hypnosis in working with children with sleeping problems is given in Chapter 8.

Post-Traumatic Stress Disorder (PTSD)

Definition

Increasingly, individuals are presenting with symptoms that characterise post-traumatic stress disorder (PTSD). Specifically, diagnostic Criterion A (DSM-IV) requires that:

> the person experienced, witnessed or was confronted with an event or events that involved actual or threatened death or injury, or a threat to the physical integrity of self or others and that the person's response involved intense fear, helplessness or horror.

Foa, Davidson and Frances (1999) list the key symptoms of PTSD as follows:

(1) Re-experiencing the traumatic event as indicated by:

- intrusive, distressing recollections of the event;
- flashbacks (feeling as if the event were recurring while awake);
- nightmares (the event or other frightening images recur frequently in dreams);
- exaggerated emotional and physical reactions to triggers that remind the person of the event.

(2) Avoidance and emotional numbing as indicated by:

- activities, places, thoughts, feelings or conversations related to the trauma;
- loss of interest;
- feeling detached from others;
- restricted emotions.

(3) Increased arousal as indicated by:

- difficulty sleeping;
- irritability or outbursts of anger;
- difficulty concentrating;
- hypervigilance;
- exaggerated startle response.

Besides these three major types of symptoms, other common symptoms include panic attacks, severe avoidant behaviour, depression, suicidal thoughts and feelings, substance abuse, feelings of alienation and isolation, feelings of mistrust and betrayal, anger and irritability, severe impairment in daily functioning and strange beliefs and perceptions. The duration of the symptoms must be more than one month in order to meet the DSM criteria for PTSD, and must also have a significant detrimental effect on social and occupational functioning.

Acute stress disorder

Acute stress disorder is similar to PTSD in the precipitating event and in symptomatology, but is time limited, up to one month after the event. Although most individuals experiencing severe trauma such as rape are initially symptomatic, the majority recover without developing PTSD.

Adjustment disorder

Adjustment disorder is also a stress-related phenomenon in which the stressor has resulted in maladaptation and symptoms that are time limited until the stressor is removed or a new state of adaptation has occurred (Strain, Newcorn, Wolf & Fulop, 1994, p. 671).

Stressful life situations

Any stressful life situation that stimulates excessive arousal by the autonomic and endocrine systems can lead to the varying clinical symptomatology of PTSD (Rossi & Cheek, 1988). Traumatic events with empirically demonstrated links to PTSD include childhood physical and sexual abuse (Duncan, Saunders, Kilpatrick, Hanson & Resnick, 1996); military combat (King et al., 1995); adult rape (Kilpatrick & Resnick, 1993); natural and technological disasters (Pynoos et al., 1993). Results of the National Comorbidity Study (Kessler, Sonnega, Bromet, Hughes & Nelson, 1995) showed that trauma exposure is a common feature of modern life.

There is increasing evidence that many people enter a dissociated state (Cardeña & Spiegel, 1993) during physical and psychological trauma that protects them from the overwhelming pain of the situation. Initially, dissociation works well at the time of the trauma, but if this defence lasts too long it inter-feres with the grief work necessary to put the experience into perspective, and reduces the likelihood of later symptomatology (Spiegel, 1994).

Rossi (1996) postulates that dissociated or state-dependent memories remain active at unconscious levels and dynamically precipitate and maintain psychosomatic symptomatology. This could explain why certain clinical syn-dromes are often the result of chronic dissociation; for example, eating dis-orders, depression, obsessive-compulsive disorder, phobias, panic disorder and dissociative identity disorder. Rossi and Cheek (1988) conclude that this leads to the provocative insight that: 'The entire history of depth psychology and psychoanalysis now can be understood as a prolonged clinical investiga-tion of how dissociated or state-dependent memories remain active at uncon-scious levels, giving rise to the complexes' (p. 112).

A recent study investigated the transgenerational effects of PTSD in babies of mothers exposed to the World Trade Center attacks during pregnancy (Yehuda et al., 2005). The authors concluded that 'the data suggest that effects of maternal PTSD related to cortisol can be observed very early in the life of the offspring, and underscore the relevance of *in utero* contributors to putative biological risk for PTSD'.

Good general reviews of PTSD are provided by Foa, Rothbaum and Molnar (1995, available at www.psychiatrist.com), Spiegel (1996), Leskin, Kaloupek and Keane (1998) and Dwivedi (2000). The reader is also referred to Holmes et al. (2005) for a discussion of PTSD and dissociation (www.sciencedirect.com), and www.trauma-pages.com for general information.

Treatment of PTSD

Two types of treatment are helpful for PTSD: psychotherapy and medication. Some people recover from PTSD with psychotherapy alone, while others need a combination of psychotherapy and medication, and some need only med-ication (Foa et al, p. 71). A survey of experts concluded that three types of psychotherapy are especially effective in treating PTSD; namely, anxiety man-agement, cognitive therapy (Foa et al., 1995; Kennerley, 1996; Harvey, Bryant & Tarrier, 2003) and play therapy (Foa et al., 1995). As well as these, it was also considered important for people with PTSD, and their families, to receive appropriate educational and supportive counselling. It was also recognised that eye movement desensitisation and reprocessing (Shapiro, 1995; Edmond & McCarty, 2004), as well as hypnotherapy and hypnoanalysis – for example, ego-state therapy (Phillips, 1993) and psychodynamic psychotherapy – may be useful in treating PTSD. Although hypnotherapy was not recommended as the treatment of choice, it could play a significant role when used adjunctively with other treatments, as well as being utilised as a significant stress-management approach. Behavioural and cognitive-behavioural methods that fall in the category of exposure therapy (i.e. desensitisation, flooding or implosion therapy) are now arguably the treatment of choice for PTSD (Keane, 1998; Leskin et al., 1998; Foa, Keane & Friedman, 2000). As Meichenbaum (1995) has observed, the entire narrative in which the traumatic event is embedded can change with retelling or re-experiencing in the direction of greater self-acceptance and more realistic assessment of the dangerousness of the environment.

Given that many people enter a dissociated state during a trauma experience, it makes sense that enabling them to enter a structured dissociative state in therapy would facilitate their access to memories of the experience. These memories must then be worked through in order to resolve the post-traumatic symptomatology.

Hypnotherapy

The hypnotherapeutic approach (Rossi, 2002) can be used to help the patient reframe the original negative traumatic experience, thus allowing for a creative transformation of the initial problem. Ideodynamic exploration can provide a systematic way to access, review and transform past experiences in a safe and creative way. Because this approach works at the level of unconscious integration and psychosomatic problem resolution, there is less chance of reopening traumatic wounds. Traumatic events can be restructured, using available adult resources, to re-experience the trauma from a different perspective while developing a general sense of mastery over the past. In other words, a recursive replaying of the traumatic experience allows the creative potential of the crisis situation to be realised. Rossi writes:

> The early memories are usually loaded with other states of being, with other aspects of personality that may have been prematurely pushed aside. These state-dependent memories and identities, when sympathetically understood, often point to potentialities within the individual's personality that have not reached their optimal development. (p. 272)

Renurturing experiences

Hypnosis can be used to provide renurturing experiences to the traumatised patient (Erickson & Rossi, 1989). In this approach, the hypnotherapist actively stimulates change through unconscious responses to direct and indirect suggestions. Another approach that allows the nurturing adult to comfort the traumatised child is to have patients imagine that they are watching a video of an earlier traumatic event. The patient is then encouraged to float into the scene and comfort the child in any appropriate manner, as well as to open up a communicative dialogue. This is a good example of the developmentally needed or reparative relationship proposed by Clarkson (2003), which was discussed in Chapter 2.

Imagery techniques

Spiegel (1994) suggests that it is useful for patients to imagine the traumatic event on an imaginary screen, which gives them some sense of distance from the experience. The screen could be divided in half (i.e. 'the split-screen technique'), having the patient picture on one side some aspect of the event (e.g. a rape victim's image of the assailant), and on the other side of the screen, something he or she did to protect him- or herself (e.g. fighting the assailant). This enables the patient to restructure his or her view of the assault, changing fear and shame into courage and control during a time of overwhelming threat. Spiegel outlines the basic principles as follows:

> The most distressing thing about a traumatic event is the sense of absolute helplessness that it engenders. This helplessness is re-enacted in a post-traumatic stress disorder through loss of control over the state of mind, with spontaneous dissociative states, startle reactions, or intrusive recollections of the event. Furthermore, such patients may tend to identify the therapist with the assailant and feel that the therapy amounts to a reinflicting of the trauma. It is crucial that the process of the therapy, especially when a technique such as hypnosis is used, be structured so that it enhances patients' sense of control. This approach can integrate the image of themselves as victims with the ongoing, more global image of themselves as persons, making the repressed material conscious and therefore less powerful, and enabling them to establish a new, more congruent self-image, absorbing the loss into the ongoing flow of their lives. (p. 1125)

Imagery can also be used to help the patient transform traumatic experiences from the past (e.g. Stanton, 1989, 1990; Hammond, 1990a). Stanton recommends a process he calls 'dumping the rubbish'. This involves having the patient imagine herself filling a laundry sink with water, dumping all her unwanted fears, anxieties and guilt from the past into the water, and then pulling the plug and watching the dark, inky water disappear down the sink.

The therapist can create similar imaginary scenes concerned with 'disposal' that fit with the attitudes and background of the patient. In the 'inner guide' technique (see Scripts 17 and 52) the patient receives advice from the advisor or 'friendly animal' on any problem of concern, including ways of resolving past experiences related to trauma and abuse (Bresler, 1990). The 'friend' can also accompany the patient whilst he or she is accessing and reviewing traumatic material.

The use of stories, jokes and metaphors can also be helpful in the 'working through' stage of treatment (Yapko, 1990b, pp. 320–22).

Catharsis

Working with the PTSD patient in trance often initiates an emotional catharsis. The patient should be informed that the traumatic experience does not need to be completely explored and resolved in one session. It should be reiterated here that the therapist must persistently educate the patient about the real possibility of retraumatisation if too much material is processed at a given time. During the session it is important to tell the patient that:

> You need only know and experience (consciously) those images, feelings and sensations that you are able to deal with appropriately at the present time . . . your unconscious mind can continue to explore these events and when it is appropriate and safe for you to know consciously then your unconscious mind will let you know . . . maybe in a dream later today or tomorrow . . . or in some other way, perhaps with a bodily sensation or a different feeling.

It is very unlikely that abreaction of traumatic experiences alone will be sufficient in working with PTSD patients (Van der Hart & Brown, 1992: available at www.trauma-pages.com). Putman (1989) points out that abreacted material must be carefully processed and worked through. What seem important in using hypnoanalysis with PTSD patients are progressive uncovering, working through and integration of the traumatic material (e.g. Van der Hart & Brown, 1992; Degun-Mather, 1997).

Another model effective in transforming dissociated traumatic experiences is the somatic experiencing approach (Levine, 1991, 1994). Levine has emphasised the importance of helping the patient renegotiate the trauma response by evoking psychophysiological resources in somatic and perceptual systems. Several hypnotic techniques can provide a somatic focus, including sensory exploration (Alman & Lambrou, 1997), the somatic bridge (J.G. Watkins, 1990) and ideosensory signalling (Erickson & Rossi, 1979).

Degun-Mather (2001) presents a case of the successful use of hypnosis in the treatment of chronic PTSD with dissociative fugues in a war veteran. Hypnosis was incorporated into the cognitive-behavioural treatment in an approach outlined by Brende (1985):

- as a supportive technique to reduce anxiety and stabilise the patient by using the 'special place' and 'anchor' in order to produce feelings of calmness;
- as an uncovering technique, whereby the patient can talk through traumatic events and transform the fragmented memories into a narrative.

Initially, the patient learned anxiety management with hypnosis, using the anchor of the special place, as well as self-monitoring to help identify triggers, after which various hypnotherapy approaches were employed. These included regression, ideodynamic questioning, ego-state therapy, post-hypnotic dream suggestions and hypnotic dream elaboration. In the ego-state therapy the older, wiser self offered the younger self any reassurance needed and alternative self-statements (cognitive restructuring). Degun-Mather concluded:

This was a successful outcome of a chronic and long-standing case of PTSD with severe and handicapping dissociative features. The whole treatment programme included psycho-education of PTSD and dissociation, cognitive-behavioural methods with hypnosis for 'grounding' and identifying triggers to his dissociative fugues. Memory integration was achieved by hypnotic recall with non-leading methods and resolving of traumatic memories by ego-state therapy approaches. Some of the memories were recovered with hypnosis and later verified as true. Dissociated feelings were also accessed by a method of hypnotically suggested dreams and hypnotic dream elaboration. Later memory integration was facilitated by writing, which was also a hypnotic experience for the client. (p. 12)

Recovered memories

Memories of child abuse are frequently uncovered during psychotherapy by clinicians using hypnosis and other procedures. In his early work, Freud believed he had discovered that sexual seduction in childhood was the cause of hysterical symptoms in grown women. In 1897 he rescinded this conclusion by reporting that such seductions had not actually happened, but were childhood 'fantasies'. This problem has again become most acute in recent times with the increasing recognition of the incidence of child abuse, as reported by many therapists in cases of dissociation and other disorders (e.g. Lamb, 1994). Since hypnotised patients are particularly suggestible, therapists who use this treatment modality must be especially cautious to avoid instilling false memories. It is therefore important that therapists have access to accurate information about the concept of 'false memory syndrome', or FMS (Toon, Fraise, McFetridge & Alwin, 1996; McNally, 2003). A discussion of the issues involved is provided by Holmes et al. (2005).

Recent reports published by the British Psychological Society (Morton et al., 1995) and the American Psychological Association (1996) concluded that recovered memories of childhood traumas – including sexual abuse – are generally reliable, but not always so. Both working parties condemned the use of suggestion-based techniques (e.g. hypnotic regression) and guided imagery as the memories elicited may be false, especially in individuals with high hypnotisability. Arguably, if the therapeutic procedures implemented are process oriented rather than content oriented, the possibility of false memories should be minimised. Also, if the therapist has sufficient understanding and experience in utilising therapeutic implication rather than suggestion, this will also help in avoiding the development of artefacts.

Phillips and Frederick (1995) remind therapists that they: 'have an obligation to remain objective in eliciting material, to avoid making suggestions or leading patients into any particular kind of memory material, to remain careful about their language, to keep open minds, and to view each case as a unique research opportunity' (p. 14).

Accusations have been made suggesting that FMS does not really exist and that it is essentially a socio-political phenomenon. Nevertheless, it certainly is the case that there have been instances where psychotherapists (including hypnotherapists) have been less than rigorous in applying an objective position when working with memory material. However, there is compelling evidence from clinical studies for the repression of abuse experiences during childhood (e.g. Herman & Schatzow, 1987). Holmes et al. (2005) conclude: 'Both American and British working parties concluded that it is possible to forget memories of abuse for a long time until remembered later and that it is possible for false memories to be created' (p. 17).

Chapter 7
Treatment of Specific Problems (2)

Have you ever thought about transformation? For example, when a block of ice starts to get warmer then the temperature gradually changes, but it stays as a solid until it reaches 0°C when it changes into water. As the temperature continues to rise the water becomes hotter and hotter, but remains as water until 100°C is reached when it changes into vapour. Each new state appears as a leap, suddenly interrupting and checking the gradual succession of temperature changes at each transition point. It is also interesting to contemplate that as the temperature increases, so the invisible particles in the ice and water move faster and faster.

Pain

Although pain is not necessarily caused by stress per se, it is often exacerbated by it, and experiencing pain can, of course, be very stressful. The use of hypnosis for pain control has a strong basis in the experimental literature as well as in numerous anecdotal reports, although until fairly recently there were few controlled studies supporting its clinical efficacy.

Hypnosis as a treatment approach provides the patient with the opportunity to develop self-efficacy whilst also developing the ability to engage in muscle relaxation, correction of dysfunctional cognitive processes and identification of maladaptive cognitive/physiological interactions. Clinicians can optimise their effectiveness by attending to both the experimental literature (e.g. increasing patients' expectations) and clinical findings; for example, by matching hypnotic suggestions to the type of pain (Patterson, 2004).

Many hypnosis procedures have been described for a wide variety of acute and chronic pain-management problems in medical and dental contexts (Bills, 1993; Evans, 1994), and good general accounts may be found in Hilgard and LeBaron (1984a), Olness and Gardner (1988), Chaves (1993), Gibson (1994); Hilgard and Hilgard (1994), Hart and Alden (1994) and Barber (1996).

Initial interview

As already discussed in Chapter 3, the initial interview is critical in establishing rapport and building the therapeutic alliance. However, some important additional information is required with respect to the 'quantity and quality' of the pain. The following questions should be asked:

- How long have you had the pain?
- Are there times when it is more comfortable than others? Close your eyes now and remember that time . . . the place, what was happening, the physical sensations . . . and now 'measure' the degree of comfort on an intensity meter . . . allowing the pointer to come to rest somewhere between 0 and 10, where 0 is the most comfortable . . . and 10 the least comfortable.

The same procedure using the visual analogue scale (VAS) (described in Chapter 2) can be used to access and obtain an intensity measure for the most uncomfortable times. This allows the patient to learn that he or she can change his or her experience of the pain. A pain-rating scale such as that published by the British Pain Society (www.britishpainsociety.org) could also be used.

> So you now know that you can alter the sensations in that part of your body because sometimes you feel more comfortable than others and you have just proved that for yourself . . . that you have the resources to feel more comfortable even though you may not know consciously how to do it, but trusting that your unconscious knows how.

- Can you describe the pain to me?

A detailed description of the pain should cover the following sensory aspects (Hammond, 1990a, p. 46):

- thermal sensations (hot versus cold);
- kinaesthetic sensations and pressure aspects (e.g. dull, sharp, itching, heavy, stabbing, etc.);
- imagery of the pain (size, shape, colour, texture, sound).

This provides the clinician with valuable information that can be utilised during the course of treatment. The following script might assist the patient.

Script 43 – Assessment of the quality of pain experience

Just close your eyes and focus on the pain for a moment . . . maybe you can see it, feel it, touch it or maybe even hear it. . . . What colour is it? What temperature is it? Is it hot or cold? And what about its shape and size? And if you could touch it what does it feel like? Is it soft or hard, rough or smooth? And maybe it can even talk and move. I wonder what it might be saying . . . perhaps if you listen very carefully you might hear what it says . . . maybe it has something very important to say to you . . . if not now, maybe later on in a dream . . . you will have to wait and wonder what might happen. Imagine that you are floating above your body so that you have a bird's-eye view of where the pain is. Perhaps the pain in your body shows up in a particular colour. . . .

Afterwards, the patient can be invited to make a drawing or painting of the pain. This can help to assess the location of the pain and may also suggest images and metaphors that may be useful as part of the treatment strategy. Hammond (1990a, p. 47) suggests that using drawings to determine the location of pain may be facilitated by giving the patient a page with a line drawing of the front and back of the body, with instructions to shade areas where pain is experienced. Mills and Crowley (1986) have children draw how the pain looks 'right now' (picture one); how the pain looks 'all better' (picture two), and what will help 'picture one' change into 'picture two'. This, as in many other instances, is both an assessment and a treatment strategy.

- How do you control the pain at the moment? Have you tried other approaches in the past? Have you experienced hypnosis before or considered using it?

If the patient has considered the possibility of using hypnosis in the past, but rejected the idea, it is important to establish the reasons for this and why the patient is now reconsidering. If the patient has tried hypnosis before, then information concerning his or her experiences might provide important information for the current treatment. The patient's attitudes, expectations and beliefs play an enormous role in determining treatment outcome and, therefore, clinicians must be concerned about the identification and proper utilisation of those variables that have the potential to enhance or to diminish expectations regarding hypnotic responding and clinical outcomes (Chaves, 1994).

- How does having this pain affect your everyday activities and your lifestyle? How would your life be different if your pain could be taken away? What would you be able to do that you can't do now?
- Are there any advantages to having this problem?

Although most patients will at first think that this is rather a pointless question, they often recognise that there may be some advantages or secondary gain associated with having the problem. For example, they may receive more attention from their spouse or avoid certain unpleasant activities.

- You have had this pain for some considerable time; why have you chosen this moment in time to see me for treatment?
- What would you like to achieve by having this treatment? Would it be all right to decrease the sensations that you have or alter the quality of the pain experience?

It is important to note here that a treatment goal for pain does not necessarily mean getting rid of the pain in its entirety. In fact, total removal may not be a good idea anyway, as pain is an important communication that usually needs to be taken seriously. Hammond (1990a) advocates having a realistic goal and retaining the signalling function of pain while decreasing the suffering and incapacitating aspects.

- Do you have your own story as to why you are experiencing this pain?

This may be fairly obvious, particularly in cases where it is related to injury or medical procedures. However, there are many cases where individuals experience pain that has no obvious or explanatory causation. In these instances the aetiology is often ascribed as psychosomatic or psychological whereas, in fact, the causes are unknown. To hear the patient's view about the reasons why he or she has the pain can provide the therapist with some useful guides for intervention.

- Did you decide to see me or did someone else make the suggestion?

The patient's attitude to a referral is important, particularly with respect to motivation and collaboration with the therapist.

To reiterate, it is extremely important to make sure that a medical doctor has examined the patient before commencing treatment. If this is not the case, the patient should be referred to a physician immediately. If a non-medical psychotherapist treats an undiagnosed pain patient, this could have serious repercussions, especially if there is a somatic basis for the problem. A headache is likely to be just a headache, but sometimes it indicates much more – a brain tumour, for instance. Similarly, back pain is occasionally a signal for bone cancer. Nevertheless, as with many of the other problems discussed in this book, working within a multidisciplinary team is the ideal. In any event, the hypnotherapist should be familiar with the methods of pain management used by other professionals.

Pain assessment

Another method, apart from using the VAS, of finding out about the way in which the patient is subjectively experiencing the pain is to use the McGill Pain Questionnaire (Melzack, 1975). For the assessment of pain in children, the Varni/Thompson Paediatric Pain Questionnaire (Varni, Thompson & Hanson, 1987) and the Children's Comprehensive Pain Questionnaire (McGrath, 1990) can be used. The ongoing monitoring of the intensity of pain, or different components of it, hour by hour and day by day whilst the patient is in therapy (Brown & Fromm, 1987), has given rise to standardised techniques such as those of Elton, Stanley and Burrows (1983, Appendix). By carrying out these initial diagnostic tasks efficiently, the therapist will come to understand the nature of the individual patient's pain experience, as far as it is possible for such an understanding to be established. In so doing, the therapist will be in a much better position to make appropriate therapeutic suggestions and to initiate optimal treatment strategies.

For example, on one occasion many years ago I requested that a young female patient, with diagnosed lumbar spondylosis, imagine that she was lying in the sun on a Greek beach (she had informed me that she had just come back from holiday). As the treatment proceeded she became increasingly agitated and remarked that her pain was getting worse because it was 'red hot'. She then informed me that she usually experienced her pain as 'red and hot'. If I had obtained this information at the beginning of the session, I would not have made such an unfortunate and inappropriate suggestion. However, once she had informed me of this, I suggested that she imagine entering the sea and allow the waves to gently bathe her until her back changed to a comfortable temperature. This suggestion worked fine as she was able to alter the quality of her pain by changing one of the important dimensions, namely temperature (and incidentally the colour of the pain). This dimension (i.e. temperature) would also have been ascertained by using the McGill Pain Questionnaire or an adaptation of it. Of course, rather than using the tests described above in a formal way, the patient could simply be asked to describe the pain (see under 'Initial interview' above), or to draw the pain and colour it.

Part of the assessment could also include an evaluation of the expression of anxiety and depression, which often accompany both acute and chronic pain. The Beck Anxiety Inventory (Beck et al., 1988) and the Beck Depression Inventory (Beck, 1967) are useful adjuncts to the clinical interview for this purpose. Patients experiencing acute pain often differ in their expression of anxiety and depression from those experiencing chronic pain, and this can suggest a differential emphasis in treatment (Vingoe, 1993). Patients with acute pain often show more anxiety than chronic-pain patients, probably due to the more predictable nature of acute pain. It is usually time limited and of less than six months' duration. Examples are pain associated with childbirth, dysmenorrhoea and medical and dental procedures such as injections, venipunctures, bone-marrow aspirations, lumbar punctures, intrauterine device insertion and surgery (Hart & Alden, 1994, p. 122). Because acute pain gradually declines in intensity, relaxation techniques and other anxiety reduction procedures are generally sufficient. Chronic pain sufferers, on the other hand, show greater expressions of depression and demoralisation (Axelrad, 1990). Examples are pain from spinal injury, lower-back pain, tension headache, migraine, irritable bowel syndrome (IBS), atypical facial pain, arthritic and rheumatic pain, and pain associated with cancer (Hart & Alden, 1994, p. 122).

Turk, Meichenbaum and Genest (1983) categorised pain into the following different types:

- acute pain (e.g. post-surgical pain, dental pain, childbirth): time limited; gradually declines in intensity; psychological factors and secondary gain not usually present; effective treatment with anxiety-reduction procedures and relaxation;
- chronic, periodic pain (e.g. migraine headaches, trigeminal neuralgia): recurs and is intense and intermittent; strong likelihood of physiological factors; treatment can focus on symptom relief;
- chronic, intractable, benign pain (e.g. lower-back pain): present most of the time; psychological factors and secondary gain may be important, including interpersonal and financial factors; treatment strategies must take account of the psychological factors;
- chronic, progressive pain (e.g. cancer pain): progressive and constant, thus placing immense demands on the patient; anxiety is often an important factor.

It can be seen that knowing what type of pain the patient has can give important indications as to the overall treatment stratagems, as well as more specific clinical hypnosis approaches.

Strategies and techniques for managing pain

Initially, it is important for the patient to give his or her 'unconscious' permission to allow the therapist to help him or her facilitate the removal of the pain. It is not enough to have the patient ask you at a conscious level to give help, because the pain may have taken on a special unconscious meaning. Many of those who treat pain in clinics have failed to recognise this hidden meaning for pain. If there are no apparent unconscious factors contributing to the pain problem (determined by using ideodynamic signalling), then some of the basic relaxation, ego-strengthening, suggestive and imagery techniques described below may be used. Whenever using pain management approaches, it is essential for the therapist to stress 'safety and appropriateness', for obvious reasons. A patient who has a painful back wants to feel more comfortable to allow him- or herself to enjoy life without the continual 'nagging' pain. However, it would probably be inappropriate if such a patient engaged in an activity such as digging the garden! It is also important to tell the patient about pain control. The following approach could be used.

Script 44 – Utilising experiences of controlling pain

Did you know that when you are worried, depressed, in pain or anticipating pain you tighten the muscles of your forehead, neck shoulders and arms . . . and when you are at peace with your world you relax these muscles and consequently you feel more comfortable? . . . It is hard to relax these muscles purposefully and intentionally . . . you need to go about it indirectly by remembering times and places where you were automatically and unconsciously relaxed . . . for example, by remembering times when you were on holiday and enjoying yourself. Curiously, when you learn to do this you also automatically improve your ability to tolerate or even ignore the factors that have been making you anxious, depressed or uncomfortable. A first step towards learning to control pain is to realise that you can pay attention to one arm and notice how heavy it feels, and not notice the heaviness of the other arm.

Olness and Gardner (1988) describe a method called the 'switchbox', in which the therapist explains to the child the idea that pain is transmitted by nerves from various parts of the body to the brain, which then sends a 'pain message' back to the body (coloured drawings can be used to facilitate this). The patient is asked to choose a switch that could turn off or modulate incoming nerve signals (e.g. a flip, dimmer or pull) situated wherever the patient wants (for example, in the brain or near the site of pain). Patients were asked to practise turning off the switches for defined periods of time, starting with 10 to 15 seconds and working towards longer periods. Hawkins, Liossi, Hatira, Ewart and Kosmidis (1998) used this technique in a programme with children who were undergoing lumbar punctures. I have also used it successfully with headache patients in an outpatients' neurology clinic.

Hammond (1990a, p. 47) presents a useful classification of hypnotic strategies and techniques for managing pain. However, to repeat, such 'lists' are not exhaustive – there are always other possibilities, and the invention of new and creative ways of intervening will depend on the ingenuity of the therapist and the intimate collaboration with the patient. As a general rule it is important to teach the patient self-hypnosis for the control of his or her pain as early as possible in the treatment programme, as this provides the patient with a sense of control and mastery that is often severely lacking in patients with chronic pain. Ego-strengthening can also be valuable with chronic-pain patients who often develop feelings of low self-esteem and low self-worth.

Another important reservation concerns the proviso that some sensory experience should always be left, except in a small number of conditions such as dental anaesthesia, childbirth, cancer pain, phantom limb pain and when hypnosis is being used for surgical anaesthesia (Hammond, 1990a, p. 49).

Relaxation

Relaxation is often very effective in controlling stress-related pain, especially acute pain, because it reduces anxiety and tension. In addition, it is relatively easy for patients to learn how to use these techniques themselves. A number of scripts are provided below and, although these are presented as discrete, they can be combined quite easily. Remember to tell the patient what you expect him or her to do before you begin the session.

Script 45 – Breathing relaxation

Firstly, be aware of your breathing . . . allowing the air to flow through your nose and into your lungs (*the therapist paces the patient by saying this as the patient is breathing in*) . . . and back out again (*the therapist says this as the patient is breathing out*) . . . just breathing away all of the residual tension in your mind and body . . . nothing you need do but to allow that to happen (*this sequence can be repeated a number of times*). . . . And the next time you breathe in, take a deep breath and hold it for a moment . . . and as you exhale allowing your body to become so relaxed just like a rag doll . . . the ripples of relaxation spreading through your body like a pebble thrown into a quiet pool on a warm summer's day . . . spreading to every part of your body from the top of your head to the tips of your toes. And, as the relaxation flows through your whole body, maybe you will notice how wonderfully comfortable every cell in your body is becoming as you discover those memories and resources you have to feel really calm and deeply relaxed.

Script 46 – Passive progressive relaxation for specific pain (modified autogenic training)

The clinician can start with an approach that helps the patient to relax his or her entire body (e.g. Script 45), and then the following can be added:

And there may be part of your body that would like to experience this deep relaxation to an even greater degree right now . . . just allowing the warmth, heaviness and relaxation to flow to that part of your body . . . bathing that part of your body in relaxing and healing energy . . . as it restores that part of your body to more optimal functioning . . . knowing at some level that you have the resources to allow that to happen . . . all by itself . . . nothing you need do consciously . . . trusting in your unconscious mind . . . to enable that part of your body to become more comfortable . . . if this is appropriate . . . into the future.

Note that no mention is made of the pain per se. The emphasis is on the total relaxation of the whole body. This is usually quite easy for the patient to do and quickly helps him or her to develop a sense of mastery and control.

Script 47 – Ball of light

This sequence can follow on from Script 46.

And as you continue to breathe slowly and effortlessly . . . you can allow a peaceful and healing ball of light to flow around your body . . . as you breathe in so it flows up your back and over the top of your head . . . and as you breathe out it flows down the front of your body . . . massaging away all of the residual tension . . . leaving your body feeling warm, heavy and relaxed . . . and this ball of light can continue to flow around your body long after you have left here . . . as long as this is appropriate for you with respect to your safety . . . , and so on.

In all of these scripts, when an appropriate level of relaxation has been achieved the patient can be asked to 'anchor' this state in some way, for example:

And when that feeling of relaxation is strong and comfortable, then put your thumb and forefinger together, and the more you rub them together the more relaxed you will become . . . and during the week when you are at home or work you can do that so that you can become comfortable and relaxed quite automatically and spontaneously . . . and you may be surprised to find how well this can work.

The VAS could also be used to facilitate reduction in pain intensity. The patient may already have been introduced to this approach during the initial interview.

Guided imagery

There are many ways of using mental imagery to help alleviate pain (e.g. Williamson, 2004). The methods used will be determined by the nature of the pain itself, the experiences and preferences of the patient and, of course, the creativity of the therapist. A number of examples are provided below to give the therapist some indication of the range of possibilities.

Alden (1992) describes a technique called the 'magic pool'. She asks the patient to imagine travelling down a path from a garden or beach and to discover a secluded and private pool with special properties to soothe and calm. The patient then imagines entering the water, allowing the magic water to wash away the pain and anxiety, leaving an invisible healing film on the skin. Alden further suggests that this technique can be used for skin disorders by suggesting that the water has a medicinal effect. I have used a similar technique called the 'magic shower'.

Script 48 – The magic shower technique

When the patient is in trance, he or she is invited to take a magic shower.

> And I would like you to know that the drops of water that come out of the shower head are very special magical drops that have very extraordinary healing properties . . . you can adjust the temperature of the water so that it is very comfortable and relaxing as it flows over your body . . . helping you to feel calmer and more relaxed . . . and as the magic water flows to every cell in your body so it massages away all the tension and discomfort . . . healing every cell and restoring it to optimal functioning . . . and there may be a part of your body that would like this special healing right now . . . allowing the magic water to flow there . . . dissolving away all the discomfort . . . as it flows away quite effortlessly . . . away out of your body. . . .

A similar technique, 'medicinal fluid', is described by Hart and Alden (1994, p. 133) in which the patient imagines drinking a special nice-tasting drink that fills his or her body and attaches itself to the pain. When the pain attaches itself to the fluid, it changes colour and consistency and can be emptied out of the body by opening taps in the fingers and toes. Of course, these techniques can be used for a whole range of psychosomatic problems, and this also applies to the following technique.

Script 49 – The magic flower

The patient is invited to visit a beautiful garden (when assessing the patient in the first session, ask whether he or she likes flowers and gardens). I often 'take' the patient to his or her favourite place first, and then into the garden.

> And as you look around your favourite place you notice the colours . . . the shapes . . . the movements . . . enjoying that experience, feeling relaxed, calm and peaceful . . . be aware of any sounds that you can hear . . . the temperature of the air on your hands and face . . . and as you look around you notice a very inviting path leading away from you . . . and I would like to invite you to follow that path until you come to six steps leading down into a very beau-

tiful garden . . . counting down from six to one as you gently proceed down the steps into the garden . . . becoming more and more relaxed as you go down and down into the garden . . . and in the garden you are aware of what you can see . . . what you can hear . . . what you experience . . . and you notice a very beautiful flower . . . and taking a deep breath and inhaling the healing fragrance . . . allowing the fragrance to flow to that part of your body that requires special healing right now . . . knowing that the healing fragrance can help to restore feelings of comfort, calm and peacefulness. . . .

During a hypnotherapy session, a patient of mine with chronic lower-back pain spontaneously had an image of a rusty door lock that was difficult to turn. He put some oil into the lock, which helped to free the mechanism. Afterwards, he volunteered that his back was very similar to the lock and that perhaps it would help if he 'gave it an infusion of oil'. Then during trance he imagined that olive oil (ingested with his food) travelled to his back and lubricated it to more efficient functioning. After the session he reported that the pain had decreased and that he could stand without stooping as much as he had before. This was obvious as he got up from the chair. He was requested to replay this image everyday throughout the week. When he arrived for the next session he reported that his back problem had considerably lessened during the week and that he was actually using olive oil in his food to a greater extent than previously! I hope that there were no iatrogenic symptoms resulting from this activity. The important issue here is that the patient himself, and not the therapist, generated the image used.

Patients can also be taught to experience themselves in another place by floating on a cloud or a magic carpet, or indeed by some other mode of travel.

Transformation of pain

Two kinds of transformations have been used:

- those in which the pain is moved (displaced) to a different part of the body;
- those in which the pain experience (e.g. temperature, colour, shape, sensations) is altered to something that is more acceptable.

In methods of transformation, the patient is not being asked to give up the pain, only to transform it. In the physical transformation of pain, the pain is moved, or displaced, to a part of the body that is less central to the patient's activities or to a part that is less significant (e.g. a pain in the hand that causes the patient problems in writing with a pen could be moved to the left ear, or a headache could be moved to the left little toe). Pain in the extremities is usually less frightening than pain in the abdomen (Karle & Boys, 1987). This procedure is particularly valuable in cases of chronic, intractable, benign pain, where there is often a psychological reason (e.g. secondary gain) for the patient to retain the pain. Barber (1990, p. 50) provides the following example of displacement:

> As you continue to pay careful attention to the discomfort in your abdomen, let me know when you first begin to notice the very slight movement of that feeling. . . . That's right, now just notice, as the movement continues, in perhaps a circular way, to increase. . . . Is it moving clockwise, or counterclockwise?. . . That's fine, now just continue to be curious as you notice how the feeling can continue to move, in an ever-increasing spiral, moving round and round your abdomen and notice which leg it begins to move into . . .

It is probably a good idea for the therapist to ask the patient to which part of the patient's body he or she would like to move the pain. Once again it must be stressed that the therapist must be very careful in adopting these procedures and consult with the physician as to the specific nature of the patient's problems.

Substituting another sensation (e.g. itching, pressure or warmth) for pain can assist in the reinterpretation. Hart and Alden (1994) suggest that success is more likely if the substituted sensation is not totally pleasant, as this would be somewhat implausible to the patient (p. 135). The patient can be asked to imagine the pain (remember that this should be part of the assessment procedure) and to change one, or more, of the most significant qualities, such as the shape, colour, size, temperature or intensity. Suggestions for hand warmth and head cooling are typically used for migraine (Alladin, 1988), and hand warmth to the stomach for irritable bowel syndrome (Whorwell, Prior & Faragher, 1984). The use of a VAS (described earlier) is an effective method for changing the intensity of pain as well as monitoring the effectiveness of the therapy.

Script 50 – Visualising the pain (adapted from Simonton, Matthews-Simonton & Creighton, 1978, p. 205)

> Focus on the pain and notice its colour . . . see its colour and shape and size very clearly . . . and as you continue to breathe slowly and effortlessly so the way the pain appears becomes very clear to you . . . it may be the size of a tennis ball . . . or a grapefruit . . . or a basketball. . . . Mentally project the ball out into space . . . maybe 10 feet away from your body. . . . Make the ball bigger, about the size of a basketball . . . and now shrink it to the size of a pea . . . and now let it become any size it chooses to be . . . letting that happen all by itself . . . and now begin to change the ball's colour, making it pink and then light green . . . now take the green ball and put it back where you originally saw it. At this point, notice whether or not your pain has been reduced

... and as you open your eyes you are now ready to resume your normal activities.

There is normally no need to hypnotise the patient first, as engaging in the visualisation will in itself induce trance.

Time distortion

It is a well-known everyday phenomenon that we distort time by slowing it down or speeding it up. This idea should be explained to the patient by using a common everyday example (e.g. watching an interesting television programme compared to waiting for a bus in the rain), emphasising the fact that he or she has the resources to slow down the passage of time when feeling comfortable, and to speed it up when experiencing an unacceptable level of pain. It is useful to ask the patient to provide a personal example, which most are able to quite readily.

Script 51 – Time distortion

And do you already know how to alter the passage of time? ... to slow it down and to speed it up even though you don't know exactly how you do that ... there are times in your life when time goes very quickly ... when you are enjoying yourself, for example ... and there are other times when time passes very slowly (*the therapist can slow down speed of talking when saying this*) ... so you already have the resources to do this without really trying to do anything ... because it just happens. ... So, maybe, you can allow time to pass more slowly when you are feeling comfortable and relaxed ... whereas when you are feeling uncomfortable you can allow the time to pass much more quickly ... and in this way you will have more time to experience feeling comfortable and relaxed ... and when you know that you can do that without trying, will your hand float? ... and when it floats towards your face, will your eyes open?

Projection

Jaffe and Bresler (1980) ask the patient to give the pain away to a 'friendly animal' for safekeeping or to ask for advice on how to cope with the pain (refer to Scripts 17 and 52). It is important for the therapist to emphasise that the patient can keep some of the pain for him- or herself, as well as the idea that the 'friendly animal' is only looking after the pain and that the patient can have it back at any time. Similar techniques include putting the pain into a box, a desk drawer or envelope, or posting the pain to a friend. I once asked a patient to put her pain into an envelope, which was sealed, labelled with the patient's name and with a brief description of the contents and placed in a locked drawer. A few days later the patient telephoned to make sure that the pain was still safely locked away, as she was rather anxious that it might 'get out' or 'get lost'. I reassured her that it was still in the drawer inside the envelope. The patient checked from time to time, and two years later the pain was still in the drawer!

Script 52 – Giving the pain away to a friendly animal

Take a deep breath and allow your body to float to your favourite outdoor place . . . noticing what you can see . . . what you can hear . . . what you smell . . . what you can touch. . . . noticing the temperature of the air on your hands and face . . . and how you are feeling right now . . . breathing in healing energy, flowing to every part of your body, massaging every cell into a feeling of total comfort and relaxation And as you continue to enjoy that effortless feeling of relaxation you notice a friendly path leading away from you, and as you look more closely you notice a peaceful ball of light at the end of the path which is moving slowly and effortlessly towards you . . . you are beginning to enjoy a calm and peace that radiates from it . . . and as it gets closer to you it begins to change into a very friendly animal or person . . . and you welcome your friend and ask their name, and you can share yours and any other personal information that is appropriate. And I would like you to know that your friend is very special and is able to help you with issues in your life including your pain . . . they can look after your pain for you for as long as you wish . . . and this will not cause them any discomfort. You can check out with them whether they can do this for you today. If the answer is positive then give them your pain in a special way knowing that you can ask for it back at any time. That's fine! And now its time to thank your friend and say goodbye knowing that you can meet them at anytime in the future . . . all you have to do is to go to your special place and notice the inviting path and the friendly ball of light. . . . And now being in your special place once more and with every breath that you take becoming lighter and lighter, spreading upwards from your feet through your body into your face and up into your eyelids, as they gently flutter open . . . that's fine . . . back into this room . . . feeling relaxed and comfortable . . . and trusting in your unconscious mind to allow you to stay like this for as long as is appropriate. You know the date, the day of the week and how old you are . . . and perhaps you could tell me how you intend to travel home after the session?

Hypnotic analgesia and anaesthesia

Analgesia and anaesthesia can be suggested directly or induced through indirect or Ericksonian methods. Resistant patients, in particular those receiving secondary gain for their pain, might resist a direct approach, but be more likely to respond to an indirect method.

Hawkins et al. (1998) used the following direct suggestions:

> We'll do some strong magic now . . . first you have to allow your lower back
> to go to sleep for few minutes. . . . I'll show you how to do it . . . I'll just put
> my hand up on your back to help it become numb . . . sleepy and numb . . .
> soft and sleepy.
>   Just imagine painting numbing medicine onto your back.
>   Imagine injecting an anaesthetic into your low back . . . feel it flow into
> your body . . . notice the change in feeling as the area becomes numb.

Kuttner (1986) describes the use of 'glove anaesthesia', or the magic glove
technique, with a child with cancer who had a strong dislike of chemotherapy. The child was asked to imagine putting a magic glove over her hand to
cover, protect and numb the hand. Once the glove was on, the needle was
inserted into the vein without difficulty. It is essential that the patient (and
parents in the above example) is adequately prepared for these approaches
as the development of a positive mindset or expectation is an important part
of the process.

Hawkins et al. (1998) used the following technique for transferring numbness from the hand to the painful area in children with cancer:

> Pay attention to your hand . . . notice how you can feel tingling feelings in
> that hand . . . let it become numb . . . when it is very numb, touch your lower
> back with that hand . . . let the numb feeling transfer from your hand to your
> back.

The patient could also be asked to remember a time when he or she received
an anaesthetic:

> Just go inside your mind and find a time in your life when a feeling of pleas-
> ant numbness flowed through your body. And do you already notice the begin-
> ning of those comfortable changes? It's very positive and comforting to know
> that you can allow those changes to happen and that your unconscious mind
> can enable you to do that whenever it is appropriate for you. That's fine, as
> you allow those feelings to flow to a specific part of your body, and you may
> be surprised to discover that any part of your body that you choose can be
> very comfortable and relaxed.

Metaphors and stories

The use of stories and metaphors are very good ways of bypassing any conscious resistance a patient may have. They should be matched carefully to the
patient's interests as well as to the problem. Hammond (1990a, pp. 45–83)
provides a number of examples.

Hypnoanalysis

In hypnoanalysis, the patient can be regressed back to the time before the pain started, or to a time when the pain was less severe, so that he or she can enjoy experiences of comfort and calmness in the areas of the body currently affected by pain.

Script 53 – Positive psychosomatic regression

Close your eyes and develop whatever degree of trance is appropriate and allow your unconscious mind to take you back to a time in your past when your body felt well and comfortable all over . . . when you could enjoy every part of your body as it felt relaxed, comfortable and very peaceful . . . and when your unconscious mind has found an experience when your whole body felt comfortable then it can move one of your fingers just to indicate that this has happened, even though you may not know it consciously just yet . . . and I think that you're going to enjoy experiencing those feelings of comfort in your whole body, including your back (*or area in which the pain problem occurs*) . . . you know that you have the resources to allow that to happen at any time in the future when it is appropriate and safe. . . . And you can acknowledge that by putting your thumb and forefinger together as a signal for this to occur whenever you want. . . . And now take these feelings and sensations into the future and experience yourself doing something appropriate that you really enjoy doing . . . feeling relaxed and comfortable.

The therapist could also proceed with an ideodynamic approach:

And I would like to ask your unconscious mind whether it is willing and able to allow you to take these positive feelings and sensations of comfort and well-being into the future . . . and to allow John's (*i.e. name of patient*) body (*or specific area*) to feel comfortable and calm when it is appropriate and safe . . . , and so on.

Asking the patient to progress in time from a point before the pain commenced could facilitate a regression to the time when the problem started:

Find a time in your life when your body was feeling comfortable and peaceful, and now progress to the time just before your body started to become less comfortable . . . and gently progress to that point in time when a part of your body became uncomfortable.

It is essential that the clinician has considerable experience in using these approaches, as significant abreaction may occur (refer to Chapter 3, and also to Kleinhauz & Beran, 1981; Carich, 1986; Hammond, 1990a).

Apart from the basic regression technique described above, the hypno-analytic methods discussed in Chapter 5 could also be used to access the unconscious dynamics that maintain or exacerbate the pain.

Hypnosis in the Treatment of Specific Pain Problems

There are many specific pain conditions that can be helped with hypnosis. Those discussed here include back pain and headaches, gastrointestinal and dermatological problems, pain associated with medical procedures (such as dressing changes and lumbar punctures) and cancer.

Back pain

The 'New Hypnosis' approach developed by Araoz (1985) encourages patients to focus on their lower back pain and to experience what thoughts, feelings, images and sensations emerge. They are encouraged to allow their rational mind to stand aside and allow 'whatever' is there to 'come up'. Often memories, psychosomatic expressions or unusual images appear. By talking through, revivifying or reframing these experiences, patients can often release much of the 'suffering' associated with the pain (Burte, Burte & Araoz, 1994, p. 100). This technique has much in common with the somatic bridge approach discussed in Chapter 5, and can be understood in terms of 'psychosomatic healing', that is, the utilisation of internal unconscious processes or what Rossi (1996) refers to as 'hypnotherapeutic work'.

Migraine and non-migraine headaches

The benefits of hypnotic relaxation and suggestion for headache patients have been reported by Cedercreutz, Lahteenmaki and Tulikoura (1976), Drummond (1981) and Carasso, Peded and Kleinhauz (1985). In the former study, three or four group sessions were usually sufficient, while in the latter, nine group and individual sessions were used and patients performed self-relaxation twice daily. However, certain refinements may be made that are specific to the pathology of this type of headache. It has been suggested (Bakal, 1975; Adams, Feuerstein & Fowler, 1980) that in the prodromal phase of migraine there is a constriction of the cranial blood vessels immediately followed by a compensatory dilation that is responsible for symptoms such as pain, nausea and dizziness. Therefore, as well as suggestions of relaxation and the regular practice of self-hypnosis, suggestions may be given, with suitable imagery, for redistribution of blood supply. Edmonston (1981) concluded that specific suggestions could be an active component in the treatment of migraine. These changes may be suggested directly by asking the patient to imagine the process of constriction of the cranial arteries (Anderson, Basker & Dalton, 1975) or by imagining the hands becoming warmer using imagery such as immersing them in warm water (Alladin, 1988). In general, procedures described as 'hypnotic' appear to give good results (Anderson et al., 1975; Friedman & Taub, 1985; Berlin & Erdmann, 1987; Davidson, 1987; Alladin, 1988; Matthews & Flatt, 1999). Gibson and Heap (1991) suggest that:

> The practitioner, then, may be confidently advised when treating migraine, to use a hypnotic procedure emphasising both general relaxation and hand-warming and perhaps appropriate vascular changes. Ego-strengthening suggestions may also be incorporated into the hypnotic script, and the hypnotic session may be recorded on tape for daily (or even more frequent) use by the patient. (p. 107)

Gastrointestinal problems

Irritable bowel syndrome (IBS)

IBS is the most common disorder of the intestine affecting 10 to 20% of adults. Patients are often caught in a cycle in which stress triggers the symptoms, which in turn exacerbate the stress. The implication of psychological factors is recognised in the onset and worsening of the symptomatology (Switz, 1976). Symptoms of IBS include abdominal pain, bloating, cramping and flatulence, as well as bouts of diarrhoea and constipation. Usually patients report anxiety and depression, although there is no relationship between IBS and specific psychological disorders (Welch, Hillman & Pomare, 1985). A number of well-documented studies have demonstrated that hypnosis can be a valuable treatment strategy for IBS (Solloway, 2005; www.ibshypnosis.com/IBSresearch.html). The earliest and perhaps the best research study in this area was published in *The Lancet* in 1984 (Whorwell, Prior, & Faragher). The study was thoroughly placebo-controlled and showed dramatic contrast in response to hypnosis treatment above the placebo group. Thirty patients with severe symptoms unresponsive to other treatments were randomly chosen to receive seven sessions of gut-directed hypnotherapy (15 patients) or seven sessions of psychotherapy plus placebo pills (15 patients). The psychotherapy group showed a small, but significant, improvement in abdominal pain and distension, and in general well-being, but not bowel activity pattern. The hypnotherapy patients showed a dramatic improvement in all central symptoms. The hypnotherapy group also showed no relapses during the three-month follow-up period.

Further research studies have confirmed these early results; for example, Whorwell, Prior & Colgan, 1987; Houghton, Heyman & Whorwell, 1996; Houghton et al., 1999; Lea et al., 2003; Cooper, Cruickshanks, Miller & Whorwell, 2003. In gut-directed hypnotherapy, hypnosis is first induced before the patient is asked to place his or her hand on the abdomen and generate feelings of warmth and comfort. This is followed by suggestions of symptom reduction and personal control over gut function. Appropriate guided imagery and metaphors are also used. Emphasis is placed on determination and a positive attitude on the part of the patient. A tape of daily autohypnosis is used for reinforcement and sessions are concluded with ego-strengthening suggestions. The suggestions are adapted to each particular condition and to the needs of the patient.

Zimmerman (2003) describes the use of hypnotically facilitated suggestion with a woman diagnosed as suffering from a functional disorder with features of IBS. In view of her lack of response to pharmacological therapy, the motivation of the patient and lack of contraindication, the use of hypnosis seemed appropriate. It should also be noted that the patient described her symptoms very clearly and vividly, using metaphors. In the first two sessions, Zimmerman instructed the patient in self-hypnosis and used guided imagery to facilitate relaxation and to enhance a sense of control, as well as establishing ideomotor signals. Although some improvement took place after these two sessions, it was not until after the third session – when a metaphor, 'cleaning up the river', was used – that a notable improvement occurred. An image of a river was used to evoke a smooth, coordinated flow through the normal digestive tract, and a normal flow in the management of the patient's emotions. The session started with an ego-strengthening metaphor using the tree as a symbol of strength and power, in which tactile contact was stressed. The patient was then encouraged to examine her own image reflected in the clear water of a peaceful stream surrounded by trees. The session culminated in the obstruction of the stream and the invitation to the patient to clear the obstacle and restore the peaceful flow. This triggered an abreaction in the patient that appeared to lead to a successful resolution of her problems. The metaphor relates both to the altered motility of the gut as well as to the emotional content of the symptoms. Zimmerman concludes that: 'The abreaction experienced by this patient as well as her comments after termination of the session suggest that unblocking her emotional response, rather than her gut, was the main factor in recovery'.

Although there is some good evidence for the use of hypnotherapy in the treatment of IBS, it should not be regarded as a panacea, as up to 25% of patients fail to respond. Even when patients do improve, conventional approaches to treatment should not necessarily be ignored. It is still important that lifestyle factors, such as diet, are also taken into account. In addition, some patients may find that an occasional loperamide or laxative, depending on the bowel habit abnormality, may be required. Nevertheless, a recent survey by Cox, de Lusignan and Chan (2004) of general practitioners in the UK indicates that over 70% of them considered that hypnotherapy may have a role in managing patients with irritable bowel disease and would consider referral to a qualified hypnotherapist.

Hypnosis has also been used to sedate patients undergoing gastrointestinal endoscopy (Zimmerman, 1998). Techniques included metaphors, relaxation, imagery and post-hypnotic suggestions.

Crohn's disease (CD)

Crohn's disease is an inflammatory bowel disease (IBD) currently defined as a nonspecific, chronic syndrome of unknown origin most commonly involving the lower part of the small intestine (ileum), the large intestine or the colon. The disease can begin at any age, but most typically starts between 15 and 30 years of age. No conventional (i.e. medical or surgical) cure exists, although recent clinical case studies and anecdotal reports have shown that the use of different forms of hypnotherapy for the treatment of Crohn's have actually resulted in cures (Abela, 1999). Recent evidence demonstrates that stress due to both psychosocial events and negative emotions is definitely implicated in disease course, if not actually disease onset (Greene, Blanchard & Wan, 1994). Studies showed that CD patients reported more feelings of being under pressure than control subjects, although CD patients experienced a lower amount of life stress than controls (von Wietersheim, Kohler & Feiereis, 1992). Moreover, other studies have demonstrated that negative emotions, especially rage and anger, are generally present and blocked at an unconscious level causing such emotions to be turned inward (Schafer, 1997). Schafer showed that hypnotherapy to psychologically control the presenting autoimmune characteristics, or achieve insight into the negative emotions, generally resulted in the complete remission of Crohn's. Hypnosis techniques used included visualisation, suggestions and metaphors in conjunction with regressive exploration to achieve insight and understanding, and resolution of the negative emotions involved. In addition, ego-strengthening, suggestions for general health and the enhancement of self-esteem were utilised. Abela (1999) concludes that hypnotherapy is indicated as a complementary therapy for Crohn's along with medical treatments; for example, corticosteroid therapy.

Ulcerative colitis

Another common form of IBD is ulcerative colitis (UC). Although many factors may be implicated in the cause of UC, it is likely that stressful events may trigger symptoms. Hypnosis may be used to reduce abdominal pain and bloating, for example by suggesting to the patient that their intestinal muscles are becoming smooth and calm.

Dermatological problems

Recent scientific studies point to the role of stress in the onset and/or exacerbation of many dermatological problems. Because of the central social and psychological role played by the skin and its appearance, skin diseases in turn can produce a host of psychological reactions, including depression, shame, social withdrawal and rage (Folks & Kinney, 1992). These studies indicate the need for stress-reduction techniques, of which hypnosis is one. Hypnotic suggestion has long been thought to be effective in the improvement of various skin disorders (Shenefelt, 2000, 2003a, 2003b). Many recent studies have shown a link between the use of hypnosis and changed skin response in certain dermatological affections such as psoriasis (Tausk & Whitmore, 1999), atopic dermatitis (Stewart & Thomas, 1995), warts (Ewin, 1992; Goldstein, 2005), alopecia areata (Thompson & Shapiro, 1996) and eczema (Mantle, 2001). Practising self-hypnosis to moderate stress has been shown to be effective for a variety of skin conditions that are exacerbated by anxiety.

Cheek (1961) explains his use of hypnotic techniques to treat various cutaneous manifestations, in particular herpes genitalis infections. According to Cheek, getting the affected skin to feel cool through the use of hypnosis can be much more effective than any pharmaceutical methods. In light hypnosis, Cheek sets up finger signals and asks for permission to get the tissues cool and to keep them cool for periods of two hours. He starts with an unimportant area for the production of a coolness sensation by having his patients imagine that they are sucking on a 'peppermint and breathing in'. With the patient in trance, he requests that the 'yes' finger lifts when the mouth feels cool, and that the patient tells him when there is a conscious awareness of the coolness. When the patient is confident about sensing the change, the therapist tells him or her to experience that same coolness in the lesioned area.

Cheek also used hypnosis to help patients develop a more positive attitude towards themselves, as well as to help them imagine themselves in the future without skin problems. He utilised hypnotic trance phenomena, such as the increased ability to focus, time distortion, amnesia, flashback memories, analgesia, catalepsy, and so on, in order to achieve these goals.

Other hypnosis techniques that can be used include a television screen tuned to the 'future channel' on which patients see their body without the current skin problem or their hair beginning to grow again, or imagining themselves using a brush to scrub away the lesions on the back or hands so as to clean and polish the body to make it healthy again. Approaches that facilitate ideosensory changes (e.g. warmth, coolness, tingling) are particularly valuable for the treatment of warts and herpes (Tasini & Hackett, 1977), but may also be helpful for other dermatological problems.

Stewart and Thomas (1995) used hypnotherapy to treat atopic dermatitis in adults and children. Twenty adults with extensive atopic dermatitis, resistant to conventional treatment, were treated with hypnotherapy, with statistically significant benefit, which was maintained for up to two years where follow-up was available. Twenty children with severe, resistant atopic dermatitis were treated by hypnosis; all but one showed immediate improvement, which was maintained at two follow-up examinations. In 12 other cases involving children, replies to a questionnaire at up to 18 months after treatment showed that 10 had maintained improvement in itching and scratching, 9 in sleep disturbance and 7 in mood.

When direct methods of hypnotherapy are ineffective, then hypnoanalytical approaches may be suggested in order to explore the unconscious dynamics.

Script 54 – General intervention for a dermatological problem

> Close your eyes and go inside your mind and find a time in your life when your skin was healthy and smooth . . . allowing all the resources that you have to enable your skin to stay smooth and healthy, flowing to that part of your body allowing your skin to become clean, healthy and soft as those healing resources massage away all the stress and tension in your life . . . allowing any images or thoughts to come into your mind as they can help you solve your problem . . . And when you know that this will continue to happen after you have left here, will one of your fingers move or an arm float all by itself? . . . that's fine, just continue to let that happen, nothing you need do. . . . Perhaps your unconscious mind can find other ways of dealing with the stress in your life, ways that are positive and life enhancing, enabling you to have a better quality of life . . . and when you know that this can happen, will another finger move or the other arm float? . . . that's really great, knowing that all these things are happening by themselves.

It can readily be seen that the intervention creates an atmosphere of hope and positive expectation even though there may not be any immediate evidence. As one of my patients put it: 'If my skin doesn't get better tomorrow or next week, there is always the possibility of it happening later. Saying this out loud makes it even clearer'. Many of the other scripts presented in the book could be adapted to dermatological problems.

Case Study 5 – Hypnosis in the Treatment of Psoriasis

The patient, Martine, was a 22-year-old student of psychology. During the initial interview, she explained that when stressed she suffered from psoriasis, which sometimes affected her whole body. She was asked to say at what level of intensity her psoriasis was at this moment in time using a scale of 0 to 10. She said that it was currently 6, but had on occasions been 10. When asked to say how low in intensity it had been, she replied it was three usually before the summer vacation. Martine also explained that the problem started when she was approximately 11 years old. The therapist then asked her during trance:

What level of intensity would be acceptable to you?

Martine replied that 2 or 3 would be acceptable. The therapist made the following comment:

When you are stressed then your skin reacts unconsciously to this so it is an important communication . . . so it is necessary for you to listen to what your skin is telling you . . . and although you can reduce the level of intensity to an acceptable and more comfortable level, perhaps your unconscious mind can find another and more effective way of dealing with the stress? And now find a time in your life when you utilised your inner resources to effect a much lower-intensity skin reaction, or to that time before you were 11 years old . . . and when your unconscious has found that time, will your finger or hand move?

Martine's right hand floated effortlessly away from her leg in a manner that indicated that it was an unconscious movement rather than an intentional one.

And now review that earlier experience from the beginning to the end and when this has finished then will your other arm lift? . . . and you don't need to know everything about that experience, only what is appropriate for you to know consciously at this moment in order to assist you in resolving the problem . . . and you may experience parts of the experience . . . maybe . . . images, . . . thoughts, . . . feelings . . . sensations . . . whatever happens by itself.

At this point she said, without being asked, that her mind was completely 'blank', but that she was experiencing tension in her upper chest.

Just put your hand on the area where you are experiencing the tension.

Martine put her hand on her upper chest and I asked her if it would be okay if I put my hand there. She nodded that this was all right.

And as I put some pressure on your chest, allow your breathing to deepen and make some sound on the out breath.

As I did this she started to sob, at which point I made the following comment:

And as you continue to allow the tears to flow, you may learn something from this with respect to your problem . . . and you can allow all the learnings and resources to flow to every part of your skin . . . smoothing and massaging it to glowing health . . . allowing it to become smooth and soft . . . and as that happens and you know that it can occur in the future all by itself . . . just as yesterday the water on the lake outside was rippling in the wind and small waves were splashing against the boats anchored in the harbour . . . but today the wind has disappeared . . . the sun is shining on the water, . . . and the water is smooth and tranquil . . . as the warm sun massages away all the movements

> to leave everything peaceful and comfortable . . . as you learn ways of dealing more effectively with the ways in which your body handles stressful times in your life . . . and when you know how to do that even though you may not know that you know . . . then will your arm float once more?

Martine's left arm gently lifted.

> And I'd like to invite you to put your thumb and forefinger together in acknowledgement that you have these resources and that you can utilise the learnings from this session . . . and in the future when you feel stressed all you need do is to find a comfortable place . . . look at your left hand . . . allowing it to lift by itself . . . and then put your thumb and forefinger together.

Afterwards Martine said that during the session she realised what had happened at the age of 11, that up until this time she used to cry when under stress, but then she stopped crying and allowed her skin to cry instead! I did not interpret her statement, but said to her that she could make sense of it consciously and unconsciously, perhaps in a dream later that day. Finally, she was asked to go through the session in trance finding all the learning experiences:

> Just close your eyes and go inside your mind and go back to the beginning of the session or even before . . . and with every learning experience allow your finger to move . . . and when this has finished will your hand float to a time in the future when the problem will be appropriately resolved? . . . and will this occur this weekend or next weekend or at some time in between? . . . and you may be wondering when it will happen . . . and when you know that, will your eyes open as your mind and body collaborate in solving this problem?

A six-month follow-up indicated that Martine's psoriasis problem had lessened considerably, and she was still continuing to use self-hypnosis.

Preparation for medical interventions and as an adjunct to medical procedures

There are a considerable number of studies that demonstrate the effectiveness of hypnotherapy for stress reduction in medical procedures, for example:

- needle injection (Medd, 2001; Gow, 2002);
- gynaecological examination (Rossi & Cheek, 1988);
- gastroendoscopy (Zimmerman, 1998);

- pregnancy and childbirth (Tibia, Balogh & Meszaros, 1980; Davidson, Garbett & Tozer, 1982; Poncelet, 1990; Jenkins & Pritchard, 1993; Mairs, 1995; Golden, 1999; Oster & Sauer, 2000; Cyna, McAuliffe & Andrew, 2004; German, 2004);
- chemotherapy (Walker, Dawson, Lolley & Ratcliffe, 1988; Hawkins et al., 1995; Edser, 2002);
- cancer interventions (Peynovska, Fisher, Oliver & Mathew, 2005);
- dermatological procedures (Shenefelt, 2003a, 2003b);
- vascular and renal procedures (Lang et al., 2000; Lang, Benotsch & Fick, 2000);
- surgery (Evans & Richardson, 1988; Montgomery, David, Winkel, Silverstein & Bovbjerg, 2002; Massarini, Rovetto & Tagliaferri, 2005);
- cardiovascular procedures (Ashton et al., 1997);
- burns (Ewin, 1979; Margolis & DeClement, 1980; Frenay, Faymonville, Devlieger, Albert & Vanderkelen, 2001).

Pinnell and Covino (2000) provide a critical review of hypnotic treatments as adjuncts to medical care for stress and anxiety related to medical and dental procedures, asthma, dermatological diseases, gastrointestinal problems, haemorrhagic disorders, nausea and emesis in oncology and obstetrics/gynaecology.

Dressing changes

The following research provides a good example of the application of hypnosis in a stressful procedure. Frenay et al. (2001) compared the efficacy of hypnosis with a stress-reducing strategy for pain management during dressing changes of burned patients. Burn dressing changes are often reported to be unbearable (Choinière, Melzack, Rondeau, Girard & Paquin, 1989), and frequently some degree of tolerance is developed to analgesic drugs (Patterson, Everett, Burns & Marvin, 1992). Frenay et al. conducted a prospective randomised study on severely burned patients, based on standardised medical protocols, reliable pain measures by means of a VAS and the use of standardised psychological support techniques (hypnosis versus stress-reducing strategies relying on pleasant life experience). The study was designed to compare the two psychological support regimens, but also to test whether psychological intervention made a difference on the patient's comfort during burn dressing change. Hypnosis was induced using eye fixation, muscle relaxation and permissive and indirect suggestions. Stress-reducing strategies included deep relaxation and breathing procedures, and recreating a pleasant memory. Pain VAS scores in the hypnosis group were consistently lower than in the stress-reducing group. Hypnosis also significantly reduced anxiety before and during dressing change. Although pain medication was still necessary, it was likely that optimal levels would be reached earlier. This study has obvious clinical implications for wound care specifically, and nursing practice in general.

Preparation for surgery

Waiting to have surgery, or other medical/dental intervention, is a very stressful time for most patients, although there will usually be advantages to having the intervention. The essential aspects of helping the patient are concerned with stress reduction prior to/during the medical intervention and to help the patient develop hope and optimism for a successful outcome. Stress reduction appears to be important in modulating the expression of proteins, which play an important role in wound healing (Stamenkovic, 2003). Hammond (1990a, p. 89) states that giving positive suggestions before and during surgery reduces complications, minimises pain (and the need for post-operative medication), facilitates appetite, reduces bleeding and enhances healing and recovery. A number of studies have demonstrated that if the patient is adequately prepared, the likelihood of a good surgical and psychological outcome is maximised (Schutz, 1998; Kessler, 1999). Schutz used hypnosis to enable the patient to overcome strong negative expectations and adverse past experiences, thus reducing anxiety.

Montgomery et al. (2002) carried out a meta-analysis of the effectiveness of adjunctive hypnosis with surgical patients and concluded that hypnosis was beneficial across six categories: negative emotion, pain, pain medication, physiological indicators, recovery time and treatment time.

In a controlled study, Massarini et al. (2005) showed that brief hypnotic treatment (primarily healing visualisations) carried out in the preoperative period leads to good results with surgery patients in terms of reducing anxiety levels and pain perception.

Script 55 – Preparation for surgery or other medical procedures

> Go inside your mind and find all those healing resources you have to make your body well, allowing those resources to flow to every cell . . . utilising all those memories . . . experiences . . . learnings . . . that can allow you to approach the forthcoming medical intervention with hope and optimism, and when your unconscious mind knows that it can assist you in this way, will one of your fingers move or a hand float? . . . that's fine! As the intervention takes place you know that you can utilise all of your resources as you imagine this happening in a very positive manner, trusting in your unconscious healing mind to enable a successful outcome, as your body recovers quickly, completely and comfortably.

Of course, the therapist will be able to develop this hypnotherapeutic procedure in ways that reflect the particular surgical intervention that the patient will have, as well as focusing more explicitly on preoperative suggestions, both direct and indirect, suggestions during the operation and post-operative verbalisations. Summaries of the uses of hypnosis in surgery and anaesthesiology can be found in Hammond (1990a, pp. 85–108), Fredericks (2001) and Montgomery et al. (2002).

Cancer

In recent years it has become increasingly clear that the diagnosis and treatment of cancer (or indeed many other chronic illnesses) are stressful experiences. A wide range of hypnotherapeutic techniques can be used to enhance the control of the physiological and psychological side-effects of a cancer diagnosis and subsequent therapy. These include the use of relaxation, imagery, ego-strengthening, direct suggestions and metaphor (Hammond, 1990a, pp. 199–216). Although Simonton (in Simonton et al., 1978) does not refer specifically to hypnosis interventions, many of the approaches he describes are relevant to hypnotherapists.

Evidence now exists that shows that psychological interventions, including hypnosis, can help to enhance the patient's quality of life as well as modulate the immune-system response (Meyer & Mark, 1995; Walker, 1998; Kiecolt-Glaser, Marucha, Atkinson & Glaser, 2001; Gruzelier, 2002a,b). The following script for enhancing immune-system functionality can be adapted for use in many situations; for example, generic stress, general medical problems, preparation for surgery and post-operative recovery, facilitating treatment regimens, and so on. It goes without saying that the clinicians utilising this approach must be judicious in their selection of patients.

Script 56 – Enhancing immune-system functioning

When you're ready, put your thumb and forefinger together and allow yourself to enter the deep trance that you experienced last session . . . and I wonder how long you will take to find that pleasant inner peace? . . . perhaps your unconscious mind can allow you to experience this before I count to five . . . one . . . two . . . three . . . four . . . five . . . that's fine! Carefully imagine the part of your body that requires extra-special healing attention . . . and I'd like you to know that the abnormal cells here are very weak, confused and disorganised . . . and you can imagine this part in any way you like . . . perhaps an image will just float into your mind. Now imagine the treatment you are receiving flowing to that part of your body and destroying those weak cells, but leaving the normal cells strong and healthy without any major side-effects . . . and your own white blood cells also cooperate by reorganising the diseased cells and destroying them . . . trusting in this process as the cancer cells gradually decrease and are flushed out of your body . . . allowing that healing process to assist your body to stay comfortable as you gradually become well. Now picture yourself on the path to recovery . . . gaining strength and resolve with everyday that passes . . . and imagine yourself in the future achieving your goals and ambitions. And your unconscious mind can enable you to do this and when you know that important changes are happening deep within you, will your eyes open?

Bejenke (2000) describes how hypnosis can be used to help cancer patients develop coping skills, as well as strategies for stress management in the preparation for surgery, chemotherapy, radiation and bone-marrow transplants. In a recent study, Peynovska et al. (2005) utilised hypnotherapy as a supplement therapy in cancer intervention. Particular attention was paid to:

• management of anxiety, depression, anger, frustration;
• management of pain, fatigue, insomnia;
• management of side-effects of chemotherapy and radiotherapy;
• visualisation to promote improved health.

The authors concluded that hypnotherapy is a valuable tool for enhancing the coping mechanisms of cancer patients, and that:

> The best time for hypnotherapy to be offered to cancer patients is right at the time of diagnosis. In that way, patients will be able to develop better coping skills much earlier in the disease process, which will help them to possibly prevent severe anxiety, depression and panic attacks from developing. They will have better treatment compliance and generally will have a more positive psychological response to their illness, which has been suggested as a good prognostic factor with an influence on survival. (p. 7)

The intensification of chemotherapy programmes has resulted in increased toxicity to cancer patients. One of the most common manifestations, nausea and vomiting, is considered to be the most stressful and debilitating side-effect that patients experience (Aapro, 1991). Far too often these symptoms become unbearable and patients are physically incapable of receiving further chemotherapy, or are so psychologically distressed that they, or their relatives, may refuse subsequent treatments (Laszlo, 1983). Over the past decade, advances in the understanding of the physiology and pharmacology of nausea and vomiting have led to a better ability to control these symptoms, along with a consequent reduction in stress and anxiety. A number of controlled studies have assessed the effectiveness of hypnotherapy in alleviating chemotherapy-related nausea and vomiting in adults (Cotanch, Hockenberry & Herman, 1985; Walker, Dawson, Pollet, Ratcliffe & Hamilton, 1988; Syrjala, Cummings & Donaldson, 1992), as well as children (Hawkins et al., 1995). Whilst research has shown that with some treatments (relaxation training and guided imagery) the positive effects lessen with each chemotherapy pulse, hypnotherapy produces a stable response over time (Walker, Dawson, Pollet, Ratcliffe & Hamilton, 1988; Walker, 2004).

A more detailed discussion of the role of hypnosis in ameliorating stress in medical procedures with children is presented in the next chapter.

Chapter 8
Children and Families

Once upon a time a little migrant bird was living in the forest through-out the summer. However, when the weather changed and became much colder, the little bird decided to stay for the winter too, rather than flying back home with her family. The weather got very cold and she thought she was going to die as her little body was frozen through. She felt very lonely being away from her friends and family. Then, one night when it snowed very hard, she collapsed into the snow and lay motionless as though she were dead. Soon after a cow passed by and defecated on the little bird, warming her frozen little body. She began to feel happier and began to sing her favourite song. As it happened a prowling cat was passing by and heard the bird singing. Though some-what perturbed at the beautiful song emanating from the pile of faeces, the cat started to paw his way into the pile and found the bird, where-upon he ate it with relish!

Hypnotherapy with Children

Working with children is an extremely rewarding task as they are usually very cooperative and readily enter hypnosis. I have found this assertion to hold true with children of all ages, including adolescents. However, it should be emphasised that many hypnotic techniques that work with adults may be of little value with younger children because they are directed at mental systems that have not developed sufficiently (Olness & Gardner, 1988; Olness & Kohen, 1996; Davies & Morgan, 1997). One important difference is that chil-dren have a less well-developed critical faculty and therefore suggestions given by the therapist are more likely to be accepted. Davies and Morgan argue that the most effective hypnotist with children will be the one who has a 'deep understanding of the child, and familiarity with the aptitudes, psychology, patterns of thought and interests of the appropriate age group'.

Erickson (1958) stated it succinctly when he wrote:

> Paediatric hypnotherapy is no more than hypnotherapy directed to the child with full cognizance of the fact that children are small, young people. As such, they view the words in a different way than does the adult, and their experiential understandings are limited and quite different from those of the adult. Therefore, not the therapy but only the manner of administering it differs.
>
> ... Children have a driving need to learn and discover, and every stimulus constitutes, for them, a possible opportunity to respond in some new way. Since the hypnotic trance may be defined, for purposes of conceptualisation, as a state of increased awareness and responsiveness to ideas, hypnosis offers to the child a new and ready area of exploration. The limited experiential background of the child, the hunger for new experiences, and the openness to new learnings render the children good hypnotic subjects. They are willing to receive ideas, they enjoy responding to them – there is only the need of presenting those ideas in a manner comprehensible to them. (p. 25)
>
> ... There should not be a talking down to the child, but rather a utilization of language, concepts, ideas and word pictures meaningful to the children in terms of their own learnings. (p. 26)
>
> ... A good hypnotic technique is one that offers to the patients, whether child or adult, the opportunity to have their needs of the moment met adequately, the opportunity to respond to stimuli and ideas, and also the opportunity to experience the satisfactions of new learnings and achievements. (p. 29)

Bernheim, over a hundred years ago, would simply close the child's eyes and say 'Sleep' in a confident and authoritative manner. It is most likely that the children involved had seen other children and adults being hypnotised and consequently they could easily imitate the 'hypnotised behaviour'.

Before using hypnosis with a child, it is important that a thorough medical and clinical assessment of the designated problem has been carried out. It is also important that the clinician has developed a trusting and caring relationship with the child. There is a divergence of opinion as to whether parents should be involved in the hypnotic treatment of their children, although I have generally found their collaboration to be extremely valuable. Often parents hold misconceived ideas about the nature of hypnosis and the therapist needs to correct these views by providing information and by allowing parents to be present when their child is hypnotised (Gardner, 1990).

General hypnotherapeutic approaches with children

There are many ways of engaging the child's attention, and the method chosen will depend on many factors, including the age and interests of the child, as well as the nature of the presenting problem. For very young children hypnosis can be described as playing a game (see Script 57), whereas older children could be invited to use their imagination to solve problems (Hart & Hart, 1996). In many instances the child will suggest the method to be utilised. On one occasion I introduced a little girl to a family of rabbits – mother and father rabbit and their two baby rabbits. The rabbits enacted a story that was related to the little girl's problem (a sleeping difficulty). In the initial conversation with the girl, it was established that she had a number of pet rabbits. Olness and Gardner (1988) suggest the following inductions for children of different ages:

- Ages 2–4: pop-up books, storytelling, puppets and dolls, imagining a favourite activity, and so on.
- Ages 4–6: imagining a favourite place or activity, storytelling; imagining a favourite television programme, and so on.
- Ages 7–11: imagining flying on a magic carpet, being in a favourite place, listening to music, imagining riding a bike, and so on.
- Ages from 11+: arm levitation and catalepsy, imagining listening to or playing music or driving a car, adult methods of induction, and so on.

Four examples of general induction procedures are provided below (Scripts 57–60) and many more are provided in standard textbooks (e.g. Gardner, Olness & Kohen, 1996).

Script 57 – The pretend game

Okay, I wonder if you can pretend that you are a strong oak tree. Your feet are the roots of the tree and stand firmly on the ground, your body is the trunk of the tree and your arms are the branches. Now I'd like you to hold out this arm (pointing to child's dominant hand). Good, this is a strong branch and very, very stiff – see the branch is getting extremely rigid, so strong and so stiff that it won't bend at all. Just think to yourself, this branch is getting firm and strong, and as you think to yourself that the branch is getting stiff and strong, it gets stiffer and stiffer and stronger and stronger, stiffer and stronger each second. . . . Now in a moment, I'm going to ask you try to bend that branch, but the more you try to bend it the stronger and more rigid it becomes so that the branch won't bend at all. Ready now, then, try to bend the branch, try, and the more you try the stiffer and stronger the branch becomes. . . . That's fine! . . . The branch is so strong now that it is so hard to bend it. . . . And now a very strong gust of wind is coming and it will make that branch sway and bend very easily . . . the gust of wind is coming, it's here, it's making the branch sway and now it bends . . . feel the branch beginning to bend, easily, effortless. That's good. (*Now proceed in any way that is appropriate, for example, by using the story of the oak tree presented in Script 20, Chapter 4.*)

Script 58 – Watching television (adapted from Davies & Morgan, 1997, p. 89)

I wonder what your favourite television programme is? Can you tell me something about that? . . . Now there isn't a TV in this room, but there is this special chair. If you sit in it and close your eyes then you will be able to see a TV and on it you will be able to see all your favourite characters. I don't know if you will be able to tune in to a new episode or a repeat . . . would you like to find out and tell me? . . . I don't want to interfere with your enjoyment of the programme by talking too much or by you having to talk at all . . . so I will be happy if you just nod or shake your head gently for 'yes' and 'no' when I ask any questions. Do you understand? . . . You'll be able to see the television very soon . . . give me a nod when you can see it . . . you can now find the channel you want to watch . . . and now you can enjoy the programme . . . that's good. (*With older children the therapist can continue with a problem solving strategy.*)

In just a moment that programme will finish and we will change the channel. You will continue moving into an even deeper state. You will be seeing a programme that will show you how to overcome that problem and get rid of it completely. . . . Your favourite programme has ended now and I'm changing the channel. You're continuing to feel more peaceful, and now you're seeing a programme that is showing what has been causing that problem, and how easily you're getting rid of that problem . . . the picture is becoming more clear . . . you're understanding it, and realising that you are overcoming the problem completely. And when you want you can change back to your favourite television channel or perhaps you would like to watch a video?

Once the child is engaged with the television programme the therapist can introduce ideas that relate to the therapeutic goal. It is important that the therapist relates well to the child and can generate imaginative, therapeutically oriented stories within the initially created context, that is, the television programme. It should also be noted that when children imagine themselves watching a favourite television programme, they are able to reorganise their experience of what is occurring (e.g. a painful procedure) and dissociate from it (i.e. the pain).

Script 59 – The magic carpet

Imagine that you are going on a picnic, going with your favourite people to a special place for a picnic. You have your favourite things to eat and drink. You can see and smell and taste them. . . . Enjoy playing games with your family and friends. Then when you are finished eating and drinking and playing games, you may see a carpet spread out there on the ground. It's your favourite colour, smooth and soft. You may sit on it, or lie on it. . . . Pretend it's a magic carpet, which can fly anywhere you want, and you are the pilot.

You are in control. You can fly just a few inches above the ground, just above the grass, or higher even above the trees if you want. You are the pilot. You can go where you want and as fast or as slow as you wish, just by thinking about it. You can land and visit your friends or family . . . or you can land at the zoo or the seaside, or anywhere you like. You're the pilot and you're in charge. You might fly by a tree and see birds in a nest. You can speed up and slow down. . . . Enjoy going where you want to go. Take all the time you need to feel very comfortable. When you are ready you can find a nice, comfortable landing spot and land your magic blanket. When you have landed, let me know by lifting one of your fingers. And you can fly your magic carpet whenever you wish, perhaps when you are trying to go to sleep or at times when you want to enjoy yourself.

Script 60 – The coin technique: an eye-fixation approach

Give the child a shiny coin to hold. I have found that a foreign coin works particularly well.

Have a look at the coin and notice what is on both sides. Do you know which country the coin comes from? (*You can give the child some information bearing in mind their age and experience.*) After we have done this then you can keep the coin, if you want. Hold the coin between your finger and thumb and keep holding it there, with your arm stretched out, whilst you listen to the sound of my voice. Now an interesting thing is going to happen. In a few moments you'll notice that arm becoming heavier and heavier whilst at the same time it begins to feel relaxed and comfortable. And as you notice the growing sensation of comfort within you, that arm gets heavier and the hand and the fingers begin to feel like lead weights – so heavy, so comfortable and so relaxed – and as soon as the coin falls from your fingers and touches the floor you will go into a wonderful deep sleep. We'll find it later so that you can take it home. But for now you can really enjoy this experience as your arms and the hands and fingers are getting so wonderfully heavy as you go deeper and deeper into a magical trance. Everything I say to you can go deep into that part of you that controls your behaviour (*relate this to the problem being treated*). That's right . . . and now you can float right back again as you become lighter and lighter and find yourself back in this room. Did you enjoy that? We can look for the coin now.

Storytelling

The use of storytelling is very advantageous in working with children (Mills & Crowley, 1986; Crowley & Mills, 1986; Hart & Hart, 1996; Thomson, 2005; Snyder, McDermott, Cook & Rapoff, in press). Fairy stories, such as *Hansel and Gretel*, deal with a range of human emotions and problems that can be used to help children cope with their fears and instil a sense of hope (Bettelheim, 1991). Therapists can use standardised stories, themes from fairy tales (e.g. *Good King Wenceslas*; Mantle, 1999, 2001), science fiction, alter existing stories or write their own. Mills and Crowley assert that children respond spontaneously and do not try to figure out the story being presented. Young children can be allowed to colour and play whilst a story is being told to them as it is assumed that their unconscious mind will make sense of it with respect to the resolution of their problem. Mills and Crowley (1986, p.64) suggest that the central features of effective stories:

- have a theme of metaphorical conflict in relation to the protagonist;
- contain heroes or helpers;
- contain learning situations parallel to those of the child, where the protagonist is successful;
- present a crisis in which the protagonist can overcome the problem;
- develop a new sense of identification for the protagonist as a result of his or her victory;
- culminate with a celebration where the protagonist's special worth is acknowledged.

Traditional stories such as *The Ugly Duckling* and *The Wizard of Oz* contain all of the above elements.

Children encounter many stressful situations in their lives and often experience psychosomatic and behavioural reactions that cause concern both to themselves and to their families. In the discussion below, six areas will be presented related to academic performance, stressful medical procedures, sleeping difficulties, nocturnal enuresis, dermatological problems and body image. Although the emphasis here is on working with children, many of the approaches can be adapted to adults with similar stress-related problems.

Comprehensive accounts of hypnosis approaches with children are provided by Olness and Gardner (1988), Wester and O'Grady (1991) and Gardner et al. (1996).

Academic problems

In middle and late childhood, children come under increasing academic pressure, with escalating demands to perform in endless exams and tests, which often causes stress. This can lead to a loss of self-esteem, sleeping difficulties and other behavioural and psychosomatic problems. As well as interventions with the child, it is usually appropriate to involve both the parents and the school. Nath and Warren (1995) describe an educational programme implemented in four comprehensive schools that helped students understand the nature of stress and to learn practical ways of coping with it. A number of hypnosis/relaxation exercises were used including the 'mental holiday procedure' (Stanton, 1989). The procedure, consisting of five steps, has already been described in Chapter 4. Overall, the results indicated that children involved in the programme felt less anxious, although the contribution of hypnosis to this effect is not known. The author has successfully worked with children and young adults using a combination of ego-strengthening, goal setting, contracting, story telling and metaphor. Further examples of hypnosis interventions are provided by Hammond (1990a, pp. 433–64).

Nocturnal enuresis

Enuresis can have a complex genesis and aetiology (Carr, 1999, p. 214), although it is likely that daytime enuresis is a urological, organic problem, that is, primary enuresis (Baumann, 1981), whereas secondary, or onset, enuresis is more likely to be the result of emotional distress or stress in a child's life (Wester & O'Grady, 1991). Olness and Gardner (1988) suggest that surgery, death of a pet and moving home or school can cause onset neurosis. When hypnosis is being considered as a possible treatment it is often as a last resort, as many other methods will have already been tried. Hypnosis approaches that essentially aim at symptom removal may be sufficient, although it is recognised that further dynamic exploration of family or school problems may be necessary (Gibson & Heap, 1991). Constructive parental involvement in the treatment of nocturnal enuresis can facilitate the child's use of self-hypnosis without being intrusive or undermining autonomy, although some children resist self-hypnosis because of such parental 'interference' (Kohen, Olness, Colwell & Heimel, 1984). Evaluations of hypnosis treatments indicate varied results, but success is more likely when hypnosis is combined with other approaches; for example, medical management, parental instruction and behavioural techniques. However, despite the variety of reports and results, it seems fairly clear that there is a role for hypnosis in the treatment of nocturnal enuresis.

It should be emphasised that all children wet the bed at some time, as enuresis can be considered a developmental variant until the age of approximately six, unless the child starts to wet the bed after having been continuously dry for at least six months.

Traditional methods of hypnosis in symptom removal can be combined with the use of ego-strengthening, direct suggestions, stories and metaphors. Elkins and Carter (1981) developed and used their own science-fiction metaphor technique in three cases of secondary onset enuresis. In each case the child was invited to imagine going for a ride on a spaceship where he or she met the characters and events that were needed to resolve the child's problem. It proved to be effective for both trance induction and treatment. Further examples are provided by Erickson (1952a) and Hammond (1990a, pp. 489–98).

I have successfully used the general approach below with a number of children. However, this should be adapted according to the age and circumstances of the individual child.

Script 61 – Nocturnal enuresis

Now, in my pocket I have a very special and magic coin that can help you to overcome the difficulties you have at night-times when you are asleep . . . would you like to have a look at it? That's right . . . you can see on one side is the Queen's head and on the other a lion who looks very strong and powerful . . . the Queen lives in a big palace and outside there are sentries that guard her and make sure that she is safe and protected, . . . and if there are any problems during the night then they can wake her up . . . and then she can go back to sleep again knowing that everything is all right and that when she wakes up in the morning she will feel very comfortable . . . and sometimes her dog helps as well and barks to wake her up when it is necessary. . . . Do you think that your dog could wake you up when you are asleep and you need to go to the lavatory? . . . you may already be wondering whether this could really happen? . . . I want you to gently rub the coin and as you do you may notice that your eyes are becoming tired and sleepy . . . and you can allow them to close whilst you listen to this story. . . . Once upon a time there was a little boy who had a very special dog to look after him during the day and also when he was asleep . . . when the boy needed to go to the lavatory in the night whilst he was asleep the dog would bark and wake him up and tell him that he should go to the bathroom . . . afterwards the boy would go back into his warm bed and in the morning his mother was extremely pleased that he had a nice dry bed, and so was he. . . . Maybe your dog could help you in the same way . . . shall we ask him? . . . I'll ask him now whilst you just listen. Now, Jack (*the dog*) I would like you to help your friend David in the following way . . . when he is asleep at night I want you to keep a constant guard so that he stays warm and comfortable . . . when you notice that his bladder is becoming full I want you to bark and wake him up so that he can go to the lavatory . . . will you do that, please? . . . I have told Jack what the plan is and he has agreed to cooperate. And when your other mind knows that it can hear Jack when you are asleep . . . and knows that Jack will look after you, will one of your fingers move or perhaps your arm will float into the air all by itself? . . . That's fantastic. . . . Well done! And this is what I want you to do when you are ready for bed . . . rub the magic coin and go fast asleep because you know that Jack will wake you up when you are ready to go to the lavatory . . . and you will wake up in the morning feeling dry and comfortable . . . and before long you will find that your bed is dry every morning and you can feel really good that you have done this all by yourself.

Any approach that results in a dry bed can be combined with a system of rewards. In the paediatric department of a local general hospital, enuretic problems were successfully treated by traditional hypnosis (eye fixation and arm levitation), relaxation, direct suggestions, imagery, ego-strengthening and a token economy system (star chart).

Stressful medical procedures

There have been reports of studies evaluating the effects of hypnosis and guided imagery on stressful medical procedures in children (e.g. Lambert, 1996). Lambert concluded that guided imagery lowered post-operative pain ratings, decreased recovery times, necessitating a shorter stay in hospital, and decreased anxiety. Considerable research has been carried out on children with cancer and these studies will provide the focus of the ensuing brief review.

Although cancer is not always painful in its own right, children with cancer undergo numerous painful procedures for diagnosis, therapy and supportive care, including lumbar puncture, bone-marrow aspiration and biopsy (Hilgard & LeBaron, 1984b). Children consider painful procedures to be the most difficult part of having cancer, and frequent repetition of procedures does not desensitise them to the distress (Weekes & Savedra, 1988; Fowler-Kerry 1990). Although procedure-related pain is often thought of as simple, it may cause suffering, loss of control and impaired quality of life. It is essential, therefore, that intervention for suffering includes concern for, and management of, the pain and distress associated with treatment procedures. Much of the data available on the management of procedure-related pain address pharmacological management rather than (adjunctive) psychological procedures.

Although hypnosis is frequently used in clinical practice, controlled studies on the clinical procedures are scarce and have produced conflicting and equivocal results (Genius, 1995; Liossi & Hatira, 1999; Wild & Espie, 2004). In a classic paper on the efficacy of hypnosis for the reduction of pain during bone-marrow aspirations, Hilgard and LeBaron (1982) reported the successful use of hypnosis to relieve the pain in 15 of 24 children ranging from 6 to 10 years of age. Zeltzer and LeBaron (1982) treating 27 subjects undergoing bone-marrow aspirations, and 22 undergoing lumbar punctures, with hypnotic and non-hypnotic techniques (e.g. deep breathing) found significant pain reduction for both techniques, with hypnosis the most effective. Kellerman, Zeltzer, Ellenberger and Dash (1983) demonstrated that hypnosis reduced pain and anxiety significantly below baseline in a variety of medical procedures, including nine bone-marrow aspirations, two lumbar punctures and seven intramuscular injections. A few studies (e.g. Katz, Kellerman & Ellenberg, 1987; Wall & Womack, 1989) found hypnosis to be of significant benefit, but no greater than that of non-hypnotic cognitive-behavioural interventions. Reports of the use of Ericksonian hypnosis approaches with paediatric haematology/oncology patients are scarce, although their applicability is discussed by Jacobs, Pelier and Larkin (1998).

Hawkins, Liossi, Hatira, Ewart and Kosmidis (1998) evaluated the use of hypnosis in the management of pain during paediatric lumbar punctures. Thirty children with leukaemia and non-Hodgkin's lymphoma who were undergoing regular lumbar punctures were 'hypnotised' using visual imagery techniques (favourite place, favourite activity). Following several minutes of hypnotic involvement, the children were given either direct suggestions or indirect suggestions. The session ended with a post-hypnotic suggestion that the hypnotic experience would be repeated in the actual treatment room and would provide comfort during the lumbar puncture. The actual lumbar punctures were scheduled to follow on the next five days. At the scheduled time, the child was accompanied to the treatment room by the therapist. During the preparation for the lumbar puncture, the child was encouraged to enter hypnosis and throughout the procedure the hypnotic involvement was actively encouraged as required. Results indicated that hypnosis was an effective strategy for managing pain during lumbar-puncture interventions with no difference between the efficacy of direct and indirect suggestions. Hart and Hart (1998) provide a valuable commentary on the paper.

In a recent paper, Wild and Espie (2004) systematically review the research conducted in the field of procedure-related pain management in paediatric oncology within the context of a nationally agreed framework for the assessment of research evidence. They conclude that there is currently insufficient evidence to recommend that hypnosis should form part of best-practice guidelines in this clinical area. However, they also conclude that there is sufficient evidence to justify larger-scale, appropriately controlled studies.

Sleeping problems

Sleeping problems in children will often compound any family difficulties, including the reduction in the number and quality of socially supportive interactions, parental depression, marital discord, deterioration in parent–child relationships, as well as having a possible impact on memory and academic performance (Stores, 1996). The most commonly referred sleeping problems are difficulties in getting to sleep and night waking, followed by nightmares, sleep terrors, sleepwalking, breathing-related problems and hypersomnia (i.e. an excessive daytime sleepiness not accounted for by an inadequate amount of sleep or prolonged transition to wakefulness). Comprehensive accounts are provided by Ferber and Kryger (1995), Schaefer (1995) and Stores (1996).

There are many examples of hypnosis being used successfully in the treatment of sleeping disorders in children (Olness & Gardner, 1988; Hartland, 1989; Hammond, 1990a; Wester & O'Grady, 1991; Kohen, Mahowald & Rosen, 1992; Kingsbury, 1993; Ford, 1995; Howsam, 1999). The techniques used in the treatment strategies included those drawn from the more direct traditional approaches as well as Ericksonian or naturalistic ones. For example, Carr (1999) has reported using guided imagery approaches to help the child relax. He requests that the child imagine the sun going down and the wind dying, or a bird flying into the distance.

Karle and Boys (1987) describe a number of approaches in which children who experience bad dreams can be taught to control the content and progression of the dream (pp. 176–77). Hearne (1993) suggests that hypnosis may be utilised in order to convert nightmares into lucid dreams, although his work does not specify whether this was with adults or children. A study carried out by the author (Hawkins & Polemikos, 2002) indicated that hypnosis was successful in resolving sleeping problems in young children who were considerably stressed as a result of major family bereavements. None of the children had been diagnosed with a psychiatric problem, but all had a range of difficulties relating to sleep, relationships, school work and social behaviour. The study focused on four items from the Southampton Sleep Management Schedule (Bartlet & Beaumont, 1998): difficulties going to bed, number of nights woken in the past seven days, time to resettle in own bed and the frequency of nightmares or night terrors. A new paradigm research methodology was used (Reason & Rowan, 1981; Reason, 1994; Heron, 1996) involving the collaborative participation of both experimenter and subjects (the children).

During the first part of the session (approximately 15 minutes) the children were able to play games or read, followed by a 'game' in which they took turns to tell the group some good things that had happened during the week. Each child was also asked to say what their favourite animal was and whether they had any pets. They were then encouraged to draw their 'sleeping problems' followed by a brief description of the representation. All the children referred to experiencing bad dreams and nightmares with most of them saying that this was a nightly occurrence. References were also made to difficulties in going to sleep, waking up frequently, being frightened of the dark, 'seeing' faces or shadows in the dark, hearing 'frightening' noises or voices and changing beds, and so on. It was suggested to the group that it would be possible for them to go to sleep and stay asleep with pleasant and enjoyable dreams throughout the night so that they would not wake up during the night (unless they had to get up to visit the lavatory). It was explained to the children that in order to do this they would have to engage in some preparation and practice so that it would work more effectively. They agreed to this and seemed quite excited at the idea. The children were taught a method of self-hypnosis ('sleeping game') utilising their favourite place and 'inner guide' (Jaffe & Bresler, 1980). They selected their favourite place, as part of a game, before the hypnosis was carried out. This approach was chosen because the age range and interests of the group were quite diverse, and managing anxiety rather than the content of the dreams was much more appropriate to the group situation. The following instructions were given to the children:

Script 62 – Sleeping problems in children: the magic cloud car

Now, close your eyes as if you were just about to go to sleep so that you begin to feel all dreamy . . . you might notice how light you feel and perhaps even a tingling sensation as if you are sitting on a big fluffy ball of wool. . . . And as you feel light, so you might notice that the cotton wool is like a fluffy white cloud. . . . Would you like to go to a special or favourite and very

safe outdoor place? . . . Then all you have to do is to imagine your fluffy floating cloud is a magic cloud car. You can steer this car quite easily and fly it
to your favourite place . . . you land your car and look around. . . . What can
you see? What can you hear? . . . Is it hot or cold? . . . Now, as you look
around you notice a very friendly animal (maybe your own pet) that comes
up to you. As you stroke your friendly animal you feel extremely sleepy
knowing that you can go to sleep and make all of your dreams enjoyable.
And if you wake up during the night, you will remember how to go to your
safe place quickly and easily in your cloud car. . . . And when you get to your
special place you will already be dreamy and sleepy so that when you stroke
your friendly animal you will fall deeply asleep, very relaxed and happy.
. . . And, the more you practise, you might not even notice that you might not
even wake up as you go to your special place . . . and there you will learn to
sleep soundly all night long with enjoyable dreams. When you wake up in
the morning you will feel wide awake and look forward to all the things that
you have to do during the day. (Adapted from Ford, 1995, pp. 204–05;
Hammond, 1990a, pp. 253–56.)

The children then practised this on their own and were instructed to do this
every night before going to sleep. Feedback from the children suggested that
they followed the general idea of the 'script', although there were considerable 'interpretations'.

At the second meeting, the general consensus of the group was that:

- the 'sleeping game' helped them to get to sleep;
- when they woke they were less afraid and could easily go to sleep again
  (one child);
- they had fewer bad dreams (one eight-year-old boy said that he could
  control his dreams and 'make' them good); and
- they felt better in the morning (one child).

There was also some indication that there were improvements in other aspects
of their lives, such as school work. Five members of the group said that they
felt less tired at school and looked forward to going there.

Dermatological problems

Stress has been implicated as an exacerbating factor in children's eczema
(Koblenzer, 1988). The skin disease itself can also generate considerable stress
as a result of embarrassment, concerns about self-image, lowered self-esteem,
anxiety, difficulties in sleeping and possible social isolation (Daud, Garralda
& David, 1993; Morgan, McCreedy, Simpson & Hay, 1997). There are few
studies into the role of hypnosis in the treatment of eczema. Sokel, Lansdown,
Atherton, Glover and Knibbs (1993) compared hypnotherapy, biofeedback
and discussion in the treatment of childhood atopic eczema. Results showed

that the amount of skin damage reported was reduced in the hypnosis and biofeedback groups, with the girls in the hypnosis group obtaining the best results. Because of the emotional and social problems that result from eczema, it is appropriate to use ego-strengthening techniques so as to enhance the child's confidence, self-esteem and feelings of mastery and autonomy. This might be done by using metaphors and stories. For example, Mantle (2002) used the story of *Good King Wenceslas* as follows:

> The patient suffers from eczema but, in spite of this, she is chosen by the king to accompany him when he goes out to give alms to the poor. The patient notices that the falling snow cools and soothes the eczema on her face and, at the king's suggestion, she applies the snow to her arms and legs. As she does she feels the benefit of its cooling effect and the skin ceases to itch. On return to the castle, the patient finds that whenever she feels like scratching her skin, she thinks about the snow and immediately the skin is soothed and the irritation goes. Because of this the patient becomes much more relaxed and does not mind getting undressed in front of the other patients, she feels more confident and enjoys joining in with their games. In addition she also finds that she sleeps better at night and is, therefore, better able to learn in school the next day. (p. 44)

There are many treatments available for the effective treatment of dermatological problems, and hypnotherapy may be a valuable adjunctive procedure. Case Study 5 – Hypnosis in the Treatment of Psoriasis, presented in Chapter 7, provides examples of suitable hypnotherapeutic interventions.

Eating issues and body image

Eating problems are common in a culture that is increasingly obsessed with fast food, dieting and body image, fashion and the celebrity cult. Teenagers may also be concerned with sport and artistic activities that emphasise thinness and competition. Body dissatisfaction and dieting can lead to unhealthy and dangerous eating behaviours, which can result in eating disorders such as bulimia nervosa and anorexia nervosa. Teenage girls are particularly prone to developing eating problems. However, boys are also concerned with issues relating to body shape and weight. There is often a preoccupation with food and body image that generates stress and anxiety as well as disruptive eating patterns.

Eating disorders are often associated with feelings of helplessness, sadness, anxiety and the need to be perfect. This can cause a person to use dieting or weight loss to provide a sense of control and stability. Family stress, dealing with life transitions such as bereavement, and school bullying, can all contribute to the development of eating disorders. Associated problems may include depression, obsessive-compulsive disorder, substance abuse or self-harm.

Since eating disorders are usually a medical and psychological problem, treatment typically involves working with a physician, nutritionist and psychologist (Siegel, Brisman & Weinshal, 1997). As with less serious eating problems, the clinician can use hypnosis for ego-strengthening to improve confidence, self-image and body image, anxiety management, as well as hypnoanalytical approaches and family therapy where appropriate.

Hypnotherapy with Families and Couples

Generally, clinical hypnosis is used in a one-to-one situation. However, in the context of family and couple therapy, the hypnosis work could be managed in a number of ways (Hawkins, 1994d):

- Individual one-to-one psychotherapy.
- One-to-one hypnotherapy within the family or couple. In this case the therapist works with a family member (in trance) with the family or partner (probably in trance) present. This also utilises the therapeutic principle of 'passive imagination', which may lead any one family member into a (silent) emotional abreaction, or into gaining insight or self-knowledge through both conscious and unconscious 'problem solving'.
- Family 'group' hypnosis, in which the therapist works with the whole family or couple at the same time, maybe using some form of relaxation, or group-guided fantasy. In this case all of the family members are 'actively' imagining, which could lead to spontaneous insights or abreaction in some or all family members. It is also assumed by some therapists that an unconscious search process will be initiated for each individual.
- Facilitating ultradian synchrony (Rossi & Nimmons, 1991), in which the family members become more aware of one another's mind–body cues of ultradian stress, and entrain their circadian and ultradian rhythms together.

Regardless of the way the therapy is conducted, it would tend to have an individual focus, whether the person is seen alone or in the family group. It is important to reiterate the point here that the hypnosis is often understood as being a facilitating or catalytic strategy, which provides a 'therapeutic context' in which the primary 'family therapy' strategies are introduced. In other words, the persons practising hypnosis are, firstly, trained professionals where the utilisation of hypnosis can enhance their professional skills. For example, family therapists who wished to explore some of the hidden conflicts in a family could utilise hypnoanalytical procedures (e.g. ideodynamic signalling or dream analysis) in order to achieve this. However, having uncovered some material the therapists have to use all of their professional skills as family therapists in order to help the family utilise these 'insights' to achieve therapeutic gains.

Although Erickson never mentions working with families or systems, many family therapists are indebted to his contributions (e.g. Haley, 1973; Lankton & Lankton, 1986; Madanes, 2001). Many of the 'traditional' hypnotherapeutic approaches can be easily adapted for working with families, and can easily be combined with Ericksonian approaches. Indirect suggestions and metaphors can be used to stimulate unconscious activity and resources for the purposes of ego-strengthening, stress management, symptom function and resolution, decision making and goal setting.

The therapist helps the family to 'construct' positive images relating to the defined target behaviours agreed with the family. The outcome is that all the family members feel more confident, with improvements in self-image and body image, and with increased feelings of hope and optimism concerning problem resolution. A basic assumption being made is that families have the answers to their problems ('the answer is within the family', that is, is already 'known' unconsciously), and that a process of unconscious search can be facilitated by the therapist in order to help the family 'find' and actualise this inner potential. It is also likely that the family will become more creative as a result of the 'group trance' and will therefore be able to consider different strategies for solving their 'family' problems. Homework assignments can be prescribed for all the family to be carried out individually or together. The whole family should be encouraged to keep diary records of dreams, unexpected thoughts, images and feelings. These can then be 'worked through' in the family therapy sessions.

Case Study 6 – Hypnosis in Family Therapy

The patient was a bulimic 16-year-old female who lived with her parents, younger brother and grandmother. The diagnosis of anorexia nervosa had been made at the age of 13, and she had been bulimic for about a year. At the age of 14 she spent some time in hospital, where she was 'treated' for the problem using behavioural methods. Her parents were very concerned about their daughter, and her mother was referred to me by the Eating Disorders Association with a view to treating the problem with a number of sessions of psychotherapy.

In presenting the case study it should be noted that only key 'hypnosis' elements of the therapy interventions are discussed, and not all of the approaches discussed earlier presented. However, it is hoped that this brief illustration will give the reader some idea of how hypnosis can be utilised within a family therapy context.

The case history that follows demonstrates many of the treatment approaches suggested by Weiss, Katzman and Wolchik (1985). The overall approach adopted is essentially one of a pragmatic integration embracing psychodynamic, behaviourist and phenomenological paradigms, along with hypnosis (both 'formal' and 'naturalistic') to enhance the therapeutic process.

The approaches used include ego-strengthening, dealing with negative emotions, assertiveness training, relaxation, reframing, hypnoanalysis, goal setting and action planning, and stress management.

Session 1

Both parents were invited to attend this session, which they readily accepted. A case history was taken, paying particular attention to: time of onset; symptoms – physiological, behavioural, cognitive and emotional; modulation of the problem within a time-frame; identification of events that precede an eating binge; consequences of bingeing; identification of any secondary-gain components and previous treatments. They were asked to identify their reactions to the problem in general, as well as specific behaviours and feelings following the discovery of any 'bulimic behaviour'. The effect on family relationships and family life in general was also discussed. Both Joanne and her parents were asked about their own explanations of the 'presenting problems', and what they thought might need to be done to find a solution. What was important in this first session was to get the family talking to each other as well as to the therapist. This helped to identify patterns of interaction and communication, as well as roles, which might be important in determining treatment strategies. Evidence for the function of the designated symptom within the family system could also be gauged.

It emerged during the session that Joanne's mother was very dominant in that she attempted to control the interactions, but at the same time she showed a very caring relationship with her daughter. The father was rather quiet and tended to agree with his wife, although his attitude regarding Joanne was less considerate; for example, he believed that Joanne's eating problem was 'her own fault', and that 'she could do something about it if she really wanted to'. The emotional tension between the mother and father with respect to this issue was considerable. What emerged during the session was that all family members were stressed by Joanne's problem, which resulted in, or exacerbated, a number of (stress-related) problems; for example, insomnia, colitis and anxiety.

The focus of the therapy was discussed with regard to the goals, timescale, fees, frequency of meetings and therapeutic approach. The family agreed to attend some sessions together (including the brother and grandmother), although occasionally Joanne would be seen alone. Explanations of hypnosis and its effects were given, and the opportunity to ask questions provided. Throughout this part of the session considerable emphasis was placed on the utilisation of language, both direct and indirect, which was designed to increase optimism, hope and expectancy as a way of enhancing therapeutic engagement and leverage, thus helping to establish a more therapeutic context.

Therapy commenced with Spiegel's 'eye-roll' method of hypnotic induction:

And the next time you breathe in just roll up your eyes, and as you breathe out closing your eyelids to a point where you feel they will not work. Hold onto that feeling and allow it to spread throughout your whole body, allowing your body to float to your favourite outdoor place. Just enjoying that as it happens. No other place to go right now. (*The session continued with an ego-strengthening sequence with the therapeutic intention of engaging an unconscious search process for solutions to the problem.*) And in this relaxing and enjoyable place you notice an inviting path leading away from you. Follow this path, and with every step that you take you travel back in your life to a time when you solved a family problem, even though you may not know how you solved it. Experience that successful event knowing that you have the unconscious resources within you to solve any problems that occur in the future. Allow the positive feeling associated with that achievement to flow through you and hold on to those feelings ... and ... now follow the path back to your favourite place, bringing with you all the positive feelings and resources, knowing that you have the ability to solve the current problems that are affecting Joanne and the whole family ... and that these solutions are being found right now even though you are unaware that this is happening.

The whole family participated in this therapeutic sequence. A short discussion followed.

Joanne was then worked with individually whilst her parents 'listened in'. Hypnosis was 'induced' with Spiegel's eye-roll method, and then ideodynamic arm levitation was elicited. When her arm was gently 'floating', Joanne was asked to say the following three statements to herself:

- For me nourishment is essential.
- I need my body to live.
- I owe my body this respect and attention.

This is an adaptation of Spiegel's approach for smoking cessation (refer to Chapter 6). Joanne practised doing this on her own, and was instructed to do this as many times a day as possible. She was then asked to imagine herself standing between two mirrors, one behind and one in front of her. In the mirror behind she was asked to experience herself with the problem – the way she looked, her feelings, the effect on her relationships, family, and so on.

Now walk away from that mirror and look at the mirror in front of you. Imagine yourself as you would like to be, feeling good and happy about that. See this reflection brighter, clearer, more colourful and walk towards it, and become that person. You know that this is already happening, even though you may not fully appreciate it yet.

Even though her parents were not asked directly to engage in this exercise they also went into trance (see 'My Friend John' technique described in Chapter 3). Although Joanne was engaged in individual therapy, her family were also significantly involved in the learning experience at both conscious and unconscious levels. The session continued with a short story, which was introduced naturally and without explanation.

> There is a story about a monk in ancient times who was feeling very depressed and sad. It was winter and he was looking out into the gardens feeling very depressed and forlorn. He became aware of the bare trees, without their beautiful foliage. It seemed to him that they were also feeling sad and depressed when he realised that they were not dead, for in spring they would grow new leaves and be even stronger than before. Although they appeared dead on the outside, they were very much alive on the inside, in their roots. Their roots, the soul of their very being, were alive, and when nourished by the spring rains and early summer sun they would blossom again. All through the winter they were growing stronger and stronger, utilising their natural healing resources and potential to develop their natural capacities.

Joanne was provided with an ego-strengthening tape, which she was asked to listen to at least once a day. It was suggested that the whole family should listen to the tape together whenever possible in order to encourage supportive collaboration in the therapeutic endeavour.

Session 2

Joanne's brother and grandmother attended the session, along with her mother and father. A brief resumé of the previous session was provided. The family reviewed what had happened during the week, which was followed by group relaxation and ego-strengthening. During the first session it had been indicated that Joanne was more likely to binge when she was 'stressed'. The family were asked to generate alternative coping strategies by 'brainstorming'. Joanne then 'checked out' the alternatives whilst in hypnosis. She selected a number of alternatives and agreed to implement them. The ways in which the other family members could help were discussed, and a contract agreed. In group hypnosis, the family then imagined themselves helping Joanne to engage in the agreed behaviours. Joanne agreed to keep a diary of these activities.

Session 3

After discussing issues arising from the homework assignments carried out during the previous two weeks, the session focused on the underlying dynamics of Joanne's eating problem. Hypnoanalytical techniques were utilised, specifically the ideodynamic finger approach (Rossi & Cheek, 1988). After three recursive cycles, Joanne's unconscious indicated (by moving a finger) that she was able to go into the future without the problem.

> As your 'yes' finger lifts as an acknowledgement that your unconscious is now able to allow you to go into the future without the problem, you can allow that lifting sensation to spread to the rest of your hand and arm causing that arm to float into the air to the date at which you can be well. . . . Your unconscious can write the date automatically on an imaginary blackboard, even though your conscious mind may choose to forget this.

Joanne 'remembered' two important 'causative' events during the ideodynamic session, both related to family experiences. These events were discussed with the family, and followed by further ego-strengthening with all the family. Some catharsis occurred during this session when Joanne's mother and grandmother both sobbed in relation to a painful family experience (which had become a not-talked-about 'family secret'). This catharsis was encouraged, and along with the associated disclosure, seemed to be therapeutically valuable.

Session 4

The main part of the session involved group hypnosis with all the family, and involved the experiencing of a favourite outdoor place.

> And you notice an inviting path leading into the distance. At the end of this path you notice a very friendly, bluish-green light that is gently moving towards you . . . as it gets closer it gradually changes into a friendly animal, your inner guide or therapist, who can help you with any problem that you may have. Please introduce yourself to your friend and tell them what your problem is . . . your friend listens very carefully and then replies . . . listen carefully to them acknowledging that you may not understand the communication completely at this moment in time . . . that the full significance of the communication may be appreciated much later, perhaps in the form of a dream later on today or next week, sooner or later. And now say goodbye to your friend knowing that you can meet them at any time by visiting your favourite place and calling their name.

The experiences were shared by the family, followed by a group dialogue between the animals (a type of gestalt experience). This proved to be very enlightening, and demonstrated a number of important relationships (e.g. aspects of control and power, resentments and jealousy, affection, etc.) between the family members.

Session 5

During this session, anger and assertiveness were explored utilising a guided imagery approach within the context of hypnosis. All of the family members were hypnotised using a focusing technique (breathing) followed by Spiegel's eye roll.

> Allowing yourself to float to the banks of a gently flowing stream . . . experience the sights . . . colours . . . shapes . . . sounds . . . feelings . . . and now follow the path along the stream back towards its source, growing younger with every step that you take . . . back to a time when you felt happy and contented . . . and now walk back to the starting place sharing any problems that you have with your friendly animal . . . and you find that the path is blocked by a very large rock . . . there is no way to get past . . . beside the rock is a large stick . . . you pick it up and start to hit the rock, and as you continue to hit this it changes into a person . . . maybe someone that you know . . . and as you continue to hit the person, then the rock gradually becomes smaller and smaller until you are able to step over it, and proceed . . . you walk towards the estuary where the stream meets the sea . . . and on your way you rest beneath an old oak tree. . . .

The story of the 'life of the oak tree' (see Script 20 in Chapter 4) was then told, providing a metaphor for growth and change. Discussion followed and was accompanied by some gestalt work involving 'empty chair' techniques and role reversal.

Sessions 6 and 7

The final two sessions largely reinforced previous work. Joanne gradually brought her bulimic behaviour under control, and sixth monthly follow-ups revealed no reoccurrence after a period of two years.

Summary

The therapist's basic assumption was that of an inner potential to reach a state of balance with respect to human functioning, at both the individual and family levels. It can be postulated that a number of curative therapeutic factors were implicated:

(1) Facilitation of 'inner healing resources', through the use of ego-strengthening and hypnotherapy (Rossi, 1996).
(2) Accessing and reviewing of repressed dynamic, leading to 'insight' (with both conscious and unconscious 'awareness'), and a consequent dissolution of this dynamic that maintained the symptomatology.
(3) Development of alternative and 'competing' behaviours and strategies.

(4) Sharing of concerns and issues between family members.
(5) Development of collaborative support and trust within the family.
(6) Opportunities for emotional catharsis within a supportive environment.
(7) Facilitation of shared hope and optimism.

The approach provided for tremendous therapeutic leverage in terms of developing between-session motivation. The whole family was 'engaged' in the therapeutic process, and all received considerable benefit from the family-therapy sessions. Joanne was able to modify her eating behaviours with the help of her family, and all family members made changes in their own func-tioning as a result of the therapeutic process. It can be stated with a good deal of confidence that this approach to Joanne's problems was enhanced by involving the whole family, although no explicit family-therapy model was being proposed. As a result the family was less stressed and able to enjoy closer family relationships. This in itself would have a considerable impact on their lives in general.

Postscript

There is a story about a cruise ship full of passengers, which was about to sail around the world. At the last moment the main engine stopped working, causing considerable consternation to the captain. He summoned the best engineers to examine the engine, which they did with all the latest technology available, but to no avail. Eventually, one of the passengers offered to help, and after a brief explanation of the problem he requested that a hammer be brought down to the engine room. He vigilantly examined the engine and listened carefully to the noise that it was making before striking a small red valve judiciously with the hammer. Immediately, the engine started to work perfectly. When asked what his fee was, the man replied that he wanted one dollar for tapping with the hammer and $999 for knowing where to tap!

This book has provided many hypnotherapy scripts for working with patients who are experiencing a wide variety of stress-related situations and symptomatologies. Hopefully, a view has been promulgated that promotes a philosophy of the uniqueness and healing qualities of each patient and, therefore, individually tailored treatments. In hypnotherapy, particular attention is paid to the quality of the therapeutic relationship as well as to the active involvement of the patient. Hypnotherapists need to be professionally trained and familiar with recent advances in both the theory and practice of specific clinical fields, but they are still essentially healers. The art of healing requires that the clinician pays particular attention to meeting the psychological needs of patients, a process that requires compassion and sensitivity. For this to happen, a high degree of personal awareness is necessary and a capacity to trust in their inner resources.

Although medical technology and pharmaceutics have advanced rapidly over the past few decades, they are often deficient in tackling some of the major problems of the human condition, frequently because the social and personal contexts are ignored. A good example is that of Viagra, which though it may well assist men in achieving a sufficient erection for sexual intercourse, does not guarantee a satisfactory sex life for either the man or his partner. Advances in medicine and neurology allow many problems of the human mind and body to be treated, but not cured. Increasingly, people are requesting alternatives to so-called conventional medicine. Complementary therapies such as acupuncture are a valuable adjunct to medical treatments and there is increasing evidence that their efficacy goes beyond the acknowledged placebo effect. For example, Parient, White, Frackowiak & Lewith (2005) found that real acupuncture has a specific physiological effect and that patients' expectations and beliefs regarding a potentially beneficial treatment modulate activity in component areas of the brain's reward system. Also, as discussed in this book, recent developments in hypnotherapy have convincingly shown that psychoneuroimmunological processes can be stimulated that can facilitate inner healing.

However, more good research is needed to demonstrate that hypnotherapy really does work, as well as for which patients and with what symptomatologies. Currently, the randomised clinical trial (RCT) is the accepted method for evaluating clinical effectiveness upon which judgements concerning evidence-based practice are made. What constitutes good research, though, is problematical. In a recent book, Steven Rose (2005) argues that much of the clever neurological research is being done using essentially crude models of the brain. Interestingly, he found that people working under stress, such as a group of nurses, had the same neurochemical profiles as the depressed, while feeling perfectly cheerful! He concludes that there is no simple chain of cause and effect linking events on the cellular and psychological levels. Even so, crude neuropharmacological interventions, such as electro-convulsive treatment or Ritalin, sometimes work, although the reasons for this are not exactly understood. McCrone (1999) likens this approach to 'smacking the side of an old vacuum tube TV set', which may do the trick. In some respects hypnotherapy is similar in that often it works, or at least attributions to this effect can be made, although the reasons why it works cannot easily be ascertained.

Of course, hypnotherapeutic interventions do not always work, even though case studies presented in books and journals often imply this as so few studies are reported that indicate failure! Caution must be exercised in claiming that hypnotherapy works when these claims cannot be reliably substantiated, particularly with reference to the specific curative factors involved. It should also be reiterated that hypnotherapy is not a panacea, and for many patients it may not provide the most beneficial treatment. In this context it should be remembered that the National Health Service (NHS) patient has the right to clear, understandable information about the treatment being offered as well as any preferable alternative treatments available (www.nhs.uk/nhsguide), and this maxim should also apply to private practice (refer to the Human Rights Act, 1998, www.hmso.gov.uk). Often, hypnotherapy can only be used with maximum effect when it is incorporated with other medical and mind–body approaches such as cognitive-behavioural therapy and, indeed, in many situations such integration is necessary. Integrating hypnotherapy with other complementary approaches such as acupuncture may also prove to be worthwhile.

Nevertheless, there is growing evidence for the efficacy of clinical hypnosis within medicine and psychotherapy through the increasing number of well-researched RCTs. Its utility is also evidenced in the burgeoning number of small-scale research studies and clinical case reports that use integrated methodologies. As the number and range of studies increase, as well as their sophistication, so the use of hypnotherapy with respect to specific techniques, individual patients and their unique personalities and symptomatologies will be refined. As yet, little research has been carried out using functional magnetic resonance imaging (fMRI) to identify and characterise the brain regions that are active during hypnotherapy. Future research will provide more substantiated knowledge concerning the neurochemical and anatomical basis for the effects of hypnotherapy on various physiological activities.

Whilst attempts are made to allow hypnotherapists to become more sophisticated, it is essential that, in the meantime, we continue to offer interventions that are as successful as possible. But it is important to remember that human beings are all unique and react to stress, and to therapeutic interventions, in different ways; sometimes their 'little red valve' is another colour and in another position, sometimes unrecognisable and sometimes it doesn't even exist! Keep tapping and notice with surprise what happens!

References

Aapro, M.S. (1991). Controlling emesis related to cancer chemotherapy. *European Journal of Cancer* **27**, 356–362.

Abela, M.B. (1999). Hypnotherapy for Crohn's Disease: A promising complementary/alternative therapy. *Integrative Medicine* **2**(2/3), 127–131.

Adams, H., Feuerstein, M. & Fowler, J. (1980). Migraine headache: Review of parameters, etiology and intervention. *Psychological Bulletin* **87**, 217–237.

Adler, R., Felton, D.L. & Cohen, N. (1991). *Psychoneuroimmunology*. San Diego, CA: Academic Press.

Alden, P.A. (1992). *The Use of Hypnosis in the Management of Pain on a Spinal Injuries Unit.* Paper presented at the 12th International Congress of Hypnosis, Jerusalem, Palestine.

Alden, P. (1995). Back to the past: Introducing the 'bubble'. *Contemporary Hypnosis* **12**(2), 59–68.

Alexander, F. & French, T. (1946). *Psychoanalytic Therapy: Principles and Applications.* New York: Ronald Press.

Alladin, A. (1988). Hypnosis in the treatment of severe chronic migraine. In M. Heap (Ed.), *Hypnosis: Current Clinical, Experimental and Forensic Practices* (pp. 159–166). London: Croome Helm.

Alman, B.M. & Lambrou, P. (1997). *Self-Hypnosis: The Complete Manual for Health and Self-Change* (3rd edn). New York: Brunner/Mazel Publishers.

American Psychiatric Association. (1980). *A Psychiatric Glossary.* Washington, DC: American Psychiatric Association.

American Psychiatric Association. (1994). *Diagnostic and Statistical Manual of Mental Disorders* (4th edn). Washington, DC: American Psychiatric Association.

American Psychological Association. (1996). *Final Report of the Working Group on Investigation of Memories of Childhood Abuse.* Washington, DC.

American Psychological Association (2005). *The Division 30 Definition and Description of Hypnosis.* Available: www.apa.org/divisions/div30/define_hypnosis.html.

Anderson, J.A.D., Basker, M.A. & Dalton, E.R. (1975). Migraine and hypnotherapy. *International Journal of Clinical and Experimental Hypnosis* **23**, 48–58.

Araoz, D.L. (1980). Clinical hypnosis in treating sexual abulia. *American Journal of Family Therapy* **8**(1), 48–57.

Araoz, D.L. (1982). *Hypnosis and Sex Therapy*. New York: Brunner/Mazel Publishers.

Araoz, D.L. (1985). *The New Hypnosis*. New York: Brunner/Mazel Publishers.

Araoz, D.L. (2005). Hypnosis in human sexuality problems. *American Journal of Clinical Hypnosis* **47**(4), 229–242.

Ashton, R.C. Jr, Whitworth, G.C., Seldomridge, J.A., Shapiro, P.A., Weinberg, A.D., Michler, R.E., Smith, C.R., Rose, E.A., Fisher, S. & Oz, M.C. (1997). Self-hypnosis reduces anxiety following coronary artery bypass surgery: A prospective randomized trial. *Journal of Cardiovascular Surgery* **38**, 69–75.

Assagioli, R. (1965/1975). *Psychosynthesis: A Collection of Basic Writings*. London: Turnstone Books.

Axelrad, A.D. (1990). The role of hypnosis in multiple convergent management of chronic pain. *Houston Medicine* **6**, 111–119.

Bach, R. (1970). *Jonathan Livingston Seagull*. New York: Macmillan Company.

Baer, P.E., Garmezy, L.B., McLaughlin, R.J., Pokorny, A.D. & Wernick, M.J. (1987). Stress, coping, family conflict, and adolescent alcohol use. *Journal of Behavioral Medicine* **10**, 449–466.

Bakal, D.A. (1975). Headache: A biopsychological perspective. *Psychological Bulletin* **62**, 306–308.

Bakich, I. (1995). Hypnosis in the treatment of sexual desire disorders. *Australian Journal of Clinical and Experimental Hypnosis* **23**(1), 70–77.

Balint, M. (1968). *The Basic Fault: Therapeutic Aspects of Regression*. London: Tavistock.

Bandler, R. & Grinder, J. (1979). *Frogs into Princes*. Moab, UT: Real People Press.

Bannister, D. (1983). The internal politics of psychotherapy. In D. Pilgrim (Ed.), *Psychology and Psychotherapy*. London: Routledge & Kegan Paul.

Bannister, P., Burman, E., Parker, I., Taylor, M. & Tindall, C. (1994). *Qualitative Methods in Psychology*. Buckingham: Open University Press.

Barabasz, A. & Watkins, J.G. (2005). *Hypnotherapeutic Techniques* (2nd edn). New York: Brunner-Routledge.

Barber, J. (1990). Techniques of hypnotic pain management. In D.C. Hammond (Ed.), *Hypnotic Suggestions and Metaphors* (pp. 50–52). London: W.W. Norton.

Barber, J. (Ed.) (1996). *Hypnosis and Suggestion in the Treatment of Pain: A Clinical Guide*. New York: W.W. Norton.

Barber, T.X. (1969). *Hypnosis: A Scientific Approach*. New York: Van Nostrand Reinhold Company.

Barber, T.X. & Wilson, S.C. (1978). The barber suggestibility scale and the creative imagination scale: experimental and clinical applications. *American Journal of Clinical Hypnosis* **21**, 84–108.

Barnier, A.J., McConkey, K. & O'Neill, L.M. (1999). Treating anxiety with self-hypnosis and relaxation. *Contemporary Hypnosis* **16**, 68–80.

Bartlet, L. & Beaumont, J. (1998). Treating the sleep disorders of children with disabilities and illness: A one-year project. *Clinical Child Psychology and Psychiatry* **3**, 591–612.

Battino, R. (2001). *Metaphoria: Metaphor and Guided Metaphor for Psychotherapy and Healing*. Bancyfelin, Carmarthenshire: Crown House Publishing.

Baum, L.F. & George, M. (1900). *The Wonderful Wizard of Oz*: George M. Hill Company.

Baumann, F. (1981). Hypnosis in the treatment of urinary and fecal incontinence: A twenty-year experience. In H.J. Wain (Ed.), *Theoretical and Clinical Aspects of Hypnosis*. Miami, FL: Symposia Specialists Incorporated.

Bayot, A. & Capafons, A. (1997). Emotional self-regulation therapy: A new and efficacious treatment for smoking. *American Journal of Clinical Hypnosis* **40**(2), 146–156.

Beck, A.T. (1967). *Depression: Clinical, Experimental and Theoretical Aspects*. New York: Holber.

Beck, A.T., Epstein, N., Brown, G. & Steer, R.A. (1988). An inventory for measuring clinical anxiety: Psychometric properties. *Journal of Consulting and Clinical Psychology* **56**, 893–897.

Becker, J.V., Skinner, L.J., Abel, G.G. & Cichon, J. (1986). Level of postassault sexual functioning in rape and incest victims. *Archives of Sexual Behavior* **15**, 37–49.

Beecher, H. (1959). *Measurement of Subjective Responses*. New York: Oxford University Press.

Beigel, H.G. (1980). The hypnotherapeutic approach to male impotence. In H.G. Beigel & W.R. Johnson (Eds), *Application of Hypnosis in Sex Therapy*. Springfield, IL: Charles C. Thomas Publisher.

Beigel, H.G. & Johnson, W.R. (1980). *Applications of Hypnosis in Sex Therapy*. Springfield, IL: Charles C. Thomas Publisher.

Bejenke, C.J. (2000). Benefits of early interventions with cancer patients. *Hypnos*, **27**(2), 75–81.

Bergin, A.E. & Garfield, S.L. (1994). *Handbook of Psychotherapy and Behavior Change* (4th edn). Chichester: Wiley.

Bergin, A.E. & Lambert, M.J. (1978). The evaluation of therapeutic outcomes. In S.L. Garfield & A.E. Bergin (Eds), *Handbook of Psychotherapy and Behavior Change* (2nd edn, pp. 139–189). New York: Wiley.

Berlin, J. & Erdmann, W. (1987). Hypnosis in the treatment of classical migraine. *Pain, Supplement*, **4**, 580.

Berne, E. (1961). *Transactional Analysis in Psychotherapy*. New York: Grove Press.

Bernheim, H. (1886/1957). *Suggestive Therapeutics: A Treatise on the Nature and Uses of Hypnotism*. Westport, CT: Associated Booksellers.

Bettelheim, B. (1991). *The Uses of Enchantment: The Meaning and Importance of Fairy Tales*. Harmondsworth: Penguin Books.

Bills, I.G. (1993). The use of hypnosis in the management of dental phobia. *Australian Journal of Clinical and Experimental Hypnosis* **21**(1), 13–18.

Black, P.H. (1994). Immune system-central nervous system interactions: Psychoneuroendocrinology of stress and its immune consequences. *Antimicrobial Agents and Chemotherapy* **38**, 7–12.

Braid, J. (1843). *Neurypnology: Or the Rationale of Nervous Sleep Considered in Relation with Animal Magnetism*. London: Churchill.

Braid, J. (1846). *The Power of the Mind Over the Body*. London: Churchill.

Braid, J. (1855/1970). The physiology of fascination and critics criticised. In M. Tinterow (Ed.), *Foundation of Hypnosis*. Springfield, IL: Charles C. Thomas Publisher.

Brandon, D. (1976). *Zen in the Art of Helping*. London: Routledge & Kegan Paul Limited.

Braun, B.G. (1984). Uses of hypnosis with multiple personalities. *Psychiatric Annals* **14**, 34–40.

Brende, J.O. (1985). The use of hypnosis in post-traumatic conditions. In W.E. Kelly (Ed.), *Post-Traumatic Stress Disorder and the War Veteran* (pp. 193–210). New York: Brunner/Mazel Publishers.

Bresler, D.E. (1990). Meeting an inner advisor. In D.C. Hammond (Ed.), *Handbook of Hypnotic Suggestions and Metaphors* (pp. 318–320). New York: W.W. Norton.

Breuer, J. & Freud, S. (1895/1955). Studies on hysteria. In J. Strachey (Ed.), *The Standard Edition of the Complete Psychological Works of Sigmund Freud* (Vol. II). New York: W.W. Norton.

Briere, J. (1992). *Child Abuse Trauma: Theory and Treatment of the Lasting Effects.* Newbury Park, CA: Sage Publications.

Brown, W. (1920). The revival of emotional memories and its therapeutic value. *British Journal of Medical Psychology* 1, 16–19.

Brown, W. (1921). *Psychology and Psychotherapy.* London: Edward Arnold.

Brown, D.P. & Fromm, E. (1987). *Hypnosis and Behavioral Medicine.* London: Lawrence Erlbaum Associates.

Budman, S.H. & Gurman, A.S. (1988). *Theory and Practice of Brief Therapy.* London: Hutchinson.

Burte, J.M. & Araoz, D.L. (1994). Cognitive hypnotherapy with sexual disorders. *Journal of Cognitive Psychotherapy* 8, 1–2.

Burte, J.M., Burte, W.D. & Araoz, D.L. (1994). Hypnosis in the treatment of back pain. *The Australian Journal of Clinical Hypnotherapy and Hypnosis* 15(2), 93–115.

Calnan, R.D. (1977). Hypnotherapeutic ego-strengthening. *Australian Journal of Clinical and Experimental Hypnosis* 5, 105–118.

Cannon, W.B. (1932). *The Wisdom of the Body.* New York: W.W. Norton.

Cappell, H. & Greeley, J. (1987). Alcohol and tension reduction: An update on research and theory. In H.T. Blane & K.E. Leonard (Eds), *Psychological Theories of Drinking and Alcoholism* (pp. 15–54). New York: Guilford Press.

Carasso, R.L., Peded, O. & Kleinhauz, Y.S. (1985). Treatment of cervical headache with hypnosis, suggestive therapy, and relaxation techniques. *American Journal of Clinical Hypnosis* 27(4), 216–218.

Cardeña, E. & Spiegel, D. (1993). Dissociative reactions to the San Francisco Bay area earthquake of 1989. *American Journal of Psychiatry* 150, 474–478.

Carey, M.P., Kalra, D.L., Carey, K.B., Halperin, S. & Richard, C.S. (1993). Stress and unaided smoking cessation: A prospective investigation. *Journal of Consulting and Clinical Psychology* 61, 831–838.

Carich, P.A. (1986). Contraindications to using hypnosis. In B. Zilbergeld, M.G. Edelstein & D.L. Araoz (Eds), *Hypnosis Questions and Answers.* New York: W.W. Norton.

Carle, E. (1974). *The Very Hungry Caterpillar.* Harmondsworth: Puffin Books, Penguin Books Limited.

Carnes, P.J. (1991). *Don't Call It Love: Recovery From Sexual Addiction.* New York: Bantam Books.

Carr, A. (1999). *The Handbook of Child and Adolescent Clinical Psychology.* London: Routledge.

Castes, M., Hagel, I., Palenque, M., Canelones, P., Corano, A. & Lynch, N. (1999). Immunological changes associated with clinical improvement of asthmatic children subjected to psychosocial intervention. *Brain and Behavioral Immunology* 13(1), 1–13.

Cedercreutz, C., Lahteenmaki, R. & Tulikoura, J. (1976). Hypnotic treatment of headache and vertigo in skull injured patient. *International Journal of Clinical and Experimental Hypnosis* **24**, 195–201.

Charlton, R.S. & Yalom, I.D. (1997). *Treating Sexual Disorders*. San Francisco, CA: Jossey-Bass.

Chaves, J.F. (1993). Hypnosis in pain management. In J.W. Rhue, S. Lynn & I. Kirsch (Eds), *Handbook of Clinical Hypnosis*. Washington, DC: American Psychological Association.

Chaves, J.F. (1994). Recent advances in the application of hypnosis to pain management. *American Journal of Clinical Hypnosis* **37**(2), 117–129.

Cheek, D.B. (1961). Possible uses of hypnosis in dermatology. *Medical Times* **89**, 76–82.

Cheek, D.B. (1976). Short-term hypnotherapy for frigidity using exploration of early life attitudes. *American Journal of Clinical Hypnosis* **19**, 20–27.

Cheek, D.B. (1994). *Hypnosis: The Application of Ideomotor Techniques*. Boston, MA: Allyn & Bacon.

Cheek, D.B. & LeCron, L.M. (1968). *Clinical Hypnotherapy*. New York: Grune & Stratton.

Cho, K. (2001). Chronic 'jet lag' produces temporal lobe atrophy and spatial cognitive deficits. *Nature Neuroscience* **4**, 567–568.

Choinière, M., Melzack, R., Rondeau, J., Girard, N. & Paquin, M.J. (1989). The pain of burns: Characteristics and correlates. *Journal of Trauma* **29**, 1531–1539.

Chwalisz, K. (2003). Evidence-based practice: A framework for twenty-first-century scientist-practitioner. *The Counselling Psychologist* **13**, 497–528.

Clarkson, P. (Ed.) (1996). *Counselling Psychology: Integrating Theory, Research and Supervised Practice*. London: Routledge.

Clarkson, P. (1998). Supervision in counselling, psychotherapy and health: An intervention priority sequencing model. *European Journal of Psychotherapy, Counselling and Health* **1**(2), 195.

Clarkson, P. (2003). *The Therapeutic Relationship* (2nd edn). London: Whurr Publishers.

Clarkson, P. & Aviram, O. (1998). Phenomenological research on supervision: Supervisors reflect on 'being a supervisor'. In P. Clarkson (Ed.), *Counselling Psychology: Integrating Theory, Research and Supervised Practice* (pp. 273–299). London: Routledge.

Cohen, S., Doyle, W.J. & Turner, R.B. (2003). Emotional style and susceptibility to the common cold. *Psychosomatic Medicine* **65**(4), 652–657.

Conner, M., Fitter, M. & Fletcher, W. (1999). Stress and snacking: A diary study of daily hassles and between-meal snacking. *Psychology and Health* **14**, 51–63.

Cooper, A. (Ed.) (2002). *Sex and the Internet: A Guidebook for Clinicians*. Florence, KY: Brunner-Routledge.

Cooper, P., Cruickshanks, P., Miller, V. & Whorwell, P.J. (2003). Gut-focused hypnotherapy normalises disordered rectal sensitivity in patients with irritable bowel syndrome. *Alimentary Pharmacological Therapy* **17**(5), 635–642.

Cornwell, J., Burrows, G.D. & McMurray, N. (1981). Comparison of single and multiple sessions of hypnosis in the treatment of smoking behaviour. *Australian Journal of Clinical and Experimental Hypnosis* **9**, 61–76.

Cotanch, P., Hockenberry, M. & Herman, S. (1985). Self-hypnosis as anti-emetic therapy in children receiving chemotherapy. *Oncology Nursing Forum* **12**, 41–46.

Covino, N.A., Jimerson, D.C., Wolfe, B.E., Franko, D.L. & Frankel, E.H. (1994). Hypnotizability, dissociation and bulimia nervosa. *Journal of Abnormal Psychology* **42**,
204–231.

Cox, S., de Lusignan, S. & Chan, T. (2004). General practitioners believe that hypnotherapy could be a useful treatment for irritable bowel syndrome in primary
care. *BMC Family Practice* **5**(1), 22.

Crasilneck, H.B. (1979). The use of hypnosis in the treatment of psychogenic impotency. *Australian Journal of Clinical and Experimental Hypnosis*, **2**, 147–153.

Crasilneck, H.B. (1982). A follow-up study in the use of hypnotherapy in the treatment
of psychogenic impotency. *American Journal of Clinical Hypnosis* **25**(1), 52–61.

Crasilneck, H.B. & Hall, J.A. (1985). *Clinical Hypnosis: Principles and Applications*.
Orlando, FL: Grune & Stratton.

Crowley, R. & Mills, J. (1986). The nature and construction of therapeutic metaphors
for children. *British Journal of Experimental and Clinical Hypnosis* **3**(2), 69–76.

Cyna, A., McAuliffe, G. & Andrew, M. (2004). Hypnosis for pain relief in labour and
childbirth: A systematic review. *British Journal of Anaesthesia* **93**, 505–511.

Damasio, A. (1994). *Descartes' Error: Emotion, Reason, and the Human Brain*. Oxford:
Oxford University Press.

Daud, L., Garralda, M.E. & David, T.J. (1993). Psychosocial adjustment in pre-school
children with atopic eczema. *Archives of Diseases in Childhood* **69**, 670–676.

Davanloo, H. (1978). *Basic Principles and Techniques in Short-Term Psychodynamic Psychotherapy*. New York: Spectrum.

Davanloo, H. (1980). A method of short-term psychodynamic therapy. In H. Davanloo (Ed.), *Short-Term Dynamic Psychotherapy*. New York: Jason Aronson.

Davidson, P. (1987). Hypnosis and migraine headache: Reporting a clinical series.
Australian Journal of Clinical and Experimental Hypnosis **15**, 111–118.

Davidson, G.P., Garbett, N.D. & Tozer, S.G. (1982). An investigation into audiotaped
self-hypnosis training in pregnancy and labour. In D. Waxman, P.C. Misra, M.
Gibson & M.A. Basker (Eds), *Modern Trends in Hypnosis*. New York: Plenum Press.

Davies, P. & Morgan, D. (1997). Hypnosis with children. *European Journal of Clinical
Hypnosis* **4**(2), 87–92.

De Benedittis, G. (1999). Hypnotically induced dreams: Rationale and techniques.
Australian Journal of Clinical and Experimental Hypnosis **27**(2), 42–49.

Degun, M.D. & Degun, G. (1982). The use of hypnosis in the treatment of psychosexual disorders: With case illustrations of vaginismus. *Bulletin of the British Society
of Experimental and Clinical Hypnosis* **1**(5), 31–36.

Degun, M.D. & Degun, G. (1988). The use of hypnotic dream suggestion in psychotherapy. In M. Heap (Ed.), *Hypnosis: Current Clinical, Experimental, and Forensic
Approaches*. London: Croom Helm.

Degun-Mather, M. (1995). Group therapy and hypnosis for the treatment of bulimia
nervosa. *Contemporary Hypnosis* **12**(2), 69–73.

Degun-Mather, M. (1997). The use of hypnosis in the treatment of post-traumatic stress
disorder in a survivor of childhood abuse. *Contemporary Hypnosis* **14**, 100–104.

Degun-Mather, M. (2001). The value of hypnosis in the treatment of chronic PTSD
with dissociative fugues in a war veteran. *Contemporary Hypnosis* **18**(1), 4–13.

Degun-Mather, M. (2003). Ego-state therapy in the treatment of a complex eating disorder. *Contemporary Hypnosis* **20**(3), 165–173.

Denzin, N.K. & Lincoln, Y.S. (1994). *Handbook of Qualitative Research*. London: Sage
Publications.

De Shazer, S. (1985). *Keys to Solution in Brief Therapy*. New York: W.W. Norton.

De Shazer, S. (1988). *Clues: Investigating Solutions in Brief Therapy*. New York: W.W. Norton.

Dhabhar, F., Satoskar, A., Bluethmann, H., David, J. & McEwen, B. (2000). Stress-induced enhancement of skin immune function: A role for gamma interferon. *Proceedings of the National Academy of Sciences* **96**, 1059–1064.

Diamond, M.J. (1974). Modification of hypnotizability: A review. *Psychological Bulletin* **81**, 180–198.

Diamond, M.J. (1977). Hypnotizability is modifiable: An alternative approach. *International Journal of Clinical and Experimental Hypnosis* **25**, 147–166.

Dimond, R.E. (1981). Hypnotic treatment of a kidney dialysis patient. *American Journal of Clinical Hypnosis* **23**, 284–288.

Drummond, F.E. (1981). Hypnosis in the treatment of headache: A review of the last 10 years. *Journal of the American Society of Psychosomatic Dentistry and Medicine* **28**(3), 87–101.

Duncan, R.D., Saunders, B.E., Kilpatrick, D.G., Hanson, R.F. & Resnick, H.S. (1996). Childhood physical assault as a risk factor for PTSD, depression, and substance abuse: Findings from a national survey. *American Journal of Orthopsychiatry* **66**, 437–448.

Dunn, K.M., Cherkas, L.F. & Spector, T.M. (2005) Genetic influences on variation in female orgasmic function: A twin study. *Biology Letter* (The Royal Society).

Dwivedi, K.N. (Ed.) (2000). *Post Traumatic Stress Disorder in Children and Adolescents*. London: Whurr Publishers.

Edgette, J.H. & Edgette, J.S. (1995). *Handbook of Hypnotic Phenomena in Psychotherapy*. New York: Brunner/Mazel Publishers.

Edmond, T. & McCarty, D. (2004). Sexual abuse survivors' perceptions of the effectiveness of EMDR and eclectic therapy. *Research in Social Work Practice* **14**(4), 259–272.

Edmonston, W.E. (1981). *Hypnosis and Relaxation: Modern Verification of an Old Equation*. New York: John Wiley & Sons.

Edser, S.J. (2002). Hypnotically-facilitated counter-conditioning of anticipatory nausea and vomiting associated with chemotherapy. *Australian Journal of Clinical Hypnotherapy and Hypnosis* **23**(1), 18–30.

Elkins, G. & Carter, B. (1981). Use of science fiction-based imagery technique in child hypnosis. *American Journal of Clinical Hypnosis* **23**, 274–277.

Ellenberger, H.F. (1970). *The Discovery of the Unconscious: The History and Evolution of Dynamic Psychiatry*. New York: Basic Books.

Elton, D., Stanley, G. & Burrows, G. (1983). *Psychological Control of Pain*. Sydney, Australia: Grune & Stratton.

Engels, F. (1939). *Anti-Dühring*. New York: International Publishers.

Engel, G.L. (1971). Sudden and rapid death during psychological stress. *Annals of Internal Medicine* **74**, 771.

Epstein, S.J. & Deyoub, P.L. (1983). Hypnotherapeutic control of exhibitionism: A brief communication. *International Journal of Clinical and Experimental Hypnosis* **31**(2), 63–66.

Erickson, M.H. (1932). Possible detrimental effects of experimental hypnosis. *Journal of Abnormal and Social Psychology* **37**, 321–327.

Erickson, M.H. (1934). A brief survey of hypnotism. *Medical Record*, 5 December, 1–8.

Erickson, M.H. (circa 1950s). Hypnosis in obstetrics: Utilizing experiential learnings, *Milton H. Erickson: Complete Works* [CD]. Phoenix, AZ: Milton H. Erickson Foundation Press [2001]. Unpublished paper.

Erickson, M.H. (1952a). Deep hypnosis and its induction. In L.M. LeCron (Ed.). *Experimental Hypnosis*. New York: Macmillan, 70–114.

Erickson, M.H. (1952b). A therapeutic double bind utilizing resistance. *Milton H. Erickson: Complete Works* [CD]. Phoenix, AZ: Milton H. Erickson Foundation Press [2001]. Unpublished paper.

Erickson, M.H. (1953). Impotence: Facilitating unconscious reconditioning. *Milton H. Erickson: Complete Works* [CD]. Milton H. Erickson Foundation Press [2001]. Unpublished paper.

Erickson, M.H. (1954). Pseudo-orientation in time as a hypnotherapeutic procedure. *Journal of Experimental and Clinical Hypnosis* 2, 261–283.

Erickson, M.H. (1956). Reorganization of unconscious thinking without conscious awareness: Two cases with intellectualized resistance against hypnosis. *Milton H. Erickson: Complete Works* [CD]. Milton H. Erickson Foundation Press [2001]. Unpublished paper.

Erickson, M.H. (1958a). Naturalistic techniques of hypnosis. *American Journal of Clinical Hypnosis* 1, 3–8.

Erickson, M.H. (1958b). Pediatric hypnotherapy. *American Journal of Clinical Hypnosis* 1, 25–29.

Erickson, M.H. (1959). Further clinical techniques of hypnosis: Utilization techniques. *American Journal of Clinical Hypnosis* 2, 3–21.

Erickson, M.H. (1960). Utilization of patient behavior in the hypnotherapy of obesity: Three case reports. *American Journal of Clinical Hypnosis* 3, 112–116.

Erickson, M.H. (1962). *Milton H. Erickson: Complete Works* [CD]. Phoenix, AZ: Milton H. Erickson Foundation Press. Unpublished paper.

Erickson, M.H. (1964a). Pantomime techniques in hypnosis and the implications. *American Journal of Clinical Hypnosis* 7, 64–70.

Erickson, M.H. (1964b). The 'Surprise' and 'My-Friend-John' techniques of hypnosis: Minimal cues and natural field experimentation. *American Journal of Clinical Hypnosis* 6, 293–307.

Erickson, M.H. (1965). Use of symptoms as an integral part of hypnotherapy. *American Journal of Clinical Hypnosis* 8, 57–65.

Erickson, M.H. (1966). The interspersal hypnotic technique for symptom correction and pain control. *American Journal of Clinical Hypnosis* 8, 198–209.

Erickson, M.H. (1973). Psychotherapy achieved by a reversal of the neurotic processes in a case of ejaculatio praecox. *American Journal of Clinical Hypnosis* 15, 217–222.

Erickson, M.H. (1977). Hypnotic approaches to therapy. *American Journal of Clinical Hypnosis* 20(1), 20–35.

Erickson, M.H. & Kubie, L.S. (1941). The successful treatment of a case of acute hysterical depression by a return under hypnosis to a critical phase of childhood. *Psychoanalytic Quarterly* 10, 583–609.

Erickson, M.H. & Rossi, E. (1975). Varieties of double bind. *American Journal of Clinical Hypnosis* 17, 143–157.

Erickson, M.H., & Rossi, E. (1976a). Two-level communication and the microdynamics of trance and suggestion. *American Journal of Clinical Hypnosis* 18, 153–171.

Erickson, M.H. & Rossi, E. (1976b). Indirect forms of suggestion. *Milton H. Erickson: Complete Works* [CD]. Milton H. Erickson Foundation Press [2001]. Unpublished paper.

Erickson, M.H. & Rossi, E.L. (1979). *Hypnotherapy: An Exploratory Casebook.* New York: Irvington.

Erickson, M.H. & Rossi, E.L. (1981). *Experiencing Hypnosis: Therapeutic Approaches to Altered State.* New York: Irvington.

Erickson, M.H. & Rossi, E. (1989). *The February Man: Evolving Consciousness and Identity in Hypnotherapy.* New York: Brunner/Mazel Publishers.

Erickson, M.H., Rossi, E.L. & Rossi, S.I. (1976). *Hypnotic Realities.* New York: Irvington.

Erikson, E. (1950). *Childhood and Society.* New York: W.W. Norton.

Evans, F.J. (1994). Hypnosis and pain control. *American Journal of Clinical and Experimental Hypnosis* **18**(1), 21–33.

Evans, B.J., Coman, G.J. & Burrows, G.D. (Eds.) (1997). *Hypnosis for Weight Management and Eating Disorders: A Clinical Handbook.* Heidelberg, Australia: Australian Journal of Clinical and Experimental Hypnosis.

Evans, C. & Richardson, P.H. (1988). Improved recovery and reduced postoperative stay after therapeutic suggestions during general anesthesia. *The Lancet* **2**, 491–493.

Everill, J.T. & Waller, G. (1995). Dissociation and bulimia: Research and theory. *European Eating Disorders Review* **3**, 129–147.

Ewin, D.M. (1979). Hypnosis in burn therapy. In G.D. Burrows, D.R. Collison & L. Dennerstein (Eds), *Handbook of Hypnosis and Psychosomatic Medicine* (pp. 269–275). New York: Elsevier Press.

Ewin, D.M. (1992). Hypnotherapy for warts (verruca vulgaris): 41 consecutive cases with 33 cures. *American Journal of Clinical Hypnosis* **35**, 1–10.

Fabbri, R. (1976). Hypnosis and behavior therapy: A coordinated approach to the treatment of sexual disorders. *American Journal of Clinical Hypnosis* **19**, 4–8.

Faria, J.C. (1906). In D.C. Delgado (Ed.), *De la cause de sommeil lucide: Ou etude sur la nature de l'homme.* Paris: Henri Jouvet.

Federn, P. (1952). *Ego Psychology and the Psychoses.* New York: Basic Books.

Fellows, B.J. (1988). The use of hypnotic susceptibility scales. In M.J. Heap (Ed.), *Hypnosis: Current Clinical, Experimental and Forensic Practices.* London: Croom Helm.

Ferber, R. & Kryger, M. (1995). *Principles and Practice of Sleep Medicine in the Child.* Philadelphia, PA: W.B. Saunders.

Foa, E.B., Davidson, J.R.T. & Frances, A. (1999). The expert consensus guideline series: Treatment of posttraumatic stress disorder. *Journal of Clinical Psychiatry* **60**(Suppl. 16), 1–79.

Foa, E.B., Keane, T.M. & Friedman, M.J. (Eds.) (2000). *Effective Treatments for PTSD: Practice Guidelines from the International Society for Traumatic Stress Studies.* New York: Guilford Publications.

Foa, E.B., Rothbaum, B.O. & Molnar, C. (1995). Cognitive-behavioral therapy of post-traumatic stress disorder. In M.J. Friedman, D.S. Charney & A.Y. Deutch (Eds), *Neurobiological and Clinical Consequences of stress: From Normal Adaptation to Post-Traumatic Stress Disorder.* Philadelphia, PA: Lippincott-Raven.

Folks, D.G. & Kinney, F.C. (1992). The role of psychological factors in dermatologic conditions. *Psychosomatics* **33**, 45–54.

Ford, R. (1995). Hypnotic treatment of a sleeping problem in an 11-year-old boy. *Contemporary Hypnosis* **12**(3), 201–206.

Fowler-Kerry, S. (1990). Adolescent oncology survivors' recollection of pain. *Paper presented at the First International Pain Symposium.* Washington, DC: Seattle.

Frank, J.D. (1973). *Persuasion and Healing* (2nd edn). Baltimore, MD: John Hopkins University Press.

Frank, R.G., Umlauf, R.L., Wonderlich, S.A. & Ashkanazi, G.S. (1986). Hypnosis and behaviour treatment in a worksite cessation program. *Addictive Behaviors* 11, 59–62.

Frederick, C. & Phillips, M. (1992). The use of hypnotic age progressions as interventions with acute psychosomatic conditions. *American Journal of Clinical Hypnosis* 35, 89–98.

Fredericks, L.E. (2001). *The Use of Hypnosis in Surgery: Psychological Preparation of the Surgical Patient.* Springfield, IL: Charles C. Thomas.

Frenay, M.C., Faymonville, M.E., Devlieger, S., Albert, A. & Vanderkelen, A. (2001). Psychological approaches during dressing changes of burned patients: A prospective randomized study comparing hypnosis against stress reducing strategy. *Burns* 27, 793–799.

Freud, S. (1900/1976). *The Interpretation of Dreams.* Harmondsworth: Pelican Books.

Freud, S. (1923). *The Ego and the ID.* New York: W.W. Norton.

Friedman, H. & Taub, H.A. (1985). Extended follow-up study of the effects of brief psychological procedures in migraine therapy. *American Journal of Clinical Hypnosis* 28, 27–33.

Friedman, M., Thoresen, C. & Gill, J. (1986). Alteration of Type A behavior and its effects on cardiac reoccurrences in post myocardial infarction patients: Summary results of the recurrent coronary prevention project. *American Heart Journal* 112, 653–665.

Fromm, E. (1956). *The Art of Loving.* New York: Harper & Row.

Gandhi, B. & Oakley, D.A. (2005). Does 'hypnosis' by any other name smell as sweet? The efficacy of 'hypnotic' inductions depends on the label 'hypnosis'. *Consciousness and Cognition* 14, 304–315.

Gardner, G.G. (1976). Hypnosis and mastery: Clinical contributions and directions for research. *International Journal of Clinical and Experimental Hypnosis* 24, 202–214.

Gardner, G.G. (1990). Helping parents see specific advantages in child hypnotherapy. In D.C. Hammond (Ed.), *Handbook of Hypnotic Suggestions and Metaphors* (pp. 477–480). New York: W.W. Norton.

Gardner, G.G., Olness, K. & Kohen, D. (1996). *Hypnosis and Hypnotherapy with Children.* New York: Guilford Press.

Gauld, A. (1992). *A History of Hypnotism.* Cambridge, MA: Cambridge University Press.

Genius, M.L. (1995). The use of hypnosis in helping cancer patients control anxiety, pain, and emesis: A review of recent empirical studies. *American Journal of Clinical Hypnosis* 37(4), 316–325.

German, E. (2004). Hypnotic preparation of a mother-to-be. *Australian Journal of Clinical and Experimental Hypnosis* 32(2), 157–169.

Gibson, H.B. (Ed.). (1994). *Psychology, Pain and Anaesthesia.* London: Chapman & Hall.

Gibson, H.B. & Heap, M. (1991). *Hypnosis in Therapy.* Hove: Lawrence Erlbaum Associates.

Gilligan, S. (1987). *Therapeutic Trances: The Cooperation Principle in Ericksonian Hypnotherapy.* New York: Brunner/Mazel Publishers.

Glaser, R., Kennedy, S., Lafuse, W., Bonneau, R.H., Speicher, C., Hillhouse, J. & Kiecolt-Glaser, J.K. (1990). Psychological stress-induced modulation of interleukin 2 receptor gene expression and interleukin gene 2 production in peripheral blood leukocytes. *Archives of General Psychiatry* **47**, 707–712.

Glaser, R., Lafuse, W., Bonneau, R., Atkinson, C. & Kiecolt-Glaser, J.K. (1993). Stress-associated modulation of proto-oncogene expression in peripheral blood leukocytes. *Behavioral Neuroscience* **107**, 525–529.

Glaser, B.G. & Strauss, A.L. (1967). *The Discovery of Grounded Theory Strategies for Qualitative Research.* New York: Aldine Press.

Golden, L. (1999). Hypnosis in obstetrics and gynecology. In R. Temes (Ed.), *Medical Hypnosis: An Introduction and Clinical Guide* (pp. 65–78). Philadelphia, PA: Churchill Livingstone.

Golden, W.L., Dowd, E.T. & Friedberg, F. (1987). *Hypnotherapy: A Modern Approach.* Boston, MA: Allyn & Bacon.

Goldstein, R.H. (2005). Successful repeated hypnotic treatment of warts in the same individual. *American Journal of Clinical Hypnosis* **47**(4), 259–264.

Gonsalkorale, W.M., Houghton, L.A. & Whorwell, P.J. (2002). Hypnotherapy in irritable bowel syndrome: A large-scale audit of a clinical service with an examination of factors influencing responsiveness. *American Journal of Gastroenterology* **97**(4), 954–961.

Gonsalkorale, W.M., Miller, V., Afzal, A. & Whorwell, P.J. (2003). Long-term benefits of hypnotherapy for irritable bowel syndrome. *Gut* **52**(11), 1623–1629.

Gorassini, D.R. & Spanos, N.P. (1999). The Carleton skill training program for modifying hypnotic suggestibility: Original version and variations. In I. Kirsch, A. Capafons, E. Cardeña-Buelna & S. Amigo (Eds), *Clinical Hypnosis and Self-Regulation.* Washington, DC: American Psychological Association.

Gottheil, E. (Ed.) (1987). *Stress and Addiction.* New York: Brunner/Mazel Publishers.

Gow, M. (2002). Treating dental needle phobia using hypnosis. *Australian Journal of Clinical and Experimental Hypnosis* **30**(2), 198–202.

Gravitz, M.A. & Page, R.A. (2002). Hypnosis in the management of stress reactions. In G.S. Everly & J.M. Lating (Eds), *A Clinical Guide to the Treatment of the Human Stress Response* (pp. 241–252). New York: Kluwer Academic Publishers/Plenum Publishing.

Green, J.P. (1996). Cognitive behavioral hypnotherapy for smoking cessation: A case study in a group setting. In S.J. Lynn, I. Kirsch & J.W. Rhue (Eds), *Casebook of Clinical Hypnosis.* Washington, DC: American Psychological Association.

Green, J.P. (1999). Hypnosis and the treatment of smoking cessation and weight loss. In I. Kirsch, A. Capafons, E. Cardeña-Buelna & S. Amigo (Eds), *Clinical Hypnosis and Self-Regulation.* Washington, DC: American Psychological Association.

Greene, W.A. (1966). The psychosocial setting of the development of leukemia and lymphoma. *Annals of the New York Academy of Sciences* **125**, 794–801.

Greenberg, L.S. (1991). Research on the process of change. *Psychotherapy Research* **1**, 3–16.

Greene, B.R., Blanchard, E.B. & Wan, C.K. (1994). Long-term monitoring of psychosocial stress and symptomatology in inflammatory bowel disease. *Behavior Research and Therapy* **32**, 217–226.

Greenleaf, E. (1969). Developmental-stage regression through hypnosis. *American Journal of Clinical Hypnosis* **12**(1), 20–26.

Greenleaf, E. (1990). Suggestions to facilitate revivification. In D.C. Hammond (Ed.), *Handbook of Hypnotic Suggestions and Metaphors.* New York: W.W. Norton.

Greenson, R.R. (1967). *The Theory and Technique of Psychoanalysis.* New York: International Universities Press.

Greer, S. & Morris, T. (1975). Psychological attributes of women who develop breast cancer. *Journal of Psychosomatic Research* **19**, 147–153.

Grof, S. (1976). *Realms of the Human Unconscious: Observations from LSD Research.* New York: E.P. Dutton & Company.

Grof, S. (1988). *The Adventure of Self-Discovery.* New York: State University of New York Press.

Gross, J. & Levenson, R.W. (1997). Hiding feelings: The acute effects of inhibiting negative and positive emotion. *Journal of Abnormal Psychology* **106**, 95–103.

Grossarth-Maticek, R., Eysenck, H.J., Vetter, H. & Frentzel-Beyme, R. (1986). The Heidelberg prospective intervention study. In W.J. Eylenbasch, A.M. Depoorter & N. van Larbeke (Eds), *Primary Prevention of Cancer* (pp. 199–212). New York: Raven Press.

Gruzelier, J. (2002a). A review of the impact of hypnosis, relaxation, guided imagery and individual differences on aspects of immunity and health. *Stress* **5**, 147–163.

Gruzelier, J. (2002b). Self-hypnosis and immune function, health, wellbeing and personality. *Hypnos: Swedish Journal of Hypnosis in Psychotherapy and Psychosomatic Medicine* **29**, 186–191.

Gruzelier, J., Levy, J., Williams, J. & Henderson, D. (2001). Self-hypnosis and exam stress: Comparing immune and relaxation-related imagery for influences on immunity, health and mood. *Contemporary Hypnosis* **18**(2), 73–86.

Haley, J. (1973). *Uncommon Therapy: The Psychiatric Techniques of Milton H. Erickson M.D.* New York: W.W. Norton.

Haley, J. (1976). *Problem-Solving Therapy.* San Francisco, CA: Jossey-Bass.

Hall, J. (2001). Cellular imaging of zif-268 expression in the hippocampus and amygdala during contextual and cued fear memory retrieval: Selective of hippocampal CA1 neurons during the recall of contextual memories. *Journal of Neuroscience* **21**, 2186–2193.

Halmos, P. (1978). *The Personal and the Political.* London: Hutchinson & Company.

Hammond, D.C. (1984). Hypnosis in marital and sex therapy. In R.F. Stahmann & W.J. Hiebert (Eds), *Counseling in Marital and Sexual Problems* (pp. 115–130). Lexington, MA: Lexington Books.

Hammond, D.C. (1985). Treatment of inhibited sexual desire. In J. Zeig (Ed.), *Ericksonian Psychotherapy, Vol. II: Clinical Applications* (pp. 415–428). New York: Brunner/Mazel Publishers.

Hammond, D.C. (Ed.). (1990a). *Handbook of Hypnotic Suggestions and Metaphors.* London: W.W. Norton.

Hammond, D.C. (1990b). Hypnotherapy with sexual dysfunctions: The master control room technique. In D.C. Hammond (Ed.), *Handbook of Hypnotic Suggestions and Metaphors* (pp. 354). London: W.W. Norton.

Hanson, M. (2004). Over and Out. *The Guardian,* 7 August, pp. 8–9.

Hart, B.B. & Alden, P.A. (1994). Hypnotic techniques in the control of pain. In H.B. Gibson (Ed.), *Psychology, Pain and Anaethesia.* London: Chapman & Hall.

Hart, C. & Hart, B. (1996). The use of hypnosis with children and adolescents. *The Psychologist* **9**(11), 506–509.

Hart, C. & Hart, B. (1998). Discussion commentary: Hypnosis in the alleviation of procedure related pain and distress in paediatric oncology patients. *Contemporary Hypnosis* **15**(4), 208–211.

Hartland, J. (1971). *Medical and Dental Hypnosis and Its Clinical Applications.* Eastbourne: Bailliere Tindall.

Hartland, J. (1989). *Medical and Dental Hypnosis.* London: Balliere Tindall.

Harvey, A.G., Bryant, R.A. & Tarrier, N. (2003). Cognitive behavior therapy for posttraumatic stress disorder. *Clinical Psychology Review* **23**(3), 501–522.

Harvey, R.F., Hinton, R.A., Gunary, R.M. & Barry, R.E. (1989). Individual and group hypnotherapy in treatment of refractory irritable bowel syndrome. *The Lancet* **1**(8635), 424–425.

Hawkins, P.J. (1986). *Catharsis in Psychotherapy.* Unpublished PhD, University of Durham, Durham, England.

Hawkins, P.J. (1990). The use of hypnosis in the treatment of bulimia. *Paper presented at the Seventh Annual Conference of the British Society of Experimental and Clinical Hypnosis,* Sheffield, England.

Hawkins, P.J. (1994a). Is this the renaissance of clinical hypnosis? *European Journal of Clinical Hypnosis* **1**(2), 4–6.

Hawkins, P.J. (1994b). Caring for carers. In M. Kaila, N. Polemikos & G. Filippou (Eds), *People with Special Needs.* Athens: Ellinika Grammata.

Hawkins, P.J. (1994c). Ideodynamic signalling in psychodynamic psychotherapy. *European Journal of Clinical Hypnosis* **2**(1), 41–44.

Hawkins, P.J. (1994d). Hypnosis in family therapy. *European Journal of Clinical Hypnosis* **1**(3), 1–7.

Hawkins, P.J. (1995). Catharsis in counselling psychology. *Counselling Psychology Review* **10**(2), 11–17.

Hawkins, P.J. (1996). Hypnosis in sex therapy. *European Journal of Clinical Hypnosis* **3**(2), 2–8.

Hawkins, P.J. (1997a). Psychodynamic psychotherapy. In P.J. Hawkins & J.N. Nestoros (Eds), *Psychotherapy: New Perspectives on Theory, Practice and Research* (pp. 97–129). Athens: Ellinika Grammata.

Hawkins, P.J. (1997b). Clinical hypnosis strategies in the treatment of sexual dysfunction. In C. Simonelli, F. Petruccelli & V. Vizzari (Eds), *Sessualita e terzo millennio: Studi e richerche in sessuologia clinica* (Vol. 1, pp. 347–361). Milan: Franco Angeli.

Hawkins, P.J. (1997c). Clinical hypnosis. In P.J. Hawkins & J.N. Nestoros (Eds), *Psychotherapy: New Perspectives on Theory, Practice and Research* (pp. 197–241). Athens: Ellinika Grammata.

Hawkins, P.J. (in press). Hypnoanalysis: An integration of clinical hypnosis and psychodynamic therapy. In E. O'Leary & M. Murphy (Eds), *New Approaches to Integration in Psychotherapy.* London: Brunner Routledge.

Hawkins, P.J., Liossi, C., Ewart, B.E., Hatira, P., Kosmidis, V.H. & Varvutsi, M. (1995). Hypnotherapy for control of anticipatory nausea and vomiting in children with cancer: Preliminary findings. *Psycho-Oncology* **4**, 101–106.

Hawkins, P.J., Liossi, C., Hatira, P., Ewart, B.E. & Kosmidis, V.H. (1998). Hypnosis in the alleviation of procedure related pain and distress in paediatric cancer patients. *Contemporary Hypnosis* **15**(4), 199–207.

Hawkins, P.J. & Polemikos, N. (2002). Hypnosis treatment of sleeping problems in children experiencing loss. *Contemporary Hypnosis* **19**(1), 18–24.

Heap, M. & Aravind, K.K. (2001). *Hartland's Medical and Dental Hypnosis.* Edinburgh: Churchill Livingstone.

Heap, M., Brown, R.J. & Oakley, D.A. (2004). High hypnotizability: Key issues. In M. Heap, R.J. Brown & D.A. Oakley (Eds), *The Highly Hypnotizable Person: Theoretical, Experimental and Clinical Issues* (pp. 5–29). London: Brunner-Routledge.

Hearne, K.M.T. (1993). Hypnosis in the conversion of nightmares to lucid dreams. *European Journal of Clinical Hypnosis* 1(1), 12–17.

Henwood, K. & Nicolson, P. (1995). Qualitative research. *The Psychologist* 8(3), 109–110.

Henwood, K. & Pidgeon, N. (1995). Grounded theory and psychological research. *The Psychologist* 8(3), 115–121.

Herman, J.L. & Schatzow, E. (1987). Recovery and verification of memories of childhood sexual trauma. *Psychoanalytic Psychology* 4, 1–14.

Herold, D.M. & Conlon, E.J. (1981). Work factors as potential causal agents of alcohol abuse. *Journal of Drug Issues* 11, 337–356.

Heron, J. (1971). *Experience and Method*. Guildford: University of Surrey.

Heron, J. (1992). *Feeling and Personhood: Psychology in Another Key*. London: Sage Publications.

Heron, J. (1996). *Co-operative Inquiry: Research into the Human Condition*. London: Sage Publications.

Heron, J. (1998a). *Catharsis in Human Development* (Rev.). Available: www.human-inquiry.com/catharsi.htm.

Heron, J. (1998b). *Co-Counselling Manual* (Rev.). Available: www.shef.ac.uk/personal/c/cci/cciuk/resources/manuals.html.

Heron, J. (2001). *Helping the Client: A Creative Practical Guide* (5th edn). London: Sage Publications.

Heron, J. & Reason, P. (1997). A participatory inquiry paradigm. *Qualitative Inquiry* 3(3), 274–294.

Hilgard, E.R. (1982). Hypnotic susceptibility and implications for measurement. *International Journal of Clinical and Experimental Hypnosis* 33, 394–403.

Hilgard, E.R. & Hilgard, J.R. (1994). *Hypnosis in the Relief of Pain* (rev. edn). Los Altos, CA: William Kaufman.

Hilgard, J.R. & LeBaron, S. (1982). Relief of anxiety and pain in children and adolescents with cancer: Quantitative measures and clinical observations. *International Journal of Clinical and Experimental Hypnosis* 30, 417–442.

Hilgard, J.R. & LeBaron, S. (1984a). *Hypnotherapy of Children with Pain*. Los Altos, CA: William Kaufman.

Hilgard, J.R. & LeBaron, S. (1984b). *Hypnotherapy of Pain in Children with Cancer*. Los Altos, CA: William Kaufmann.

Hilliard, R.B. (1993). Single-case methodology in psychotherapy process and outcome research. *Journal of Consulting and Clinical Psychology* 61(3), 373–380.

Hoareau, J. (1998). Hypnosis in France. In P.J. Hawkins & M. Heap (Eds), *Hypnosis in Europe*. London: Whurr Publishers.

Hollander, E., Simeon, D., & Gorman, J.M. (1994). Anxiety disorders. In R.E. Hales, S.C. Yudofsky & J.A. Talbott (Eds), *Textbook of Psychiatry* (2nd edn). Washington, DC: American Psychiatric Press.

Holmes, E.A., Brown, R.J., Mansell, W., Pasco Fearon, R., Hunter, E.C.M., Frasquilho, F. & Oakley, D.A. (2005). Are there two qualitatively distinct forms of dissociation? A review and some clinical implications. *Clinical Psychology Review* 25, 1–23.

Holmes, T.H. & Rahe, R.H. (1967). The social readjustment rating scale. *Journal of Psychosomatic Research* 11, 213–218.

Houghton, L.A., Heyman, D.J. & Whorwell, P.J. (1996). Symptomatology, quality of live and economic features of irritable bowel syndrome – the effect of hypnotherapy. *Alimentary Pharmacology Therapeutics* **10**(1), 91–95.

Houghton, L.A., Larder, S., Lee, R., Gonosalcorale, W.M., Whelen, V., Randles, J., Cooper, P., Cruikshanks, P., Miller, V. & Whorwell, P.J. (1999). Gut focused hypnotherapy normalizes rectal hypersensitivity in patients with irritable bowel syndrome (IBS). *Gastroenterology* **116**, A1009.

House of Lords Select Committee (2000). *Select Committee on Science and Technology: Sixth Report*, 21 November.

Howsam, D.G. (1999). Hypnosis in the treatment of insomnia, nightmares, and night terrors. *Australian Journal of Clinical and Experimental Hypnosis* **27**(1), 32–39.

Hull, C. (1933/1968). *Hypnosis and Suggestibility*. New York: Appleton-Century-Crofts.

Humphries, A. (1988). Applications of hypnosis to anxiety control. In M. Heap (Ed.), *Hypnosis: Current Clinical, Experimental and Forensic Practices*. London: Croom Helm.

Iphofen, R., Corrin, A. & Ringwood-Walker, C. (2005) Design issues in hypnotherapeutic research. *European Journal of Clinical Hypnosis* **6**(2), 30–37.

Illich, I. (1975). *Medical Nemesis*. London: Calder Boyars.

Irons, R. & Schneider, J.P. (1997). Addictive sexual disorders. In N.S. Miller (Ed.), *Principles and Practice of Addictions in Psychiatry* (pp. 441–457). Philadelphia, PA: W.B. Saunders.

Jack, M.M. (1999). The use of hypnosis for a patient with chronic pain. *Contemporary Hypnosis* **16**(4), 231–237.

Jacobs, E., Pelier, E. & Larkin, D. (1998). Ericksonian hypnosis and approaches with pediatric hematology oncology patients. *American Journal of Clinical Hypnosis* **41**(2), 139–154.

Jaffe, D.T. & Bresler, D.E. (1980). The use of guided imagery as an adjunct to medical diagnosis and treatment. *Journal of Humanistic Psychology* **20**(4), 45–59.

Janet, P. (1907). *The Major Symptoms of Hysteria*. New York: Macmillan Publishing.

Janov, A. (1973). *The Primal Scream*. London: Sphere.

Jencks, B. (1984). Using the patient's breathing rhythm. In W.C. Wester & A.H. Smith (Eds), *Clinical Hypnosis: A Multidisciplinary Approach* (pp. 29–41). Philadelphia, PA: Lippincott.

Jenkins, M.W. & Pritchard, M.H. (1993). Hypnosis: Practical applications and theoretical considerations in normal labour. *British Journal of Obstetrics and Gynaecology* **100**, 221–226.

Johnson, J.H. (1986). *Life Events as Stressors in Childhood and Adolescence*. Newbury Park, CA: Sage Publications.

Johnson, V.C., Walker, L.G., Heys, S.D., Whiting, P.H. & Eremin, O. (1996). Can relaxation training and hypnotherapy modify the immune response to stress, and is hypnotizability relevant? *Contemporary Hypnosis* **13**(2), 100–108.

Jung, C. (1902/1957). *The Collected Works of C.G. Jung: Vol.1, Psychiatric Studies*. Princeton, NJ: Princeton University Press.

Jung, C.G. (1938/1969). Psychology and religion, *The Collected Works of C.G. Jung: Vol. 11, Psychology and Religion, West and East*. (pp. 64–105). Princeton, NJ: Princeton University Press.

Jung, C. (1943/1966). The synthetic or constructive method. In R.C.F. Hull (trans.). *The Collected Works of Jung: Vol. 7, Two Essays on Analytical Psychology* (pp. 80–89). Princeton, NJ: Princeton University Press.

Jung, C. (1954). The practical use of dream analysis. In H. Read, M. Fordham & G. Adler (Eds), *The Collected Works of C.G. Jung: Vol 16, The Practice of Psychology* (pp. 139–161). Princeton, NJ: Princeton University Press.

Jung, C.G. (1969). A review of the complex theory. *Collected Works of C.G. Jung: Vol 8, The Structure and Dynamics of the Psyche*. Princeton, NJ: Princeton University Press.

Kanner, A.D., Coyne, J.C., Schaefer, C. & Lazarus, R.S. (1981). Comparison of two modes of stress measurement: Daily hassles and uplifts versus major life events. *Journal of Behavioral Medicine* 4, 1–39.

Kaplan, H.S. (1974). *The New Sex Therapy: Active Treatment of Sexual Dysfunctions*. New York: Brunner/Mazel Publishers.

Kaplan, H.S. (1979). *Disorders of Sexual Desire and Other New Concepts and Techniques in Sex Therapy*. New York: Brunner/Mazel Publishing.

Kaplan, H.S. (1988). *The Illustrated Manual of Sex Therapy* (2nd edn). New York: Brunner-Routledge.

Kaplan, H.S. (1995). *Sexual Desire Disorders: Dysfunctional Regulation of Sexual Motivation*. New York: Brunner/Mazel Publishing.

Karasek, R. & Theorell, T. (1990). *Healthy Work, Stress, Productivity and the Reconstruction of Working Life*. New York: Basic Books.

Karle, H.W.A. (1988). Hypnosis in the management of tinnitus. In M. Heap (Ed.), *Hypnosis: Current Clinical, Experimental and Forensic Practices*. London: Croom-Helm Limited.

Karle, H. & Boys, J.H. (1987). *Hypnotherapy: A Practical Handbook*. London: Free Association Books.

Katz, N.W. (1979). Comparative efficacy of behavioural training, training plus relaxation, and sleep/trance hypnotic induction in increasing hypnotic susceptibility. *Journal of Consulting and Clinical Psychology* 47, 119–127.

Katz, E.R., Kellerman, J. & Ellenberg, L. (1987). Hypnosis in the reduction of acute pain and distress in children with cancer. *Journal of Pediatric Psychology* 12(3), 379–394.

Kaufer, D., Friedman, A., Seidman, S. & Soreq, H. (1998). Acute stress facilitates long-lasting changes in cholinergic gene expression. *Nature* 393, 373–377.

Keane, T.M. (1998). Psychological and behavioral treatment of posttraumatic stress disorder. In P. Nathan & J. Gorman (Eds), *Treatments That Work*. Oxford: Oxford University Press.

Kellerman, J., Zeltzer, L., Ellenberger, L. & Dash, J. (1983). Adolescents with cancer: Hypnosis for the reduction of acute pain and anxiety associated with medical procedures. *Journal of Adolescent Health Care* 4, 76–81.

Kennerley, H. (1996). Cognitive therapy of dissociative symptoms associated with trauma. *British Journal of Clinical Psychology* 35, 325–340.

Kessler, R. (1999). The consequences of individual differences in preparation for surgery and invasive medical procedures. *Australian Journal of Clinical and Experimental Hypnosis* 27(1), 40–53.

Kessler, R., Sonnega, A., Bromet, E., Hughes, M. & Nelson, C.B. (1995). Posttraumatic stress disorder in the National Comorbidity Survey. *Archives of General Psychiatry* 52, 1048–1060.

Kiecolt-Glaser, J.K. & Glaser, R. (1986). Psychological influences on immunity. *Psychosomatics* 27, 621–624.

Kiecolt-Glaser, J.K. & Glaser, R. (1992). Psychoneuroimmunology: Can psychological interventions modulate immunity? *Journal of Consulting and Clinical Psychology* **60**, 569–575.

Kiecolt-Glaser, J.K., Marucha, P., Atkinson, C. & Glaser, R. (2001). Hypnosis as a modulator of cellular immune dysregulation during acute stress. *Journal of Consulting and Clinical Psychology* **69**, 674–682.

Kilpatrick, D.G. & Resnick, H.S. (1993). Posttraumatic stress disorder associated with criminal victimization in clinical and community populations. In J.R.T. Davidson & E.B. Foa (Eds), *Posttraumatic stress disorder: DSM-IV and beyond* (pp. 113–143). Washington, DC: American Psychiatric Press.

King, A.C., Blair, S.N. & Bild, D.E. (1992). Determinants of physical activity and intervention in adults. *Medicine and Science in Sports and Exercise* **24**, S221–S237.

King, D.W., King, L.A., Gudanowski, D.M. & Vreven, D.L. (1995). Alternative representations of war zone stressors: Relationships to posttraumatic stress disorder in male and female Vietnam veterans. *Journal of Abnormal Psychology* **104**, 184–196.

Kingsbury, S.J. (1993). Brief hypnotic treatment of repetitive nightmares. *American Journal of Clinical Hypnosis* **35**(3), 161–169.

Kirsch, I. & Lynn, S.J. (1995). The altered state of hypnosis: Changes in the theoretical landscape. *American Psychologist* **50**(10), 846–858.

Kirsch, I., Montgomery, G.H. & Sapirstein, A. (1995). Hypnosis as an adjunct to cognitive-behavioral psychotherapy: A meta-analysis. *Journal of Consulting and Clinical Psychology* **63**, 214–220.

Kissen, D.M. (1966). The significance of personality in lung cancer in men. *Annals of the New York Academy of Sciences* **125**, 820–826.

Kissen, D.M. (1967). Psychosocial factors, personality, and lung cancer in men aged 55–64. *British Journal of Medical Psychology* **40**, 69.

Kissen, D.M., Brown, R.I.F. & Kissen, M.A. (1969). A further report on personality and psychological factors in lung cancer. *Annals of the New York Academy of Sciences* **164**, 535–545.

Kleinhauz, M. & Beran, B. (1981). Misuses of hypnosis: A medical emergency and its treatment. *International Journal of Clinical and Experimental Hypnosis* **29**, 148–161.

Kleinplatz, P. (Ed.). (2001). *New Directions in Sex Therapy: Innovations and Alternatives.* Florence, KY: Brunner-Routledge.

Kluft, R.P. (1988). On treating the older patient with multiple personality disorder: 'Race against time' or 'Make haste slowly'. *American Journal of Clinical Hypnosis* **30**, 257–266.

Koblenzer, C. (1988). Stress and the skin: Significance of emotional factors in dermatology. *Stress Medicine* **4**, 21–26.

Kohen, D.P., Mahowald, M.W. & Rosen, G.M. (1992). Sleep-terror disorder in children: The role of self-hypnosis in management. *American Journal of Clinical Hypnosis* **34**, 233–244.

Kohen, D., Olness, K., Colwell, S. & Heimel, A. (1984). The use of relaxation-mental imagery (self-hypnosis) in the management of 505 pediatric behavioral encounters. *Developmental and Behavioural Pediatrics* **5**, 21–25.

Kopp, R.R. (1995). *Metaphor Therapy.* New York: Brunner Mazel Incorporated.

Kroger, W.S. (1952). Natural childbirth: Is the Reid method of 'natural childbirth' waking hypnosis? *Medical Times* **80**, 152.

Kroger, W.S. (1977). *Clinical and Experimental Hypnosis in Medicine, Dentistry and Psychology.* Philadelphia, PA: Lippincott.

Kuttner, L. (1986). *No Fears No Tears: Children With Cancer Coping With Pain* [video guide production]. Vancouver: Canadian Cancer Society.

Laing, R.D. (1983). *The Voice of Experience.* Harmondsworth: Penguin Books Ltd.

Lake, F. (1981). *Tight Corners in Pastoral Counselling.* London: Darton, Longman and Todd Limited.

Lamb, M.E. (1994). The investigation of child sexual abuse: An interdisciplinary consensus statement. *Child Abuse and Neglect* **18**(12), 1021–1028.

Lambert, M.J. (1992). Psychotherapy outcome research: Implications for integrative and eclectic therapists. In J.C. Norcross & M.R. Goldfried (Eds), *Handbook of Psychotherapy Integration* (pp. 94–129). New York: Basic Books.

Lambert, S.A. (1996). The effects of hypnosis/guided imagery on the postoperative course of children. *Journal of Developmental and Behavioral Pediatrics* **17**(5), 307–310.

Lambert, M.J. & Bergin, A.E. (1994). The effectiveness of psychotherapy. In S.L. Garfield & A.E. Bergin (Eds), *Handbook of Psychotherapy and Behavior Change* (4th edn, pp. 143–189). New York: Wiley.

Lang, E.V., Benotsch, E.G. & Fick, L.J. (2000). Adjunctive non-pharmacological analgesia for invasive medical procedures: A randomised clinical trial. *The Lancet* **355**(9214), 1486–1490.

Lankton, S. (1980). *Practical Magic.* Cupertino, CA: Meta Publications.

Lankton, S.R. & Lankton, C.H. (1983). *The Answer Within: A Clinical Framework for Ericksonian Hypnotherapy.* New York: Brunner/Mazel Publishing.

Lankton, S.R. & Lankton, C.H. (1986). *Enchantment and Intervention in Family Therapy.* New York: Brunner/Mazel Publishing.

Lankton, S. & Lankton, C. (1987). *Enchantment and Intervention.* New York: Brunner/Mazel Publishing.

Laszlo, J. (1983). *Antiemetics and Cancer Chemotherapy.* Baltimore, MD: Williams & Wilkins.

Laudenslager, M.L., Ryan, S.M., Drugan, R.C., Hysen, R.L. & Maier, S.F. (1983). Coping and immunosuppression: Inescapable but not escapable shock suppresses lymphocyte proliferation. *Science* **221**, 568–570.

Lazarus, R.S. (1975). A cognitively oriented psychologist looks at biofeedback. *American Psychologist* **30**, 553–561.

Lazarus, R.S. & Cohen, F. (1973). Active coping processes, coping dispositions, and recovery from surgery. *Psychosomatic Medicine* **35**, 375–389.

Lazarus, R.S. & Cohen, F. (1977). Environmental stress. In L. Altman & J.F. Wohlwill (Eds), *Human Behavior and the Environment: Current Theory and Research* (Vol. 2, pp. 89–127). New York: Plenum Publishing.

Lazarus, R.S. & Folkman, S. (1987). Transactional theory and research on emotions and coping. *European Journal of Personality* **1**, 141–170.

Lea, R., Houghton, L.A., Calvert, E.L., Larder, S., Gonsalkorale, W.M., Whelan, V., Randles, J., Cooper, P., Cruikshanks, P., Miller, V. & Whorwell, P.J. (2003). Gut focused hypnotherapy normalizes disordered rectal sensitivity in patients with irritable bowel syndrome. *Alimentary Pharmacology Therapeutics* **17**(5), 635–642.

LeCron, L. (1954). A hypnotic technique for uncovering unconscious material. *Journal of Experimental and Clinical Hypnosis* **2**, 76–79.

Leiblum, S.R. & Rosen, G.M. (2000). *Principles and Practice of Sex Therapy* (3rd edn). New York: Guilford Press.

LeShan, L.L. (1977). *You Can Fight for Your Life*. New York: M. Evans & Company.

Leskin, G.A., Kaloupek, D.G. & Keane, T.M. (1998). Treatment for traumatic memories: Review and recommendations. *Clinical Psychology Review* 18(8), 983–1002.

Levenson, H. & Butler, S.F. (1994). Brief dynamic individual psychotherapy. In R.E. Hales, S.C. Yudofsky & J.A. Talbott (Eds), *Textbook of Psychiatry* (2nd edn, pp. 1009–1033). Washington, DC: American Psychiatric Press.

Levine, P. (1991). The body as healer: A revisioning of trauma and anxiety. In M. Sheets-Johnstone (Ed.), *Giving the Body its Due* (pp. 85–108). Stonybrook, NY: State University of New York Press.

Levine, P. (1994). *Encountering the Tiger: How the Body Heals Trauma*. Lyons, CO: Ergo Institute Press.

Levit, H.I. (1971). Marital crisis intervention: Hypnosis in impotence-frigidity cases. *American Journal of Clinical Hypnosis* 14(1), 56–60.

Lichtenstein, E., Weiss, S.M. & Hitchcock, J.L. (1986). Task force 3: Patterns of smoking relapse. *Health Psychology* 5(supplement), 29–40.

Liossi, C. & Hatira, P. (1999). Clinical hypnosis versus cognitive behavior training for pain management with pediatric cancer patients undergoing bone marrow aspirations. *International Journal of Clinical and Experimental Hypnosis* 47, 104–116.

Lowen, A. (1975). *Bioenergetics*. London: Coventure Limited.

Luborsky, L. (1995). Are common factors across different psychotherapies the main explanation for the Dodo bird verdict that 'Everyone has won so all shall have prizes'? *Clinical Psychology: Science and Practice* 2, 106–109.

Luborsky, L., Crits-Christoph, R., Alexander, L., Margolis, M. & Cohen, M. (1983). Two helping alliance methods of predicting outcomes of psychotherapy. *Journal of Nervous and Mental Disease* 171, 480–491.

Lynn, S. & Hallquist, M.N. (2004). Toward a scientifically based understanding of Milton H. Erickson's strategies and tactics: Hypnosis, response sets and common factors in psychotherapy. *Contemporary Hypnosis* 21(2), 63–78.

Lynn, S.J., Neufeld, V., Rhue, J.W. & Matorin, A. (1994). Hypnosis and smoking cessation: A cognitive behavioural treatment. In S.J. Lynn, J.W. Rhue & I. Kirsch (Eds), *Handbook of Clinical Hypnosis*. Washington, DC: American Psychological Association.

Mackinnon, C. (1998). Working with adult survivors of child sexual abuse. *European Journal of Clinical Hypnosis* 4(4), 190–195.

Madanes, C. (2001). The therapist as humanist, social activist, and systemic thinker. *Paper presented at the 8th International Congress on Ericksonian Approaches to Hypnosis and Psychotherapy*, Phoenix, AZ.

Maddi, S. & Kobasa, S.G. (1984). *The Hardy Executive: Health Under Stress*. Homewood, IL: Dow Jones-Irwin.

Mair, M. (1989). *Between Psychology and Psychotherapy: A Poetics of Experience*. London: Routledge.

Mairs, D.A.E. (1995). Hypnosis and pain in childbirth. *Contemporary Hypnosis* 12(2), 111–118.

Malan, D. (1963). *A Study of Brief Psychotherapy*. New York: Plenum Publishing.

Malarkey, W., Glaser, R., Kiecolt-Glaser, J.K. & Marucha, P. (2001). Behavior: The endocrine-immune interface and health outcomes. *Advances in Psychosomatic Medicine* 22, 104–115.

Mantle, F. (1999). Hypnosis in the management of eczema in children. *Paediatric Nursing* 11(5), 24–26.

Mantle, F. (2001). Hypnosis in the management of eczema in children. *Nursing Standard* **15**(51), 41–44.

Margolis, C.G. & DeClement, F.A. (1980). Hypnosis in the treatment of burns. *Burns* **6**, 253–254.

Marlatt, G.A. & Gordon, J.R. (1985). *Relapse Prevention: Maintenance Strategies in the Treatment of Addictive Behaviors.* New York: Guilford Press.

Maslow, A.H. (1973). *The Farther Reaches of Human Nature.* Harmondsworth: Penguin Books.

Massarini, M., Rovetto, F. & Tagliaferri, C. (2005). Preoperative hypnosis: A controlled study to assess the effects on anxiety and pain in the postoperative period. *European Journal of Clinical Hypnosis* **6**(1), 8–15.

Masters, W.H., Johnson, V.E. & Kolodny, R.C. (1995). *Human Sexuality.* New York: Longman Group.

Matthews, M. & Flatt, S. (1999). The efficacy of hypnotherapy in the treatment of migraine. *Nursing Standard* **14**(7), 33–36.

McCrone, J. (1999). *Going Inside: A Tour Round a Single Moment of Consciousness.* London: Faber & Faber.

McDaniel, J.S., Moran, M.G., Levenson, J.L. & Stoudemire, A. (1994). Psychological factors affecting medical conditions. In R.E. Hales, S.C. Yudofsky & J.A. Talbott (Eds), *Textbook of Psychiatry* (Vol. 2). Washington, DC: American Psychiatric Press.

McDermott, D. & Snyder, C.R. (1999). *Making Hope Happen.* Oakland/San Francisco, CA: New Harbinger Press.

McGrath, P.A. (1990). *Pain in Children: Nature, Assessment and Treatment.* London: Guilford Press.

McLeod, J. (1994). *Doing Counselling Research.* London: Sage Publications.

McNally, R.J. (2003). *Remembering Trauma.* Cambridge, MA: Belknap Press/Harvard University Press.

McNeal, S. & Frederick, C. (1993). Inner strength and other techniques for ego-strengthening. *American Journal of Clinical Hypnosis* **35**, 170–178.

Medd, D.Y. (2001). Fear of injections: The value of hypnosis in facilitating clinical treatment. *Contemporary Hypnosis* **18**(2), 100–106.

Meichenbaum, D. (1995). *A Clinical Handbook/Practical Therapist Manual for Assessing and Treating Adults with Post-Traumatic Stress Disorder.* Waterloo, Canada: Institute Press.

Melzack, R. (1975). The McGill Pain Questionnaire: Major properties and scoring methods. *Pain* **1**, 277–299.

Meyer, T.J. & Mark, M.M. (1995). Effects of psychological interventions with adult cancer patients: a meta-analysis of randomised experiments. *Health Psychology* **14**, 101–108.

Michaud, C., Kahn, J.P. & Musse, N. (1990). Relationships between a critical life event and eating behaviour in high-school students. *Stress Medicine* **6**, 57–64.

Mills, J.C. & Crowley, R.J. (1986). *Therapeutic Metaphors for Children and the Child Within.* New York: Brunner/Mazel Publishing.

Milne, G. (1985). Hypnorelaxation for essential hypertension. *Australian Journal of Clinical and Experimental Hypnosis* **13**, 113–116.

Montgomery, G.H., David, D., Winkel, G., Silverstein, J.H. & Bovbjerg, D.H. (2002). The effectiveness of adjunctive hypnosis with surgical patients: A meta-analysis. *Anesthesia and Analgesia* **94**, 1639–1645.

Moos, R.H. & Schaefer, J.A. (1984). The crisis of physical illness: An overview and conceptual approach. In R.H. Moos (Ed.), *Coping with Physical Illness: New Perspectives* (Vol. 2, pp. 3–35). New York: Plenum Publishing.

Moos, R.H. & Swindle, R.W. (1990). Stressful life circumstances: Concepts and measures. *Stress Medicine* **6**, 171–178.

Moreno, J.L. (1946). *Psychodrama* (Vol. 1). New York: Beacon House Incorporated.

Morgan, A.H. & Hilgard, J.R. (1978a). Stanford hypnotic clinical scale for adults. *American Journal of Clinical Hypnosis* **21**, 134–147.

Morgan, A.H. & Hilgard, J.R. (1978b). Stanford hypnotic clinical scale for children. *American Journal of Clinical Hypnosis* **21**, 148–168.

Morgan, M., McCreedy, R., Simpson, J. & Hay, R.J. (1997). Dermatology quality of life scales – a measure of the impact of skin diseases. *British Journal of Dermatology* **133**, 202–206.

Morimoto, R. (2001). *Stress Induced Gene Expression.* Available: www.grc.uri.edu/programs/2001/stress.htm.

Morton, J., Andrew, B., Bekerian, D., Brewin, C.R., Davies, G.M. & Mollon, P. (1995). *Recovered Memories.* Leicester: British Psychological Society.

Murcott, T. (2005). *The Whole Story.* Basingstoke: Macmillan Publishing.

Nath, S. & Warren, J. (1995). Hypnosis and examination stress in adolescence. *Contemporary Hypnosis* **12**(2), 119–124.

Nestoros, J.N., Vasdekis, V.G.S., Patakou-Parassiri, V. & Sfakianakis, G. (1998). Hypnosis in Greece. In P.J. Hawkins & M. Heap (Eds), *Hypnosis in Europe.* London: Whurr Publishers.

Neylan, M.D., Reynolds, C.E. & Kupfer, D.J. (1994). Sleep disorders. In R.E. Hales, S.C. Yudofsky & J.A. Talbott (Eds), *Textbook of Psychiatry* (2nd edn, pp. 833–855). Washington, DC: American Psychiatric Press.

Nichols, M.P. & Zax, M. (1977). *Catharsis in Psychotherapy.* New York: Gardner Press.

Oakley, D., Alden, P. & Degun-Mather, M. (1996). The use of hypnosis in therapy with adults. *The Psychologist* **9**(11), 502–505.

Ogden, J. (2000). *Health Psychology* (2nd edn). Buckingham: Open University Press.

O'Leary, E. (1993). Empathy in the person centred and gestalt approaches. *British Gestalt Journal* **2**, 111–115.

Olness, K.N. & Gardner, G.C. (1988). *Hypnosis and Hypnotherapy with Children.* London: Grune & Stratton.

Olness, K. & Kohen, D. (1996). *Hypnosis and Hypnotherapy with Children* (3rd edn). New York: Guilford Press.

Oster, M.I. & Sauer, C.P. (2000). Hypnotic methods for preparing for childbirth. In L.M. Hornyak & J.P. Green (Eds), *Healing from Within: The Use of Hypnosis in Women's Health Care* (pp. 161–190). Washington, DC: American Psychological Association.

Panksepp, J. (2004). *Affective Neuroscience: The Foundations of Human and Animal Emotions.* Oxford: Oxford University Press.

Parient, J., White, P., Frackowiak, R.S.J. & Lewith, G. (2005). Expectancy and belief modulate the neuronal substrates of pain treated by acupuncture. *NeuroImage* **25**(4), 1161–1167.

Patterson, D.R. (2004). Treating pain with hypnosis. *Current Directions in Psychological Science* **13**(6), 252–255.

Patterson, D.R., Everett, J.J., Burns, G.L. & Marvin, J.A. (1992). Hypnosis for treatment of burn pain. *Journal of Consulting and Clinical Psychology* **60**, 713–717.

Pederson, L., Scrimjeour, W. & Lefcoe, N. (1975). Comparison of hypnosis plus counseling, counseling alone, and hypnosis alone in a community service smoking withdrawal program. *Journal of Counseling and Clinical Psychology* **43**, 920.

Pekala, R.J. (1995a). A short, unobstrusive hypnotic procedure for assessing hypnotizability level: I. Development and research. *American Journal of Clinical Hypnosis* **37**(4), 271–283.

Pekala, R.J. (1995b). A short unobtrusive hypnotic induction for assessing hypnotizability: II. Clinical case reports. *American Journal of Clinical Hypnosis* **37**(4), 284–293.

Perkins, K.A., Grobe, J.E., Stiller, R.L., Fonte, C. & Goettler, J.E. (1992). Nasal spray nicotine replacement suppresses cigarette smoking desire and behavior. *Clinical Pharmacology and Therapeutics* **52**, 627–634.

Perls, F.S. (1969). *Gestalt Therapy Verbatim.* Moab, UT: Real People Press.

Perls, F., Hefferline, R.F. & Goodman, P. (1951). *Gestalt Therapy: Excitement and Growth in the Human Personality.* New York: Dell Publishing.

Perry, C., Gelfand, R. & Marcovitch, P. (1979). The relevance of hypnotic susceptibility in the clinical context. *Journal of Abnormal Psychology* **89**, 598–603.

Perry, C. & Mullin, G. (1975). The effects of hypnotic susceptibility on reducing smoking behavior treated by an hypnotic technique. *Journal of Clinical Psychology* **31**, 498–505.

Pertot, S. (2005). *Perfectly Normal: A Woman's Guide to Living With Low Libido.* New York: Rodale Institute.

Petrie, K.J., Booth, R.J. & Pennebaker, J.W. (1998). The immunological effects of thought suppression. *Journal of Personality and Social Psychology* **75**, 1264–1272.

Peynovska, R., Fisher, J., Oliver, D. & Mathew, V.M. (2005). Efficacy of hypnotherapy as a supplement therapy in cancer intervention. *European Journal of Clinical Hypnosis* **6**(1), 2–7.

Phillips, M. (1993). The use of ego-state therapy in the treatment of posttraumatic stress disorder. *American Journal of Clinical Hypnosis* **35**(4), 241–249.

Phillips, M. & Frederick, C. (1995). *Healing the Divided Self: Clinical and Ericksonian Hypnotherapy for Post-Traumatic and Dissociative Conditions.* New York/London: W.W. Norton.

Pierce, R.A., Nichols, M.P. & DuBrin, J.R. (1983). *Emotional Expression in Psychotherapy.* New York: Gardner Press.

Pietrofesa, J.J., Hoffman, A. & Splete, H.H. (1984). *Counseling: An Introduction* (2nd edn). Boston, MA: Houghton Mifflin.

Pinnell, C.M. & Covino, N.A. (2000). Empircal findings on the use of hypnosis in medicine: A critical review. *International Journal of Clinical and Experimental Hypnosis* **48**, 170–194.

Pirsig, R. (1974). *Zen and the Art of Motorcycle Maintenance.* London: Bodley Head.

Poncelet, N.M. (1990). An Ericksonian approach to childbirth. In D.C. Hammond (Ed.), *Handbook of Hypnotic Suggestions and Metaphors* (pp. 382–386). New York: W.W. Norton.

Price, M.I., Mottahedin, I. & Mayo, P.R. (1991). Can hypnotherapy help patients with psoriasis? *Clinical and Experimental Dermatology* **16**, 114–117.

Progoff, I. (1977). *The Well and the Cathedral* (2nd edn). New York: Dialogue House Library.

Progoff, I. (1982). *At a Journal Workshop: The Basic Text and Guide for Using the Intensive Journal Process.* New York: Dialogue House Library.

Putman, F.W. (1989). *Diagnosis and Treatment of Multiple Personality Disorder.* New York: Guilford Press.

Pynoos, R.S., Goenjian, A.K., Tashjian, M., Karakashian, M., Maniikian, R., Manoukian, G., Steinberg, A.M. & Fairbanks, L.A. (1993). Post-traumatic stress reactions in children after the 1988 Armenian earthquake. *British Journal of Psychiatry* **163**, 239–247.

Reason, P. (Ed.) (1988). *Human Inquiry in Action: Developments in New Paradigm Research.* London: Sage Publications.

Reason, P. (1994). Three approaches to participative inquiry. In N.K. Denzin & Y.S. Lincoln (Eds), *Handbook of Qualitative Research* (pp. 324–339). Thousand Oaks, CA: Sage Publications.

Reason, P. & Bradbury, H. (Eds). (2001a). *Handbook of Action Research, Participative Inquiry and Practice.* London: Sage Publications.

Reason, P. & Bradbury, H. (2001b). Inquiry and participation in search of a world worthy of human aspiration. In P. Reason & H. Bradbury (Eds), *Handbook of Action Research, Participative Inquiry and Practice* (pp. 1–14). London: Sage Publications.

Reason, P. & Heron, J. (1995). Co-operative inquiry. In R. Harre, J. Smith & L. Van Langenhove (Eds), *Rethinking Methods in Psychology* (pp. 122–142). London: Sage Publications.

Reason, P. & Heron, J. (1996). *A Layperson's Guide to Cooperative Inquiry.* Centre for Action Research in Professional Practice, University of Bath. Available: www.bath.ac.uk/carpp/LAYGUIDE.htm.

Reason, P. & Rowan, J. (Eds). (1981). *Human Inquiry: A Sourcebook of New Paradigm Research.* Chichester: John Wiley & Sons.

Reich, W. (1961). *The Function of the Orgasm.* New York: Farrar, Straus & Giroux.

Reik, T. (1948). *Listening with the Third Ear.* New York: Farrar.

Rennie, D.L. & Toukmanian, S.G. (1992). Explanation in psychotherapy process research. In S.G. Toukmanian & D.L. Rennie (Eds), *Psychotherapy Process Research* (pp. 234–251). London: Sage Publications.

Ribeiro, S., Goyal, V., Mello, C. & Pavlides, C. (1999). Brain gene expression during REM sleep depends on prior waking experience. *Learning and Memory* **6**, 500–508.

Rice, L.N. & Greenberg, L.S. (Eds). (1984). *Patterns of Change.* New York: Guilford Press.

Roberts, L.M. (2005). Trial design in hypnotherapy: Does the RCT have a place? *European Journal of Clinical Hypnosis* **6**(1), 16–19.

Rogers, C. (1951). *Client-Centered Therapy.* London: Constable.

Rogers, C. (1971). *Freedom to Learn.* Columbus, OH: Charles Merril.

Rogers, C. (1980). *A Way of Being.* Boston, MA: Houghton Mifflin.

Rose, S. (2005). *The 21st Century Brain: Explaining, Mending and Manipulating the Mind.* London: Jonathan Cape.

Rossi, E. (1972). *Dreams and the Growth of Personality: Expanding Awareness in Psychotherapy.* New York: Pergamon.

Rossi, E. (1982). Hypnosis and ultradian cycles: A new state(s) theory of hypnosis? *American Journal of Clinical Hypnosis* **25**(1), 21–32.

Rossi, E. (1986/1993). *The Psychobiology of Mind–Body Healing: New Concepts of Therapeutic Hypnosis* (rev. edn). New York: W.W. Norton.

Rossi, E. (1990). From mind to molecule: More than a metaphor. In J. Zeig & S. Gilligan (Eds), *Brief Therapy: Myths, Methods and Metaphors.* New York: Brunner/Mazel Publishing.

Rossi, E. (1995a). The essence of therapeutic suggestion: Part one. The basic accessing question and ultradian dynamics in single session psychotherapy. *European Journal of Clinical Hypnosis* **2**(3), 6–17.

Rossi, E. (1995b). The essence of therapeutic suggestion: Part two. Ultradian dynamics of the creative process in psychotherapy. *European Journal of Clinical Hypnosis* **2**(4), 4–16.

Rossi, E.L. (1996). *The Symptom Path to Enlightenment.* Palisades, CA: Palisades Gateway.

Rossi, E. (1997). The symptom path to enlightenment: The psychobiology of Jung's constructive method. *Psychological Perspectives* **36**, 68–84.

Rossi, E. (2000). In search of a deep psychobiology of hypnosis: Visionary hypotheses for a new millenium. *American Journal of Clinical Hypnosis* **42**(3/4), 178–207.

Rossi, E.L. (2002). *The Psychobiology of Gene Expression.* New York and London: W.W. Norton.

Rossi, E. (2003a). Gene expression, neurogenesis, and healing: Psychosocial genomics of therapeutic hypnosis. *American Journal of Clinical Hypnosis* **45**(3), 197–216.

Rossi, E. (2003b). *A Dream Series Reflecting Stroke Rehabilitation Via Activity-Dependent Gene Expression and Neurogenesis.* Available: www.ernestrossi.com.

Rossi, E. (2005) The ideodynamic action hypothesis of therapeutic suggestion: Creative replay of the psychosocial genomics of therapeutic hypnosis. *European Journal of Clinical Hypnosis* **6**(2), 2–12.

Rossi, E. & Cheek, D.B. (1988). *Mind–Body Therapy.* New York: W.W. Norton.

Rossi, E., Lippencott, B. & Bessette, A. (1994). The chronobiology of mind–body healing: Ultradian dynamics in hypnotherapy. Part 1. *European Journal of Clinical Hypnosis* **2**(1), 10–20.

Rossi, E., Lippencott, B. & Bessette, A. (1995). The chronobiology of mind–body healing: Ultradian dynamics in hypnotherapy. Part 2. *European Journal of Clinical Hypnosis* **2**(2), 6–14.

Rossi, E. & Nimmons, D. (1991). *The Twenty-Minute Break: The Ultradian Healing Response.* New York: Zeig, Tucker, Theisen.

Ruzyla-Smith, P., Barabasz, A., Barabasz, M. & Warner, D. (1995). Effects of hypnosis on the immune response: B-cells, T-cells, helper and suppressor cells. *American Journal of Clinical Hypnosis* **38**, 71–79.

Sackett, D.L., Rosenberg, W.M.C. & Gray, J.A. (1996). Evidence-based medicine: What it is and what it isn't? *British Medical Journal* **312**, 71–72.

Salmon, P. (1983). A personal approach to teaching psychology. In D. Pilgrim (Ed.), *Psychology and Psychotherapy.* London: Routledge & Kegan Paul.

Samad, T., Moore, K., Sapirstein, A., Billet, S., Allchorne, A., Poole, S., Bonventre, J.V. & Woolf, C.J. (2001). Interleukin-1-mediated induction of Cox-2 in the CNS contributes to inflammatory pain hypersensitivity. *Nature* **410**, 471–475.

Schaefer, C. (1995). *Clinical Handbook of Sleep Disorders in Children.* Northvale, NJ: Jason Aronson Publishers.

Schafer, D.W. (1997). Hypnosis and the treatment of ulcerative colitis and Crohn's disease. *American Journal of Clinical Hypnosis* **40**, 111–117.

Scheff, T. (1979). *Catharsis in Healing, Ritual, and Drama.* Berkeley, CA: University of California Press.

Schmale, A.H. & Iker, H. (1966). The psychological setting of uterine cervical cancer. *Annals of the New York Academy of Sciences* **125**, 807–813.

Schneck, J.M. (1970). The psychotherapeutic use of hypnosis: Case illustrations of direct hypnotherapy. *International Journal of Clinical and Experimental Hypnosis* **18**(1), 15–24.

Schneider, J.P. & Irons, R. (1998). Addictive sexual disorders: Differential diagnosis and treatment. *Primary Psychiatry*, April, 65–70.

Schultz, J.H. & Luthe, W. (1959). *Autogenic Training: A Psychophysiological Approach in Psychotherapy.* New York: Grune and Stratton.

Schultz, J.H. & Luthe, W. (1969). *Autogenic Therapy: Vol. 1 – Autogenic Methods.* New York: Grune and Stratton.

Schutz, J. (1998). Preparation for surgery using hypnosis. *Australian Journal of Clinical and Experimental Hypnosis* **26**(1), 49–56.

Schwartz, B. (2005). *The Paradox of Choice: Why More is Less.* New York: HarperCollins.

Selye, H. (1956). *The Stress of Life.* New York: McGraw-Hill.

Shapiro, F. (1995). *Eye Movement Desensitisation and Reprocessing: Basic Principles, Protocols, and Procedures.* New York: Guilford Press.

Shenefelt, P.D. (2000). Hypnosis in dermatology. *Archives of Dermatology* **136**(3), 393–399.

Shenefelt, P.D. (2003a). Biofeedback, cognitive-behavioral methods, and hypnosis in dermatology: Is it all in your mind? *Dermatologic Therapy* **16**, 114–122.

Shenefelt, P.D. (2003b). Hypnosis-facilitated relaxation using self-guided imagery during dermatologic procedures. *American Journal of Clinical Hypnosis* **45**(3), 225–232.

Shone, R. (1994). From Epidaurus' temples to Ericksonian therapists. *European Journal of Clinical Hypnosis* **1**(4), 46–50.

Siegel, M., Brisman, J. & Weinshal, M. (1997). *Surviving an Eating Disorder: New Perspectives and Strategies for Family and Friends.* New York: HarperCollins.

Siegfried, J., Bourdeau, H., Davis, A., Luketich, J. & Shriver, S. (2000). Expression of gastric-releasing peptide receptor, but not neuromedin B receptor, is related to sex, smoking history, and risk for lung cancer. *Proceedings of the American Association of Cancer Research* **41**, 147.

Sifneos, P.E. (1979). *Short-Term Dynamic Psychotherapy.* New York: Plenum Publishing Corporation.

Simonton, O.C., Matthews-Simonton, S. & Creighton, J. (1978). *Getting Well Again.* Los Angeles, CA: J.P. Tarcher Incorporated.

Simren, M., Ringstrom, G., Bjornsson, E. & Abrahamsson, H. (2004). Treatment with hypnotherapy reduces the sensory and motor component of the gastrocolonic response in irritable bowel syndrome. *Psychosomatic Medicine* **66**(2), 233–238.

Singer, J. (1973). *Boundaries of the Soul: The Practice of Jung's Psychology.* New York: Anchor Press.

Singer, J.L. (1974). *Imagery and Daydream Methods in Psychotherapy and Behavior Modification.* New York: Academic Press.

Smith, J.A., Jarman, M. & Osborn, M. (1999). Doing interpretive phenomenological analysis. In M. Murray & K.A. Chamberlain (Eds), *Qualitative Health Psychology: Theories and Methods* (pp. 218–240). London: Sage Publications.

Snyder, C.R., McDermott, D., Cook, W. & Rapoff, M. (in press). *Hope for Journeys: Giving Children Stories to Grow On.* Boulder, CO: Westview/HarperCollins.

Snyder, C.R. & Taylor, J.D. (2000). Hope as a common factor across psychotherapy approaches: A lesson from the 'Dodo's Verdict'. In C.R. Snyder (Ed.), *Handbook of*

Hope: Theory, Measures, and Applications (pp. 89–108). San Diego, CA: Academic Press.

Sokel, B., Lansdown, R., Atherton, D.J., Glover, M. & Knibbs, J.A. (1993). A comparison of hypnotherapy and biofeedback in the treatment of childhood atopic eczema. *Contemporary Hypnosis* **10**(3), 145–154.

Solloway, K. (2004a). Where is the evidence? Hypnotherapy research index 2003–2004. *European Journal of Clinical Hypnosis* **5**(4), 56–58.

Solloway, K. (2004b). Can clinical hypnosis prevent stress-related immune deficiency? *European Journal of Clincial Hypnosis* **5**(5), 44–56.

Solloway, K. (2005). Irritable bowel syndrome (IBS) and other functional gastrointestinal (GI) disorders. *European Journal of Clinical Hypnosis* **6**(1), 31–36.

Solms, M. (2004). Freud returns. *Scientific American* **290**(5), 57–63.

Spiegel, D. (1994). Dissociative disorders. In R.E. Hales, S.C. Yudofsky & J.A. Talbott (Eds), *Textbook of Psychiatry* (2nd edn). Washington, DC: American Psychiatric Press.

Spiegel, D. (1996). Hypnosis in the treatment of post-traumatic stress disorder. In S.J. Lynn, I. Kirsch & J.W. Rhue (Eds), *Casebook of Clinical Hypnosis* (pp. 99–112). Washington, DC: American Psychological Association.

Spiegel, D., Bloom, J.R., Kramer, H.C. & Gottheil, E. (1989). Effect of psychological treatment on survival of patients with metastatic breast cancer. *The Lancet* **2**(8668), 888–891.

Spiegel, H., Greenleaf, M. & Spiegel, D. (2000). Hypnosis. In B. Sadock & V. Sadock (Eds), *Comprehensive Textbook of Psychiatry* (Vol. 2, 7th edn). Philadelphia, PA: Lippincott Williams & Wilkins.

Spiegel, H. & Spiegel, D. (1978). *Trance and Treatment: Clinical Uses of Hypnosis*. New York: Basic Books.

Spiegle, H. & Spiegel, D. (2004). *Trance and Treatment: Clinical Uses of Hypnosis* (2nd edn). Arlington, VA: American Phychiatric Publishing, Inc.

Stamenkovic, I. (2003). Extracellular matrix remodelling: The role of matrix metalloproteinases. *Journal of Pathology* **200**(4), 448–464.

Stanton, H.E. (1979). Increasing internal control through hypnotic ego-enhancement. *Australian Journal of Clinical and Experimental Hypnosis* **7**, 219–223.

Stanton, H.E. (1989). Ego-enhancement: A five-step approach. *American Journal of Clinical Hypnosis* **31**, 192–198.

Stanton, H.E. (1990). Ego-enhancement: A five-step approach. In D.C. Hammond (Ed.), *Handbook of Hypnotic Suggestions and Metaphors*. New York: W.W. Norton.

Stanton, H.E. (1991). The reduction in secretarial stress. *Contemporary Hypnosis* **8**(1), 45–50.

Stein, C. (1963). The clenched fist technique as a hypnotic procedure in clinical psychotherapy. *American Journal of Clinical Hypnosis* **6**, 113–119.

Steptoe, A., Wardle, J. & Marmot, M. (2005). Positive affect and health-related neuroendocrine, cardiovascular, and inflammatory processes. *Proceedings of the National Academy of Sciences* **102**(18), 6508–6512.

Stevenson, C. & Cooper, N. (1997). Qualitative and quantitative research. *The Psychologist* **10**(4), 159–160.

Stewart, A.C. & Thomas, S.E. (1995). Hypnotherapy as a treatment for atopic dermatitis in adults and children. *British Journal of Dermatology* **132**, 778–783.

Stone, A.A., Cox, D.S., Valdimarsdottir, H., Jandorf, L. & Neale, J.M. (1987). Evidence that secretary IgA antibody is associated with daily mood. *Journal of Personality and Social Psychology* **52**, 988–993.

Stoney, C.M., Mathews, K.A., McDonald, R.H. & Johnson, C.A. (1990). Sex differences in acute stress response: Lipid, lipoprotein, cardiovascular and neuroendocrine adjustments. *Psychophysiology* **12**, 52–61.

Stores, G. (1996). Practitioner review: Assessment and treatment of sleep disorders in children and adolescents. *Journal of Child Psychology and Psychiatry* **37**, 907–925.

Strain, J.J., Newcorn, J., Wolf, D., & Fulop, G. (1994). Adjustment disorder. In R.E. Hales, S.C. Yudofsky & J.A. Talbott (Eds), *Textbook of Psychiatry* (2nd edn). Washington, DC: American Psychiatric Press.

Strupp, H.H. (1983). *Psychotherapy: Clinical, Research and Theoretical Issues*. New York: Jason Aronson Publishers.

Strupp, H.H. & Binder, J.L. (1984). *Psychotherapy in a New Key: A Guide to Time-Limited Dynamic Psychotherapy*. New York: Basic Books.

Switz, D.M. (1976). What the gastroenterologist does all day? *Gastroenterology* **70**, 1048–1050.

Syrjala, K., Cummings, C. & Donaldson, G. (1992). Hypnosis or cognitive behavioural training for a reduction of pain and nausea during cancer treatment: A controlled clinical trial. *Pain* **48**, 137–146.

Tasini, M.F. & Hackett, T.P. (1977). Hypnosis in the treatment of warts in immuno-deficient children. *American Journal of Clinical Hypnosis* **19**, 152–154.

Tausk, F. & Whitmore, S.E. (1999). A pilot study of hypnosis in the treatment of patients with psoriasis. *Psychotherapy and Psychosomatics* **68**(4), 221–225.

Thomson, L. (2005). *Harry the Hypno-Potamus: Metaphorical Tales for Pediatric Problems*. Bancyfelin, Carmarthenshire: Crown House Publishing.

Thompson, W. & Shapiro, J. (1996). *Alopecia Areata: Understanding and Coping With Hair Loss*. Baltimore, MD: John Hopkins University Press.

Tibia, J., Balogh, I. & Meszaros, I. (1980). Hypnotherapy during pregnancy, delivery, and childbirth. In I. Pajntar, I. Roskav & A. Lavnic (Eds), *Hypnosis, Psychotherapy and Psychosomatic Medicine* (pp. 39–56). Ljubljana: University Press.

Toon, K., Fraise, J., McFetridge, M. & Alwin, N. (1996). Memory or mirage? The FMS debate. *The Psychologist* **9**(2), 73–77.

Treacher, A. (1983). On the utility or otherwise of psychotherapy research. In D. Pilgrim (Ed.), *Psychology and Psychotherapy: Current Trends and Issues*. London: Routledge.

Truax, C.B. & Carkhuff, R.R. (1967). *Toward Effective Counseling and Psychotherapy: Training and Practice*. New York: Aldine.

Tsuji, Y. & Kobayashi, T. (1988). Short and long ultradian EEG components in daytime arousal. *Electroencephalography and Clinical Neurophysiology* **70**, 110–117.

Turk, D.C., Meichenbaum, D. & Genest, M. (1983). *Pain and Behavioral Medicine: A Cognitive-Behavioral Perspective*. New York: Guilford Press.

Udolf, R. (1981). *Handbook of Hypnosis for Professionals*. New York: Van Nostrand Reinhold.

Van der Hart, O. & Brown, P. (1992). Abreaction re-evaluated. *Dissociation* **5**(3), 127–140.

Varni, J.W., Thompson, K.L. & Hanson, V. (1987). The Varni/Thompson Pediatric Pain Questionnaire: 1. Chronic musculoskeletal pain in juvenile rheumatoid arthritis. *Pain* **28**, 27–38.

Verny, T. (1982). *The secret life of the unborn child*. London: Sphere.

Vingoe, F.J. (1993). Anxiety and pain. In H.B. Gibson (Ed.), *Psychology, Pain and Anaesthesia*. London: Chapman & Hall.

Violanti, J., Marshall, J. & Howe, B. (1983). Police occupational demands, psychological distress and the coping function of alcohol. *Journal of Occupational Medicine* **25**, 455–458.

von Wietersheim, J., Kohler, T. & Feiereis, H. (1992). Relapse-precipitating life events and feelings in patients with inflammatory bowel disease. *Psychotherapy and Psychosomatics* **58**(2), 103–112.

Walker, L.G. (1992). Hypnosis with cancer patients. *American Journal of Preventative Psychiatry and Neurology* **3**, 42–49.

Walker, L.G. (1998). Hypnosis and cancer: Host defences, quality of life and survival. *Contemporary Hypnosis* **15**(1), 34–38.

Walker, L.G. (2004). Hypnotherapeutic insights and interventions: A cancer odyssey. *Contemporary Hypnosis* **21**(1), 34–45.

Walker, L.G., Dawson, A.A., Lolley, J. & Ratcliffe, M.A. (1988b). Sick to death of it: Some psychological aspects of chemotherapy side effects. *Aberdeen Postgraduate Medical Bulletin* **22**, 11–17.

Walker, L.G., Dawson, A.A., Pollet, S.M., Ratcliffe, M.A. & Hamilton, L. (1988). Hypnotherapy for chemotherapy side effects. *British Journal of Experimental and Clinical Hypnosis* **5**(2), 79–82.

Walker, L. & Eremin, O. (1995). Psychoneuroimmunology: A new fad or the fifth cancer treatment modality? *American Journal of Cancer* **170**, 2–4.

Walker, L.G., Johnson, V.C. & Eremin, O. (1993). Modulation of the immune response to stress by hypnosis and relaxation training in healthy volunteers: A critical review. *Contemporary Hypnosis* **10**, 19–27.

Walker, L.G., Heys, S.D., Walker, M.B., Ogston, I.D., Hutcheon, A.W. Starker, T.K., Ah-See, A.K. & Eremin, O. (1999). Psychological factors can predict the response to primary chemotherapy in patients with locally advanced breast cancer. *European Journal of Cancer* **35**(13), 1783–1788.

Wall, V.J. & Womack, W. (1989). Hypnotic versus cognitive strategies for alleviation of procedural distress in pediatric oncology patients. *American Journal of Clinical Hypnosis* **31**(3), 181–191.

Watkins, H.H. (1980). The silent abreaction. *International Journal of Clinical and Experimental Hypnosis* **23**(2), 101–113.

Watkins, H.H. (1990a). Suggestions for raising self-esteem. In D.C. Hammond (Ed.), *Handbook of Hypnotic Suggestions and Metaphors.* New York: W.W. Norton.

Watkins, H.H. (1990b). Watkins' silent abreaction technique. In D.C. Hammond (Ed.), *Handbook of Hypnotic Suggestions and Metaphors.* New York: W.W. Norton.

Watkins, H.H. (1993). Ego state therapy: An overview. *American Journal of Clinical Hypnosis* **35**(4), 232–240 .

Watkins, H.H & Watkins, J. (1979). The theory and practice of ego state therapy. In H. Grayson (Ed.), *Short-Term Approaches to Psychotherapy.* New York: National Institute for the Psychotherapies & Human Sciences Press.

Watkins, J.G. (1971). The affect bridge: A hypnoanalytical technique. *International Journal of Clinical and Experimental Hypnosis* **19**, 21–27.

Watkins, J.G. (1978). *The Therapeutic Self.* New York: Human Sciences Press.

Watkins, J.G. (1990). Watkins' affect or somatic bridge. In D.C. Hammond (Ed.), *Handbook of Hypnotic Suggestions and Metaphors* (pp. 523–534). New York: W.W. Norton.

Watkins, J.G. (1992). *The Practice of Clinical Hypnosis, Vol. II: Hypnoanalytic Techniques.* New York: Irvington Publishers.

Watkins, J.G. (1995). Hypnotic abreactions in the recovery of traumatic memories. *International Society for the Study of Dissociations* **13**(6), 1–6. www.Clinicalsocialwork. com/letter.html

Watkins, J.G. & Johnson, R.J. (1982). *We the Divided Self.* New York: Irvington Publishers.

Watkins, J.G. & Watkins, H.H. (1986). Hypnosis, multiple personality and ego states as altered states of consciousness. In B.B. Wolman & M. Ullman (Eds), *Handbook of States of Consciousness.* New York: Van Nostrand.

Watkins, J.G. & Watkins, H.H. (1990). Dissociation and displacement: Where goes the 'ouch?' *American Journal of Clinical Hypnosis* **33**(1), 1–10.

Watkins, J.G. & Watkins, H.H. (1993). Accessing the relevant areas of maladaptive personality functioning. *American Journal of Clinical Hypnosis* **35**(4), 277–284.

Watkins, J.G. & Watkins, H.H. (1997). *Ego-state Theory and Therapy.* New York: W.W. Norton.

Watson, J.P. & Davies, T. (1997). Psychosexual problems. *British Medical Journal,* **315**, 239–242.

Waxman, D. (1981). *Hypnosis: A Guide for Patients and Practitioners.* London: George Allen & Unwin.

Waxman, D. (1986). Hypnosis 1788–1986: Its history, development and status within the United Kingdom. *Proceedings of the British Society of Medical and Dental Hypnosis* **6**, 3–8.

Weekes, V.J. & Savedra, M.C. (1988). Adolescent cancer: Coping with treatment-related pain. *Journal of Pediatric Nursing* **3**(5), 318–328.

Weiss, E. (1960). *The Structure and Dynamics of the Human Mind.* New York: Grune and Stratton.

Weiss, L., Katzman, M. & Wolchik, M. (1985). *Treating Bulimia.* New York: Pergamon Press.

Weitzenhoffer, A. (1957). *General Techniques of Hypnotism.* New York: Grune & Stratton.

Welch, G.W., Hillman, L.C. & Pomare, E.W. (1985). Psychoneurotic symptomatology in the irritable bowel syndrome: A study of reporters and non-reporters. *British Medical Journal* **291**, 1382–1384.

Wester, W.C. (1984). Preparing the patient. In W.C. Wester & A.H. Smith (Eds), *Clinical Hypnosis: A Multidisciplinary Approach.* Philadelphia, PA: Lippincott.

Wester, W.C. & O'Grady, D.J. (1991). *Clinical Hypnosis with Children.* New York: Brunner/Mazel Publishing.

Wester, W.C. & Smith, A.H. (Eds) (1984). *Clinical Hypnosis: A Multidisciplinary Approach.* Philadelphia, PA: Lippincott.

Whorwell, P.J. (1991). Use of hypnotherapy in gastrointestinal disease. *British Journal of Hospital Medicine* **45**, 27–29.

Whorwell, P.J., Prior, A. & Colgan, S.M. (1987). Hypnotherapy in severe irritable bowel syndrome: Further experience. *Gut* **28**, 423–425.

Whorwell, P.J., Prior, A. & Faragher, E.B. (1984). Controlled trial of hypnotherapy in the treatment of severe refractory irritable bowel syndrome. *The Lancet* **2**, 1232–1234.

Wiebe, D.J. & McCallum, D.M. (1986). Health practices and hardiness as mediators in the stress-illness relationship. *Health Psychology* **5**, 425–438.

Wijesinghe, B.A. (1977). A case of frigidity treated by short-term hypnotherapy. *International Journal of Clinical and Experimental Hypnosis* **25**, 63–67.

Wild, M. & Espie, C. (2004). The efficacy of hypnosis in the reduction of procedural pain and distress in pediatric oncology: A systematic review. *Journal of Developmental and Behavioral Pediatrics* **25**(3), 207–213.

Wilkinson, J.B. (1988). Hypnosis in the treatment of asthma. In M. Heap (Ed.), *Hypnosis: Current Clinical, Experimental and Forensic Practices*. London: Croom-Helm.

Williams, J.M. & Hall, D.W. (1988). Use of a single session hypnosis for smoking cessation. *Addictive Behaviors* **13**, 205–208.

Williamson, A. (2002). Chronic psychosomatic pain alleviated by brief therapy. *Contemporary Hypnosis* **19**(3), 118–124.

Williamson, A. (2004). A case of herpetic neuralgia treated with self-hypnosis and imagery. *Contemporary Hypnosis* **21**(3), 146–149.

Wills, T.A. (1985). Supportive functions of interpersonal relationships. In S. Cohen & S.L. Syme (Eds), *Social Support and Health*. Orlando, FL: Academic Press.

Wilson, S. (2005). Trial design in hypnotherapy: Does the RCT have a place? *European Journal of Clinical Hypnosis* **6**(1), 20.

Wilson, J.E. & Barkham, M. (1994). A practitioner–scientist approach to psychotherapy process and outcome research. In P. Clarkson & M. Pokorney (Eds), *The Handbook of Psychotherapy*. London: Routledge.

Wincze, J.P. & Carey, M.B. (2001). *Sexual Dysfunction: A Guide for Assessment and Treatment*. New York: Guilford Press.

Wolberg, L.R. (1964). *Hypnoanalysis*. New York: Grune & Stratton.

Wolberg, L.R. (1980). *Handbook of Short-Term Psychotherapy*. New York: Thieme-Stratton.

Wright, M.E. & Wright, B.A. (1987). *Clinical Practice of Hypnotherapy*. New York: Guilford Press.

Wybraniec, A. & Oakley, D.A. (1996). Dietary restraint, hypnotizability and body image. *Contemporary Hypnosis* **13**, 150–155.

Yapko, M.D. (1990a). *Trancework: An Introduction to the Practice of Clinical Hypnosis*. New York: Brunner/Mazel Publishing.

Yapko, M.D. (1990b). Responsibility to a fault: A metaphor for overresponsibility. In D.C. Hammond (Ed.), *Handbook of Hypnotic Suggestions and Metaphors* (pp. 320–322). New York: W.W. Norton.

Yehuda, R., Engel, S.M., Brand, S.R., Seckl, J., Marcus, S.M. & Berkowitz, G.S. (2005). Transgenerational effects of posttraumatic stress disorder in babies of mothers exposed to the World Trade Center attacks during pregnancy. *Journal of Clinical Endocrinology and Metabolism*. Available: www.jcem.endojournals.org/.

Young, D. (1995). The use of hypnotherapy in the treatment of eating disorders. *Contemporary Hypnosis* **12**(2), 148–153.

Zeig, J.K. (Ed.) (1980). *A Teaching Seminar with Milton H. Erickson*. New York: Brunner/Mazel Publishers.

Zeltzer, L. & LeBaron, S. (1982). Hypnosis and nonhypnotic techniques for reduction of pain and anxiety during painful procedures in children and adolescents with cancer. *Journal of Pediatrics* **101**(6), 1032–1035.

Zilbergeld, B. & Hammond, D.C. (1988). The use of hypnosis in treating desire problems. In S.R. Leiblum & R.C. Rosen (Eds), *Sexual Desire Disorders* (pp. 192–225). New York: Guilford Press.

Zimmerman, J. (1998). Hypnotic technique for sedation of patients during upper gastrointestinal endoscopy. *American Journal of Clinical Hypnosis* **40**(4), 284–287.

Zimmerman, J. (2003). Cleaning up the river: A metaphor for functional digestive disorders. *American Journal of Clinical Hypnosis* **45**(4), 353–359.

Index